The Letter of Violence: Essays on Narrative and Theory,
    by Idelber Avelar

Intellectual History of the Caribbean,
    by Silvio Torres-Saillant

Forthcoming titles

None of the Above: Contemporary Puerto Rican Cultures and Politics,
    edited by Frances Negrón-Muntaner

Puerto Ricans in America: 30 Years of Activism and Change,
    edited by Xavier F. Totti and Félix Matos Rodríguez

Remembering Maternal Bodies

Melancholy in Latina and Latin American Women's Writing

Benigno Trigo

REMEMBERING MATERNAL BODIES
© Benigno Trigo, 2006.

First published in 2006 by
PALGRAVE MACMILLAN™
175 Fifth Avenue, New York, N.Y. 10010 and
Houndmills, Basingstoke, Hampshire, England RG21 6XS
Companies and representatives throughout the world.

PALGRAVE MACMILLAN is the global academic imprint of the Palgrave Macmillan division of St. Martin's Press, LLC and of Palgrave Macmillan Ltd. Macmillan® is a registered trademark in the United States, United Kingdom and other countries. Palgrave is a registered trademark in the European Union and other countries.

ISBN 1–4039–6469–6

Library of Congress Cataloging-in-Publication Data is available from the Library of Congress.

A catalogue record for this book is available from the British Library.

Design by Newgen Imaging Systems (P) Ltd., Chennai, India.

First edition: January 2006

10 9 8 7 6 5 4 3 2 1

Printed in the United States of America.

Contents

Acknowledgments

I wish to express my gratitude to Irene Vilar for pointing out the connection between the body and writing, between philosophy and literature in her memoir. To Naomi Lindstrom for her careful reading of the chapter on Clarice Lispector that helped me to rewrite it. To Mara Negrón-Marrero for asking questions that have led me to continue to read Lispector differently. To Earl Fitz, for his generous and open disposition and his encouragement to continue to use Julia Kristeva as an interpretive lens to read Lispector. To Cathy Jrade for her precise reading of the chapter on Julia Alvarez that encouraged me to continue striving for clarity in my writing. To William Luis for his warm welcome to a new professional home and for his helpful remarks regarding reverse temporality and Latin American literature that helped me to revise the chapter on Alvarez. To Betty Josephs for an illuminating conversation about migration and temporality and for her recommendation that I look at Guha's work on this subject. To Rubén Ríos Avila for his insightful reminder to tend to the psychoanalytic tension between the Laws of the Mother and the Father in the work of Rosario Ferré. To Doris Sommer for her keen study of bilingual expression, which brought to my attention a number of texts that are similar to Ferré's in their movement through the waters of language. To Norma Alarcón for her insistence to tend to the sexuality and the bodily drives in the metaphors of Cherríe Moraga. To John Ochoa for recommending that I look at Moraga's work on motherhood in the first place. To Román de la Campa for his insistence on raising the concepts of mourning and melancholy to a level beyond the personal and for his wise recommendations on contemporary critical readings along this line. To Lou Charnon Deutsch for her pointed questions about Kristeva and feminine writing that led me to develop and better define what I call maternal writing. And to my colleagues at the Hispanic Languages and Literature department at Stony Brook, in particular to my dear friends Daniela and Adrián, for providing the necessary supportive environment without which writing would be impossible.

I also want to thank Cristina Mathews (now my colleague) for our discussions in my graduate seminars and over the course of several years regarding the presence and the absence of the mother figure in Garro and Vilar. I owe my heartfelt thanks to Aura Colón and Jason Meyler too for their assistance in compiling and photocopying the bibliography for individual chapters. Thank you also to Gretchen Susan Selcke for her help with the Index. I am also grateful to my editor at Palgrave-Macmillan, Gabriella Pearce, for her patience and sustained commitment to the project, which kept me focused and productive.

Earlier versions of chapters 2 and 3 appeared in *Revista Canadiense de Estudios Hispánicos* 29.2 (2005), and in *Posdata* 18 (2004): 25–35. I am grateful to the editors for permission to reprint the articles in revised form.

And my grateful thanks to my most dedicated reader, Kelly, without whose generosity (in every sense of that word) and love, without whose patient listening, careful reading, unwavering confidence and constant encouragement this book would never have been finished. And to Rosario, Mami, for reminding me to persevere, for teaching me how to listen, and above all, for writing.

Introduction

A recent trend toward demystifying the mother in the literature of the Americas prompted me to write this book. It is a trend perhaps exemplified by the collection of short pieces published in 2000 under the title of *Las Mamis: Favorite Latino Authors Remember Their Mothers* and edited by Esmeralda Santiago and Joie Davidow. In that edited collection, male and female writers from the Americas (broadly defined to include countries such as Cuba, Mexico, Chile, Nicaragua, and Colombia, as well as the United States, and all manner of borderlands in between) come together to remember their mothers, and they end up writing about the power that their mothers hold over them. These authors, whose works cut across racial boundaries, sexual divides, and social class, write about the mother and they acknowledge the mother's force, even as they demystify that power.[1]

I also noticed that the ubiquity of this cultural trend was matched by the difficulty of giving an account of the mother and her power. One of the editors of *Las Mamis*, Joie Davidow, vividly summarizes this difficulty in her Foreword:

> We were surprised that so many writers declined our invitation. One writer told me frankly that it wasn't worth the risk of invoking his *mami*'s displeasure. For others, the relationship was too wounded to be laid bare on a page without spilling blood and tears, or so fragile that any attempt to capture it in a web of words, however delicately constructed, might shatter it. A few writers gladly accepted, only to become paralyzed when they realized what they were about to do. (viii)

Rosario Ferré, the author of the novel *Eccentric Neighborhoods* (originally published in 1998), and my mother, admits to a similar obstacle. She says that she found it impossible to deal with the subject of the death of her mother until she began to write in English, almost thirty years later (Navarro 1988, 2). In her memoir, *The Ladies'*

Gallery (1996), Irene Vilar also poignantly voices the difficulty of broaching the subject of her mother and even suggests the existence of an opposition between the mother and writing. Vilar writes about her mother Mirna: "Mother has died, therefore I am. Not a nation, but a presence that remains. A book" (323). Obviously, both Ferré and Vilar are deeply affected by the death of their mothers. Their comments suggest, however, that it is not just the death of the mother—a poignant and significant moment to be sure—but the conflict between the mother's power and the repression of that power within patriarchal discourses that troubles them and the relationship to their mother.

In this book, I argue that Ferré and Vilar, along with six other Latina and Latin American women writers not only demystify, but also bear witness to, a powerful experience that clearly goes beyond the individual lives of their biological mothers. My claim is that they also attempt to give voice to a maternal speaking body and by doing so they try to change the shape of, what I call, a patriarchal maternal imaginary.[2] They do so by writing in the space between language and the body, which I call maternal writing.[3] They also do so by reinscribing and thereby rescuing the maternal speaking body buried under the patriarchal maternal imaginary. The difficulty that this effort poses is but a measure of the degree to which our patriarchal discourses, myths, and fantasies about motherhood and maternity are entrenched. The difficulty described by these authors is a testament to the strength and heterogeneity of forces that resist their attempts toward demystifying the mother or toward reinscribing the imaginary that inflects her.[4]

The Maternal Imaginary

Following Teresa de Lauretis's (1994) definition of the maternal imaginary, I understand that our experience of maternity, motherhood, and/or the maternal is phantasmatic and symbolic as well as libidinal and organic. And in all of these dimensions, I suggest that we experience the mother, motherhood, or maternity only in discourse.[5] I suggest that these authors engage in an ethical project of compassion and connection whose principal object is to rethink female subjectivity in terms of the maternal imaginary. I do not accept, however, de Lauretis's fundamental distinction between feminist heterosexual and postfeminist homosexual modalities of the maternal imaginary. Instead, I focus on the combined effect of what are similarly troubling, but always specific, reinscriptions of patriarchal maternal imaginaries.[6] In this book, I argue that Clarice Lispector, Elena Garro, Rosario

Ferré, Irene Vilar, and Julia Alvarez, as well as Norma Alarcón, Gloria Anzaldúa, and Cherríe Moraga give an account of motherhood and maternity that avoids what de Lauretis identifies as the pitfalls of the feminist heterosexual maternal imaginary. I argue that at the same time their account of motherhood and maternity resists the symbolic matricide implied by de Lauretis's suggestion that desire is "absolutely unrealizable" because subjectivity is built on the "impossible" foundation of a structural maternal absence (200–201). Rather than lament a maternal absence, on the one hand, or celebrate a primary maternal presence or sameness, on the other, these authors complicate such dichotomies by giving voice to different modalities of maternity thereby recreating the maternal imaginary.

As the reader of this book will quickly realize, this collection of case studies owes an important debt to the psychoanalytic work of Julia Kristeva. A closer reading of the book will further reveal that Kelly Oliver's philosophical interpretation and elaboration of Kristeva's work also significantly influences it. Specifically, it is informed by Oliver's emphasis on Kristeva's attempt to bring "the speaking body" back into language, into theory, and into discourse (Oliver 2002, viii, xvi). More particularly still, the book is influenced by what is at stake in Kristeva's attempt to bring the speaking body back into language. As Oliver suggests, Kristeva's work is important, and even necessary, because it enables (and also practices) the reinscription of our most familiar stories. Kristeva rewrites our fantasies, theories, discourses, and figures for the maternal speaking body. Indeed, Kristeva's work is very relevant to our current condition, and speaks most eloquently to us, when it brings to the forefront of our consciousness, interrogates, and most importantly rewrites the constellation of fantasies, theories, discourses and figures that revolve around the "black sun" of the maternal speaking body. It seems that within patriarchal discourse "the only way available for women to reestablish their identities with the maternal body is through becoming mothers themselves"; and Oliver emphasizes that instead "we need an image of maternity that can found, rather than threaten, the social relationship" (Oliver 2002, 297).

The central claim of *Remembering Maternal Bodies* is that Latina and Latin American women writers take us in this direction, even if they do so from different moments of our recent history and from different geographical locations. Indeed, several of the women writers showcased in this book are engaged in the attempt to reestablish their identities with the maternal body through writing rather than by becoming mothers themselves—a reinscription that Julia Alvarez calls "imagining motherhood" (1999, 96). This writing is a mode of transposition, sublimation, or idealization that I call maternal writing. In other words, in their works all of these writers interrogate, interpret, elaborate, and rewrite a patriarchal maternal imaginary that results in a symbolic, discursive, and phantasmatic matricide that in turn threatens to leave us permanently depressed and melancholic, if not suicidal.

In this book, I explore the ways in which what I call the maternal imaginary transverses the maternal body and its social inscription. The maternal body is a speaking body; and what I call maternal writing attempts to give voice to this maternal space in between body and language. Indeed, the images of the mother, maternity, and motherhood that appear in the work of the Latina and Latin American writers discussed in this book, confirm that the maternal imaginary is both a linguistic and an organic process that makes but at the same time troubles meaning, identity, and subjectivity. Garro, for example, ascribes the speaking memory of a matriarchal town as the origin of the vexed desires and incestuous phobias of its inhabitants in her 1963 novel *Recollections of Things to Come*. Not surprisingly, the inhabitants of the town defensively displace its libidinal power over them into violence and cruelty against "women, stray dogs, and Indians" (1991, 58). Similar examples of the maternal as a place in between organic and linguistic forces can be found in the work of the other women writers studied in this book. Moraga describes the maternal speaking body as a wounded and wounding writing, while Anzaldúa and Alarcón refer to it as an interface and an interstice. Ferré suggests that her mother tongue is an ancestral and troubling impulse, an angry sound, rhythm, music, an essential ambiguity and indifferentiation that destabilizes the subject and must be translated. Vilar describes her mother and grandmother as the keepers of a radically unstable or lost material at the origins of identity, an obscure knowledge that she represents as the song of the Sirens. Alvarez describes her mother's command as an archaic pulse that is both depressive and constitutive of subjectivity. And Lispector calls for a witness to the matricide that results from the separation of body from language.

If it is true, however, that these narratives confirm the fact that the maternal imaginary is an organic and linguistic process that gives rise to a vexed subject; it is also true that they often point to a dead body at the center of the maternal imaginary. Garro's novel, for example, begins with the death of the town's matriarch, Doña Ana Moncada. Moreover, the novel is the "treacherous" memory of the lost matriarchal town, a memory that "brings us to a dark inlet where nothing happens" (Garro 1991, 192). And Lispector's short story "Happy Birthday," about the powerful effect of a catatonic matriarch on her family, ends with the patriarchal certainty that "death was her mystery" (1997, 87). Other examples include Ferré speaking of the death of her mother 30 years after the fact, Vilar putting into words the horrifying suicide of her mother in her memoir, Alvarez representing time and again the death of maternal figures in her work, including her own in her latest book of poems. Alarcón, Anzaldúa, and Moraga reflect in turn on the role played by the violence against mythical maternal figures (Malintzín, Coatlicue, The Hungry Woman, La Llorona, etc.) in the constitution of a Chicana subject. What is the meaning of this recurring loss that either marks or threatens the speaking body that is at the center of the maternal imaginary? And what is the effect of this recurring loss on the emerging subject-in-process?

Matricidal Drive

Kristeva argues that we all experience a form of symbolic matricide, and indeed that matricide is the condition of possibility of our individuation. In other words, following Freudian psychoanalysis Kristeva argues that we become subjects only through a violent symbolic separation from the mother. Disagreeing with Freudian psychoanalysis, however, Kristeva also argues that this separation is not the effect of the phallic threat of castration. Instead, she argues that it is the result of a reciprocal ambivalent process with the speaking maternal body. In *Powers of Horror* (originally published in 1980), Kristeva emphasizes that this separation is ambivalent by famously calling the maternal object the abject. Abjection is a foundational symbolic act that eroticizes the lost object and produces the maternal abject: a phobic object that remains both repulsive and attractive to the subject. Kristeva repeats her emphasis on the ambivalent nature of the matricidal separation and the need to recover the lost maternal object in *Black Sun* (originally published in 1987). There, she states that "Matricide is our *vital* necessity, the sine-qua-non condition of our individuation, *provided* that it takes place under optimal circumstances and can be eroticized" (1989, 27 [My emphasis]). In other words, Kristeva implicitly distinguishes between matricide and matricidal *drive*. Only the latter is our *vital* necessity. Only the matricidal *drive* recovers the lost maternal object by eroticizing it. Lispector's transformative witness, Gregoria's lesson in Garro's novel, Ferré's translation, Moraga's accident, Anzaldúa's interface, Alarcón's interstice, Vilar's *memoria*, and Alvarez's temporally uncanny poetry, are all different modes of the transformation of the phobic abject by writers who tend to this matricidal drive.

Oliver elaborates Kristeva's remarks about matricidal drive and she suggests "that sexual difference is a result of differing relations to the maternal body" (Oliver 2002, 299). Oliver states that, as Kristeva describes it, the eroticization of the lost maternal object is only the experience of the male heterosexual subject: "Kristeva suggests that her description of the process of abjection as a splitting of the mother into sublime and terrifying in *Powers of Horror* applies only to males . . . Females do not split the mother, but merely try (unsuccessfully) to rid themselves of her. [Kristeva] diagnoses female sexuality as a melancholy sexuality in *Black Sun*" (Oliver 2002, 226). And indeed, Kristeva suggests that sexual difference, or the development of a male versus a female, or a heterosexual versus a homosexual subject, depends on the different forms of recovery of the lost maternal object. Eroticization of abjection, for example, makes possible male heterosexuality. The male heterosexual subject can overcome this identification with the maternal body through abjection and the subsequent eroticization of its fascinating or sublime aspect. Therefore, he need not identify with its terrifying repulsive aspect. The same is not true of the female heterosexual subject, however, whose identification with the maternal body is more immediate and totalizing and therefore requires a different mode of eroticization, according to Kristeva. She calls this mode of eroticization "transposition" and describes it as an "unbelievable symbolic effort" (1989, 28).

In *Black Sun*, Kristeva discusses the different effects of hindering the matricidal drive for male and female and homosexual and heterosexual subjects. Hindering the matricidal drive turns the drive against the self in all of them. The male heterosexual subject, for example, responds to the blockage of this drive by threatening to kill itself rather than kill the mother. This suicidal posture, however, is but a screen for an even more categorical form of matricide. For Kristeva, the suicidal posture requires the unconscious fantasy not only of the mother but also of the Feminine as the very image of death. In other words, the suicidal pose of the male heterosexual subject is really an explosive mood. Following Freud's description of the melancholic economy, Kristeva argues that self-hatred hides another form of hatred, one that is actually projected outside the self. This explosive mode of melancholy is the unconscious defense that prevents the male heterosexual self from pulverizing itself in the absence of a matricidal drive.

In *Black Sun*, Kristeva also discusses the effect of hindering the matricidal drive on the female heterosexual subject. Kristeva argues that the female heterosexual subject experiences an implosive mode of melancholy. She experiences identification with the mother that is more immediate by virtue of their analogous sexualities (according to Kristeva) and by virtue of social convention (according to Oliver).[7] So she does not combine the inversion of the matricidal drive with the fantasy of a death bearing Feminine or maternal figure. She cannot project her hatred outside her self. Therefore, she enters the melancholy economy that follows the hindering of the matricidal drive with a different set of unconscious defenses. She accompanies her permanent bitterness and bouts of sadness with a dark hope. This dark hope is the fantasy of feminine immortality in and beyond death that contains an anesthetized form of pain, a suspended form of *jouissance*, or a deadened self. This fantasy has the effect of weakening the aggressive affect toward the other and the despondent affect toward the self. But it does not stop the series of sustained self-inflicted physic and moral blows that constitute the imploding life of the female heterosexual subject.

It is, then, imperative for Kristeva that the matricidal drive not be hindered. It is essential to allow, and even support, the flow of the matricidal drive between the loss and the erotic recovery of the speaking maternal body. In an interview with Rosalind Coward, Kristeva suggests a counter punctual reading of her books that brings out these complementary poles of her work. Referring to *Tales of Love* (originally published in 1983), Kristeva writes "In this book I stressed more idealization and love and it can appear that I have in mind only this part of the cure. But I have already written another book called *The Powers of Horror* where the problem of negativity, rejection, hostility has been the dominant problem. So in order to have a complete image of what happens in the cure we have to read the two books" (Oliver 2002, 356). The restoration of the matricidal drive either through idealization (or transposition) and love, or negativity and abjection, is the "cure" for the explosive and implosive modes of melancholia that haunt the contemporary subject. But, Kristeva also emphasizes the daunting problem of implosive melancholia that requires elaboration, idealization, or the transposition of the lost maternal object into a sexual object of an other sex, a necessary task that nevertheless is nothing short of "gigantic" (1989, 30).

Oliver has dedicated much of her own work to emphasize the cultural dimension of the obstacles that hinder the matricidal drive: the matricide carried out by patriarchal culture, its erasures of the maternal speaking body, its rituals of defilement, and its matricidal accounts of the maternal imaginary. Oliver has also elaborated the task of overcoming this matricide by reinscribing sublimation and idealization back into the matricidal drive of the maternal imaginary.[8] Drawing from Freud's account of sublimation, Kristeva's references to idealization and transposition, and from Shoshana Felman and Dori Laub's (1992) work on testimony and witnessing, Oliver diagnoses this cultural matricide as a crisis of witnessing and calls for a restorative sublimation that she names a transformative mode of witnessing.

Matricidal Limit-Event

In *Testimony: Crises of Witnessing in Literature, Psychoanalysis, and History* (1992), Felman and Laub search for a form of "truth-bearing" testimony. In that book, Felman and Laub examine recordings from the Video Archives for Holocaust Testimonies at Yale University as well as artistic works like the film *Shoah* (1985) by Claude Lanzmann and they describe them as efforts to contain but also to go beyond what they see as an epistemological crisis in Western thought. These works are a form of witnessing the Holocaust in between historical accuracy and truth. Felman and Laub describe this form of witnessing as a dynamic movement between the inside and the outside of the Holocaust. They argue that such witnessing can bring the dead back to life and can expose the surviving core within the dead. Paradoxically, according to Felman and Laub, these works bear witness to the impossibility of witnessing after the Holocaust, an example of what Felman calls a "limit-experience whose overwhelming impact constantly puts to the test the limits of the witness and of witnessing, at the same time that it constantly unsettles and puts into question the very limits of reality" (205).

They also maintain that such testimony is an active and costly resistance to a force that insists on forgetting, erasing, burying, and covering over not only the witness to the Holocaust, but the process of witnessing itself. They argue that the Holocaust, the songs taught by the Nazi concentration camp commanders to their Jewish prisoners, and the purifying rituals that followed (e.g., the insistence by some historians on accuracy to the point of documentary obsession) produce two slightly different modes of a widespread amnesia. The Holocaust and its purifying rituals leave behind them a shadow that continues to actively and violently erase all memory of the limit-event, of the witnesses to the event, and of the process of witnessing the event. But it also has a different effect on the survivor and on the culture at large.

Following Lanzmann, Felman compares the limit-experience to a black sun, and the erasure of memory in the survivor to the effect of that stellar body on light. "The journey toward the film, the struggle toward a narration of the Holocaust *in light*, is thus not simply a historical, unprecedented journey toward erasure, but a journey, at the same time, both into and outside of the black sun inside oneself" (253). For the survivor, the Holocaust always comes back to the same place and he lives in the shadow of its imminent return. "Trauma survivors live not with memories of the past and its wake, but with an event that could not and did not proceed through to its completion, has no ending, attained no closure, and therefore, as far as its survivors are concerned, continues into the present and is current in every respect" (68–69). The effect of the Holocaust on Western culture is somewhat different, but no less traumatic according to Felman and Laub. They suggest that we react to the transvaluation of values perpetrated by the Holocaust and to the subsequent melancholy of the survivor by producing instead a "defensive fierceness," a "relentless productivity," a "historical diversion, a trivialization, a philosophical escape from, and a psychological denial of, the depth and the subversive power of the Holocaust experience" (73–74). We cannot bear to listen to the troubling and uncanny testimony of the witness, we cannot bear to live in the shadow of the limit-event, and by resisting to do so we set the conditions of possibility for its return.

Both Felman and Laub propose that we try to escape this trap by listening for the truth in the inaccuracies and in the silences of artistic and intellectual production about and following the Holocaust. Unlike the songs of the concentration camps, the systematic leveling of the camps, or the purifying religious ceremonies performed after the limit-event, many of the cultural works chosen by Felman paradoxically bear witness to the impossibility of bearing witness to it. And the artistic and intellectual works that really hold Felman and Laub's attention are those that consciously insist on testifying to this impossibility. Felman and Laub read between the lines of these insistent works. They listen for the "passwords" within their inaccuracies and silences in an effort to transform the crisis in Western epistemology produced by the Holocaust.

In her book *Witnessing: Beyond Recognition* (2001), Oliver diagnoses contemporary theories of subjectivity based on recognition and misrecognition as symptoms of traumatic events that are analogous to the Holocaust in force and effect, but also different in kind from that limit-event.[9] Following Felman and Laub, Oliver argues that these ever-more catastrophic limit-events include slavery and the World Wars, but she also suggests that these limit-events are preceded (and perhaps are even prepared) by an archaic and symbolic matricide that constitutes us as subjects. Oliver exposes a maternal imaginary where the symbolic mother is separate from language and where (as a result) the subject must endure and accept a violent intervention of paternal authority in order to separate from her natural antisocial body and achieve sociality. Oliver describes her own writing in the book as an attempt to reverse this archaic matricide by rewriting the patriarchal maternal imaginary. "This work is itself an attempt to make the social space in which maternal affects can be symbolized in order to demythologize the natural antisocial image of maternity upheld by patriarchy" (2001, 81). In that work, she warns us that the philosophical, cultural, and critical models of subject formation that follow from this matricidal imaginary guarantee the foreclosure of witnessing to this process as well as to the limit-events that follow in its wake. Left unexamined, the archaic matricide produces two modes of melancholy witnessing that resonate with the psychic economies of Kristeva's (male) explosive and (female) implosive melancholy subjects as well as with Felman and Laub's different traumatic responses to the Holocaust.

Maternal Writing or Transformative Witnessing

Archaic matricide can produce the fiercely defensive and relentlessly productive witness described by Felman and Laub in their book. This melancholy witness to the returning loss of the maternal body suffers from a depression set off by the pain of losing the maternal speaking body, but also by denial, disavowal, or negation, which are defenses against that loss. The depressed witness rechannels or reorients the lost object or the process of loss itself outward to an "other," to an "external" object. The male melancholy subject releases (rather than incorporate) the lost object and reduplicates it. In other words, he creates a displaced facsimile of the lost object outside the self and charges it with social, artistic, or intellectual value: the myths, fantasies, and figures that together constitute a patriarchal maternal imaginary (what Laub refers to as a "historical diversion, a trivialization, a philosophical escape and a psychological denial" of the limit-event [74]).

But this economy of witnessing also produces solitary subjects. These depressed witnesses are either driven by the lack of the maternal speaking body to a ferocious and insatiable hunger or they suffocate under the weight of their narcissistic walls.

This economy of witnessing also produces the explosive subjects that populate the symbolic landmarks of the Western literary canon with dangerous, violent, deadly, and homicidal figures for the Feminine and the mother. Some examples of these recalcitrant images include Euripides' *Medea*, Homer's Helen or Circe in the *Odyssey*, the biblical stories of Salomé and Herodias, and Sodom and Gomorrah, as well as modern and modernist texts such as Frank Kafka's "The Sirens," and Sigmund Freud's infamous essay on the head of the Medusa. But this economy is also very much a part of the literary tradition of the Americas. This tradition includes "La Chingada" in Octavio Paz's *The Labyrinth of Solitude* (originally published in 1950), "Rosario" in Alejo Carpentier's *The Lost Steps* (1953), the "mother" in Gabriel García Márquez's *Big Mama's Funeral* (originally published in 1962), Rudolfo Anaya's *The Legend of la Llorona* (1984), and the grandmother and mother figures in Richard Rodríguez's *Hunger of Memory* (originally published in 1982), to name but a select few. This tradition produces nationalistic, authoritarian, identitarian, and fortifying fantasies that together constitute a patriarchal maternal imaginary in an (always unsuccessful) attempt to defend the subject against the uncanny and unstable ground of the maternal speaking body, an attempt that unwittingly produces dissatisfied or suicidal modes of being.

Remembering Maternal Bodies describes the efforts of some Latina and Latin American women writers to reverse this archaic matricide by interrogating and rewriting the maternal imaginary. Moraga, Anzaldúa, and Alarcón question and bridge the symbolic split created between the prostitute and the Virgin mother, two favorite markers of matricide. Vilar demystifies the praise heaped on the Mother of the Nation by Nationalist discourse, and exposes the analogous caricatured maternal fantasies of television's late capitalism. "No one could live on the basis of having vomited or of having seen someone vomit," says Martim, the main character from Lispector's *The Apple in the Dark* (originally published in 1961). Similar to Lispector, the other writers examined in this book also interrogate the rituals of defilement that circumscribe the maternal speaking body to biology, to antisocial nature, or conversely turn it into a metaphysical moment of Annunciation or Immaculate Conception. Alvarez suggests the epitaphial nature of this tradition, which she tries to invert through a negative mode of writing. And Garro troubles the matricidal tropes of Paz's *The Labyrinth of Solitude* with the image of a matriarchal town imprisoned inside a petrified labyrinth and condemned to repeat forever the same moment in time.

The second melancholy subject position produced by the limit-event of matricide suffers a more radical solitude due to the absence of any social support.[10] Its plight is analogous to the condition of the survivor of the Holocaust as described by Felman and Laub, and to the implosive mode of melancholy described by Kristeva. Coincidentally, both Felman and Kristeva use the metaphor of the black sun to describe the limit-event at the center of this melancholic subject position. They both describe the darkening effect of the black sunlight on the life or the "light" of the subject. Lispector diagnoses this double oblivion of matricide and then the silencing or repression of that matricide in her short story "Happy Birthday," from her collection of stories *Family Ties* (originally published in 1960). The wrathful matriarch, Anita, in that story catatonically sits as a warning of the danger of this mode of silencing matricidal violence. At least the male heterosexual subject enjoys the support of the patriarchal maternal imaginary for its fantasies. But this second witness cannot rechannel or reorient the lost maternal body outward because the existing fantasies of Feminine death, the patriarchal maternal imaginary, forces her to violently repress and incorporate rather than separate and disavow the symbolic maternal cadaver.

This second mode of melancholy witness risks succumbing to the fantasies of the patriarchal maternal imaginary. It produces a constellation of monstrous returns of the repressed that affect women most dramatically. These also include the powerful phallic mothers of Ferré's fiction. She calls them "Kamikaze mothers" who defend the patriarchal law to the point of self-erasure or suicide—the melancholic's call to self-sacrifice or the Sirens of Vilar's memoir, the revolutionary and matriarchal counter societies of Garro's novel, and the vengeful and silencing maternal command described by Alvarez. They also include Lispector's extremes of motherhood that go from the punishing Vitória in *The Apple in the Dark*, to Laura or (the Virgin Mother) in "The Imitation of the Rose" (1960). Together they constitute a menacing "ladies' gallery" of what recent works of Feminist criticism has called "gatekeepers" (Kafka 2000; Tate 2003).

For these melancholy forms of witnessing to be positively transformed, there must be room for yet another subject-position, the position that

Oliver calls transformative witnessing, and later calls sublimation and idealization (2004). Following Felman and Laub, she describes this position as opening up the possibility of a response to the matricide, by creating and nurturing an inner-witness to that limit-event. It is a defense against the catastrophic force of matricide founded on disinterring, sublimating, transposing, or transforming the maternal cadaver deeply interred in the crypt of the self and monumentally visible at the center of the matricidal imaginary. Following the images of the poet Nerval, Kristeva suggests the need to recognize that the archaic limit event is also the source of a dazzling light that must be transformed, transposed, idealized or sublimated. "Melancholia belongs in the celestial realm. It changes darkness into redness or into a sun that remains black, to be sure, but is nevertheless the sun, source of dazzling light" (1989, 151). The position of the transformative witness requires vigilance for the light inside this darkness, a careful listening for a barely audible voice, rhythm, music, and pulse in the deadened world of the patriarchal imaginary. It is a position that depends on working through and transforming the insistent impossibility of bearing witness to the limit-event that is matricide. It is an exploration of what Kristeva calls an intimate revolt, the search for a minimalist impulse that nevertheless keeps alive the instability, the ambiguity, and the revolutions that make up the maternal speaking body. It is the attempt to rewrite our maternal imaginary, its system of moral values, its codes, and phantasmatics, into what Kristeva calls a herethics, in an effort to stop its petrifying, stultifying, and murderous effects on all of us. "Herethics is undeath [a-mort], love . . . *Eia mater, fons amoris*" (1987, 263).

All the authors showcased in this book develop one form of this transformative, sublimational witnessing or herethics that I call maternal writing. They all react against the matricidal limit-event by rewriting the maternal imaginary and by modeling their writing after the remembered maternal speaking body. In other words, they liberate the symbolic maternal body from the matricidal phantasmatics in which it has been imprisoned. They develop a mother tongue that emphasizes instead the connection between the maternal body and language in their works. They emphasize the productive aspect of the ambiguous or aporetic maternal and express it in their writing. Writing, then, becomes the pursuit of the accident (the precarious fragility of fantasy) for Moraga; the distillation of the aporia of the maternal experience, the embrace and transformation of *jouissance* for Garro; the translation of the negative, othered, censored voices in the case of Ferré; and

Lispector's witnessing to a limit-event. Conversely, the maternal speaking body becomes a protective tissue-like porous membrane for both Ferré and Moraga. It transforms into a *memoria*, the mournful narrative that remembers the radically unstable or lost material at the center of identity for Vilar and Garro. Its revolting injunctions give rise to a mode of poetic writing that aims to contain its intimate revolt in *The Woman I Kept to Myself* (2004) by Alvarez.

Perhaps more than the others, Lispector's writing complicates Kristeva's male and female and implosive and explosive binary and shows how the move from the melancholy position to the position of transformative witnessing requires the constant flux between the male and the female sexualities between the explosive and implosive subject positions. Her world is in fact peopled by characters that move the reader continuously from an insatiable and ferocious hunger in the case of the professor in her story "The Crime of the Mathematics Professor," to a sustained nausea that ends in a bulimic purging, as happens in the case of Vitória, the female protagonist of *The Apple in the Dark*. Lispector's work is an example of maternal writing, an attempt to write the event at the limits of body and language, an effort to write the maternal speaking body rather than fetishize, reify, or exclude it. It is also a call for an inner-witness, for a third subject position, the position of the reader, of the sympathetic and empathic interpreter of her difficult works.

Psychoanalysis in Latin American, Chicana, and Latina Feminist Criticism

Remembering Maternal Bodies is part of a tradition of critical thought that some 20 years ago turned the attention of Feminists in the field of Latin American and Chicana literature away from an insistence on an analysis of modes of production, and toward a concern with modes of representation.[11] Structuralist and post-structuralist modes of feminist analysis emphasized the role of language as the driving force in a process of subject formation. Discursive networks based on language models were perceived as the forces determining conduct, role-playing, and sociosexual behavior. The existence of what was once called real or what existed outside our language based consciousness was called into question. Reality was revealed to be a linguistic construct that at best hid arbitrary patterns and at worse consolidated power by subordinating certain races, genders, or social classes.

Authoritarian systems of government and their univocal discourses were revealed to emerge in reaction to the arbitrariness of language. The sociosexual scripts of patriarchy, its metaphors, symbols, and tropes (in particular its division of symbolic space into a private and a public sphere) were discovered to preserve privilege in the hands of the masculine few. Moreover, both authoritarian systems and the patriarchy were shown to cover over the linguistic nature of their power with a veneer of naturalness and normativity. Feminist criticism successfully showed how the natural was deployed as a mask for the fictions, master-narratives, plots, discourses, and sociosexual scripts of authoritarian and patriarchal systems of life and government.[12]

Feminist criticism of Latin American and Chicana literatures seemed to offer two solutions to this plight of women and women writers. Some called for readings and interpretations that would reveal the arbitrary nature of these linguistic constructs.[13] Presumably, this had the potential of leveling the field of representation once again, opening it up to alternative constructs. Others called for, and applauded, the effort to gain control over the modes of representation, sometimes praising the work of women writers as in itself valuable merely for occupying the position of subject in the all important sentence structures supporting the script of sociality.[14] Either way, Feminist criticism of all varieties placed the work of women writers under the general rubric of strategic resistance, oblique or direct, against authoritarian and patriarchal modes of representation.

More recently, Feminist criticism has focused on the contribution of women writers to the nation-building projects of Latin America, questionable as that project may be.[15] In this way, Latin American Feminist criticism raises our awareness of the inclusion of women and women writers in the public sphere. Much of this critical work is entangled in discussions of subaltern, dissident, and subversive modes of subjectivity, where sexuality, desire, pleasure, and the body, are part and parcel of the discussion, even when psychoanalytic criticism is not mentioned or given its due.[16] The legacy of psychoanalytic modes of analysis has an even stronger presence in the work of Chicana criticism dating as far back as the famous 1981 anthology by Moraga and Anzaldúa *This Bridge Called My Back*.

But the Feminist assault on modes of representation often inflected by psychoanalytic concepts, techniques, and master narratives has not been without its critics.[17] And from its inception, both defenders and critics of this approach have voiced strong reservations about discussing the work of women writers from a psychoanalytic perspective, questioned the existence of a "feminine" mode of writing, and warned against taking allusions and descriptions to the maternal experience as an object of study.[18] It is repeatedly suggested that such critical practices risk naturalizing and essentializing a difference that has kept women's writing apart, keeping it imprisoned within the walls of the private sphere.

Despite these warnings, the maternal reappears in these Feminist works of criticism, sometimes obliquely, as in the repeated references to the Mothers of the Plaza de Mayo in Argentina.[19] And many studies even focus on the mother figure, or on what has become known as the mother–daughter plot, coined by Marianne Hirsch in her influential 1989 book *The Mother/Daughter Plot: Narrative, Psychoanalysis, Feminism.* Teresa Hurley's recent book *Mothers and Daughters in Post-Revolutionary Mexican Literature* (2003) is a representative example of this trend in Feminist criticism. In her book, Hurley suggests that some women writers recuperate a maternal mode of being in their novels that has the potential of enabling the healthy psychic development of sons and daughters within a patriarchal society. She suggests that these writers make plain the need for mothers to develop a nurturing relationship to their children and she models this relationship after the "good-enough" mother described by the pediatrician Donald Winnicott during the 1940s and 1950s (i.e., a mother who helps her child create an identity, integrate into society, and separate from the mother). She further argues that there is now general agreement on the fact that this nurturing mode of being is necessary, despite the protestations of feminists against the social implications of Winnicot's theories (Hurley 2003, 4).

Similar to Hurley, and to other Feminist writing on the maternal along this vein, I also find compelling the possibility of having an effect on social reality by addressing representation. Indeed, this possibility puts into question the dubious distinction between reality as a cause and representation as an effect. The challenge to that distinction has certainly proven to be of great heuristic value to our contemporary thought. But this challenge can also be misleading. It can make social change appear to be the only legitimate and benign aim (or motivation) of critical commentary and it can also suggest that this aim is easily obtained. Such comforting conclusions ignore the contradicting reality that we are not always masters of our behavior (or of our writing for that matter) and that our motivations are always compromised and vexed. Hurley's positivist faith in developmental and behavioral models of analysis, for example, disregards the symbolic dimension of a problem that she nevertheless locates in literature. Indeed, her approach appears to forget the paradoxical nature of the problem: the matricidal effect of the maternal position within the patriarchal system for example. Paradoxes that give way to counter-intuitive and even self-destructive modes of behavior and representation instead call for modes of analysis that similarly allow the possibility that we may be repeating the problem in attempting to address it. In other words, such problems posit a hermeneutical obstacle that feminist criticisms in the field of Latin American studies of the past 20 years has been doggedly trying to address.

Perhaps the continuing interest of Latin American, Chicana, and Latina Feminist criticism in psychoanalysis despite the censure leveled against it is due to the promise of its central concepts such as the unconscious in our continuing effort to overcome this hermeneutical obstacle. What is certain is that interest in Kristeva's psychoanalytic work has not waned in 20 years, and that her inquiries into the role of the semiotic, negation, and abjection in subject formation continue to have critical currency in today's theoretical practice. Her work was positively reviewed and deployed in early pieces by Castro-Klaren (1984), Méndez Rodenas (1985), and Norma Alarcón (1989). And despite warnings from Kaminsky (see her "The Uses and Limits of Foreign Feminist Theory" in *Reading the Body Politic*, 77–95) and Bruzelius (1999) among others, Kristevan concepts (mostly from her early works *Revolution in Poetic Language* (originally published in 1974), *Powers of Horror* (originally published in 1980), and her 1977 essay "Women's Time," collected in *Tales of Love* (1983)) have been provocatively used in separate essays by critics from all sides of Feminist criticism in and of Spanish.[20]

Of this heterogeneous group, René Prieto's latest book *Body of Writing* (2000) stands out for its compelling departure of the way Kristeva has been recently read, as well as for being perhaps the most suggestive deployment to date of Kristevan psychoanalysis in the effort to theorize the relationship between the body and writing in Latin American literature.[21] Unlike misguided critics who search in Kristeva for the theoretical underpinnings of a Feminine writing, Prieto is right to return us to Alarcón and Castro-Klaren's emphasis on Kristeva's contribution to a critique of the vexed nature of our symbolic discourses. But Prieto's turn to Hélène Cixous's notion of "writing said to be feminine," a turn based on a ludic notion of *jouissance* as unproblematized excess at the end of his book, combined with his account of desire (following Peter Brooks) as "the desire for a body 'that may substitute for *the* body, the mother's, the lost object of infantile bliss' " return him to the patricidal maternal imaginary, and performs yet another version of the matricide diagnosed in this book (2000, 4). One wonders how Prieto's book might have changed had he ventured farther into the body of Kristeva's work to include readings of *Black Sun*, *Tales of Love*, and *Intimate Revolt* (originally published in 1996).

Prieto's book reminds us once again that despite these frontal assaults on the modes of representation driving the inequalities, injustice, and oppression against women (now known as subaltern subjects) and despite all our precautions against our inclinations, the effects of a symbolic matricide and a recalcitrant patriarchal maternal imaginary continue to determine the way we write and read, even when we think we are doing it differently. This recalcitrance has led some Feminist critics to a more careful examination of the discoursive process of indi-viduation, or subject formation, in an effort to reveal the paradoxes, contradictions, or complexity that might explain the resistant nature of these forces that affect our conduct.

Critical race theory, postcolonial and queer criticism have gone some distance in this direction, revealing the contradictory and paradoxical ways in which we exist and conduct ourselves within these discoursive networks. The fantasies that rule over and overdetermine our social behavior and conduct have been revealed to be not only precariously controlled by the master, if at all, but even the result of our complicit if vexed interaction with him (Bhabha 1994; Molloy 1991). Some modes of postcolonial criticism have revealed these fantasies to be the symp-toms of an interiorized subordination, and the effect of the complex fluidity of the positions of master and slave (de la Campa 1999; Spivak 1994). Queer and lesbian theory has also called attention to the hetero-geneity of desire as a persistent and insistent negativity, which can become a productive disavowal nevertheless (de Lauretis 1994; Fiol Matta 2002). Rather than reading the literature of women as examples of resistance, this constellation of critics tends to characterize it as symp-tomatic of the contradictory forces that precariously bind us together. Their readings are not a call for action (reading and writing) in a certain ideological direction. Instead, they practice a mode of reflective medita-tion, focusing on the difficulty of the problems that constitute literature, even as they simultaneously insist on the potential for creativity in what might sometimes appear to be an outright impossible and intractable condition. Writing becomes less an act of resistance than an open promise that these critics often displace into the future.

Similar to many contemporary critics, Jean Franco has made a compelling case that women writers have struggled over time for control of their destiny by wrestling for, what she calls, interpretative power by producing their own dissident subjects in language. But the maternal writing practice described and studied throughout this book is a testimony to something that is more than language, something that cannot be circumscribed to the body either, and something that resists the efforts to create so-called tame and domestic social subjects of good conduct. The maternal writing practice of the women writers showcased in this book testifies to the existence of a register (in and of language, in and of discourse, and its practices) that uncouples and destabilizes the best laid out personal projects of dissidence from (or collusion with) fortifying and defensive agendas. Their efforts bear witness to an aporetic and resistant force that Nikolchina calls a "reverberation," that Molloy calls a "*pulsión*," that Freud calls "the unconscious," and that Kristeva calls "love" and more recently "intimate revolt." Like these women have done in their writing, we must attend to this heterogeneous force. As Oliver reminds us, we must continue to name it, to engage with it, to wrestle with it, and most importantly to transform it. To do so might allow us to mobilize rather than fix or fetishize repeating constellations and networks of forces that are both repressive and oppressive, both symbolic and semiotic, both private and public—discoursive in short. Perhaps by modeling our writing after this remembered and uncanny force we will disturb the webs that we unwittingly continue to weave around our melancholy selves, much like the women showcased in this book have done in (and with) their novels, short stories, plays, and poems.

The Selection of the Texts

Remembering Maternal Bodies includes a selection of texts of varied geographical origin, nationality, and language. It is a corpus adjusted to the broad, hemispheric, transnational, Latin Americanist scope, perhaps best described by de la Campa in his 1999 book. In my study, I looked for a variety of literary genres (novels, short stories, poetry, and plays), as well as a diversity of social class and sexual self-definition. But I was also looking for a common thread. These are all texts from the second half of the twentieth century that interrogate a predominant nationalist master narrative, and suggest their suspicion of the concept of the master narrative itself. These are texts that (one way or another) tend to the complex role of the maternal speaking body in the patriarchal maternal imaginary. Moreover, these are all texts that focus on the contradictions of the maternal imaginary and the maternal speaking body as a significant piece of the complex puzzle of subject formation.

I chose texts that helped me to point to the limits of "dissident" critical approaches that forget the body in general and the maternal body in particular. In their desire for mastery, these critics miss the arbitrary (and performative) nature of our symbolic constructs and/or social practices. But I also chose texts that were remarkable for their vexed and intense attempts to balance the intimate with the social spheres. They speak to, and call for, a similar mode of analysis: a mode of analysis that does not abandon the goal of improving our under-standing of a material reality, but that struggles to gain some distance from our suspicious drive to master and to have authority over the world. All of these texts call for a creative response. I realize that this more speculative mode of criticism threatens to leave some critics gasping for air, as a colleague of mine once poignantly put it. It is a response that might seem suffocating to critics that speak from meta-physical certainties that privilege the so-called hard facts of historical materialism. Still, it is clear to me that the most promising and enabling aspects of these texts will remain inaudible as long as we con-tinue to stifle their calls for a different mode of analysis. Perhaps it is in our best interest to transform the battle cry of these critics for an elusive mastery, authority, and power into something more resonant with the maternal speaking body. Perhaps there are benefits to indulging in what Molloy self-consciously (but also ironically) once described as the "shameful pleasures of the critic" (1985, 69).

The fact that I selected for analysis only texts by women writers is both arbitrary and deliberate. On the one hand, it is a deliberate testi-mony to the contribution of feminist discourses or writings that engage in one way or another with feminist debates and practices; a field of knowledge that continues to be traveled and inhabited mostly by intellectuals and writers that happen to be women (see Kaminsky 1993, on this). On the other hand, it is also an arbitrary selection because it is becoming increasingly clear that the population of this changing field is very diverse, particularly as feminisms engage with queer studies and postcolonial analysis. In so far as it is arbitrary, my selection of writers can be interpreted as a partial sign of the true potential of a field of inquiry that affects all of us, and that we all continue to engage with, regardless of gender or sexuality.

Finally, I must also tend to the intimate aspect of this project. The informed reader will recognize that this book is deeply indebted to my reading of, and engagement with, the work both of my mother Rosario Ferré, and of my wife Kelly Oliver. As Ferré says, "one writes as one can, and not as one would wish." I realize that I am in no position to explain this choice, but perhaps I can motivate it in terms of the double nature of my analytical approach. I can point to the fact that I have tried (perhaps unsuccessfully) to illuminate the very personal, intimate, and troubling dimension or aspect of this project by reconciling and weaving it together with social, literary, and professional concerns. I should also point out, that it is my belief that this autobiographical aspect of the book is not so much the origin of the project as it is the force that propelled it forward—and that will continue to help me write as long as I keep interpreting its intimate *pulsión*. It is also my suspicion that I am not alone in the increasingly autobiographical (and perhaps sometimes dangerously confessional and nostalgic) nature of today's critical practice. In the last 20 years, it appears that literary and cultural criticism has gradually eroded the formerly "invisible wall" that gave criticism an aura of authority by separating the critic from the text and from the world. Perhaps this development is a good thing, I do not know. What is clear to me, however, is that this tendency gives no sign of abating, and to the contrary is becoming commonplace. It is as if today, in order to write critically about our world we are also driven inward, to write not obliquely as before, but quite directly now about ourselves. Could Kristeva be correct in suggesting that we are at a point in our place and time when we feel it is necessary to tap the diminishing reserves of our most intimate revolt? What is certain is that this is a widespread phenomenon that deserves more sustained attention than I can give it in this introduction.

The Chapters of the Book

Remembering Maternal Bodies is divided into six chapters.

Chapter one, "Transformative Witnessing: Clarice Lispector's Dark Ties," focuses on two works by Clarice Lispector. It examines Lispector's study of a world where witnessing to something that can't be seen but that paradoxically must be accounted for in order to preserve humanity is no longer possible. It answers the questions: What collapses the process of witnessing? And why is it urgent that we continue to find a witness to this dark core that we traditionally house within the maternal body: the limit-event of matricide?

Chapter two, "Maternal *Jouissance*; Elena Garro's *Recuerdos*" focuses on Elena Garro's first novel, *Los Recuerdos del Porvenir*.

It studies the novel's account of two different identifications with the maternal body as well as its attempt to interpret them by means of a figurative antidote to the plight of female subjectivity. The novel performs a struggle against incestuous and fetishistic identifications and presents the figure of a racially othered female servant as the necessary support to work through them.

Chapter three, "The Mother Tongue: Rosario Ferré's Ec-centric Writing" is a study of the work of Rosario Ferré. It poses and answers three questions. What makes writing about the loss of the mother difficult and even impossible? Why is it so important and even necessary to write about that loss? And what does it mean that Ferré can write about that loss only by displacing her mother tongue?

Chapter four, "Memoirs for the Abject: Irene Vilar's *Memoria*," focuses on Irene Vilar's 1996 memoir. It makes two principal claims: that Vilar's book mourns the loss of origins while transforming the abject rhythms of that loss into a more human voice and that Nationalist discourse produces melancholy and even suicidal subjects. It explores the necessary passage between memoir and memory and between remembering and forgetting in the effort to bridge the space that separates us from the maternal experience.

Chapter five, "Accidents of Chicana Feminisms: Norma Alarcón, Gloria Anzaldúa and Cherríe Moraga," focuses on Chicana Feminist practices. It brings together the work of Alarcón, Anzaldúa, and Moraga as repeated efforts to articulate body and language into the unstable and porous space of maternal writing. Moraga's autobiographical works, and in particular her account of her willful lesbian pregnancy in a heteronormative and heterosexist society is perhaps the most poignant example of an attempt to make visible the accidental and enabling nature of the maternal speaking body.

Chapter six, "From Revenge to Redemption: Julia Alvarez's Open Secrets" is an analysis of the work of Julia Alvarez that highlights her attempt to turn what she describes as a violent negative maternal injunction to keep writing to herself into an enabling poetic pulse, a sound, a rhythm with which she inflects her novels, essays, and poetry. In this chapter, I focus on a temporal mode of this rhythm, which I associate with the uncanny temporality, the inversions, and the temporal reversals of Alvarez's maternal writing.

Transformative Witnessing: Clarice Lispector's Dark Ties

And so the mathematics professor had renewed his crime forever. The man then looked around him and up to the skies, pleading for a witness to what he had done.

—*Clarice Lispector,* Family Ties

"But why me?" he exclaimed furiously. "Because I need a witness!" she replied in the desperation of rage. "Don't think that my life is just this."

—*Clarice Lispector,* The Apple in the Dark

Pleading, desperate, and angry, characters from Clarice Lispector's fiction not only ask for an eyewitness to something beyond sight, they ask for someone to bear witness to a limit-event: the unseen in vision and the unspoken in speech, a dark crime and a secret life.[1] The mathematics professor and Vitória are both victims and perpetrators of a symbolic matricide that leaves one with an insatiable appetite and the other with an intolerable nausea. It leaves both of them asking for a witness to what they have done and to what has been done to them. A witness, however, never arrives to see or hear the testimony of these characters. Moreover, the works themselves suggest the impossibility of bearing witness to a limit-event. Indeed, the collapse of witnessing (in the double sense of seeing with one's own eyes as well as bearing witness to something beyond sight) is a crucial theme in Lispector's popular book of short stories *Family Ties*, and in her novel *The Apple in the Dark*.[2] But if it is true that these works are about the collapse of witnessing, it is also true that Vitória's angry desperation in the *Apple*, and the professor's pleading tone in *Family Ties* suggest Lispector's urgency to make witnessing possible again.

Writing these two books, however, seems to have had a silencing effect on Lispector. She was unable to write another novel for eight years.[3] What led her to stop writing? And why is it urgent to continue to write? Lispector's life holds some of the answers to these questions, though we must also move beyond the biographical to answer them. Like Vitória, Lispector shrouded a part of her life in secrecy. She was born in 1920 but was famously unreliable about her date of birth and about her early childhood. She was so secretive that even her tombstone does not register the date of her birth (Peixoto 1994, xvi). She was similarly ambivalent about her name, signing herself Clarice Lispector Gurgel Valente, Clarice Gurgel Valente, Clarice G. Valente, Clarice Lispector, C.L., and even Wife of the consul Maury Gurgel Valente (Gotlib 1995, 60). Moreover, she never referred to her family's struggle against anti-Semitism. Her parents, Pedro and Marieta Lispector, were Ukrainian Jews, spoke Yiddish and Russian at home, and observed Jewish traditions. They fled their native Ukraine escaping the Russian Revolution's anti-Semitic violence. In fact, Clarice Lispector was born in Tchechelnik, Ukraine, on the way out of the country.

Her family's transition to the new country was difficult. After World War II, Brazil was an anti-Semitic, nationalistic, and xenophobic nation. Their experiences influenced the writing of Lispector's older sister. In her 1948 autobiographical novel *In Exile*, Elisa Lispector describes the family's displacement as part of a Jewish Diaspora, and suggests that they adapted to Brazil only with difficulty.[4] Unlike Elisa, Clarice Lispector made no reference to her family's struggle against anti-Semitism or their difficult adaptation to Brazil. In the words of Naomi Lindstrom, "in Lispector's writing, her Jewishness remains submerged, covert, and ambiguous . . . While Lispector did not deny being Jewish, she downplayed the significance of this fact for her identity and her writing" (1999, 111–112). Indeed, she seemed to go out of her way to erase traces of her origins, her own difficulties with her adopted country and its language.[5] But the experiences of her family seem to have had an influence on Lispector's work; and the absence of references to her Jewish background could be in and of itself a revealing trace of this influence as Lindstrom has suggested.[6]

Lispector began to write *Family Ties* and *Apple* in 1948 (Gotlib 1995, 268) and in 1950 (Gotlib 1995, 277) respectively, although they were both published in the early 1960s. She was married to a Brazilian diplomat and resided for a long time in Switzerland, England, and the United States. This is when she wrote her two books, *Family Ties* and *Apple*. Maury Gurgel Valente was a consul under the military dictatorship of Getúlio Vargas. The dictatorship was known as the New State and it became infamous for its violent repression and torture. The New State has also been described as a nationalist and populist attempt to struggle against neocolonialism, and to make Brazil an economically independent nation through State-driven industrialization and modernization. Its disciplinarian government promoted a paternalist image and Vargas was called the "Father of the Poor" by government controlled trade unions. It is not surprising that the constitution of the New State was fashioned after fascist European models. Tolerant of domestic fascist movements that denounced Democrats, Communists, Masons, and Jews as "enemies of the state," the violent regime began in 1930 and ended in 1954 (the year of Getúlio Vargas's suicide, Keen 1992, 350). It lasted some 25 years.[7] Arguably, Lispector was a survivor of this regime and the obscurity of her work could also be interpreted as the melancholy effect of the dictatorship on her voice as a writer. In fact, she finished writing one of the densest and darkest stories of her collection ("The Crime of the Mathematics Professor") the same year as that of Vargas's suicide, and she finished writing *The Apple in the Dark* only two years after that, in 1956. Perhaps not coincidentally, she separated from her husband and returned to Brazil in 1959. But the reader is hard pressed to find references to the repressive political environment of Getúlio Vargas's New State in the two works by Lispector that occupy us here. Only oblique references to the dictatorship and traces of its silencing effect remain in her work. For example, Anita, the catatonic matriarch that presides over her family in the short story "Happy Birthday," dramatically expresses her disgust for her children by silently calling them "A bunch of communists, that's what they were—communists" (80).

While traces of the effect of anti-Semitism and dictatorship on Lispector can be found in her troubled and troubling work, the bulk of her work also points the reader in the direction of a different limit-event: matricide. Elisa Lispector's autobiographical novel describes the early years of the Lispector family as shadowed by her mother's deteriorating health and death, according to Peixoto (1994, xvii). Marieta was afflicted with a nervous disorder that left her suffering with a progressive paralysis. According to her biographer, Gotlib, Lispector associated her own birth with her mother's fatal disease and she carried the burden of that guilt all her life (1995, 68). Moreover, her mother's death had a devastating impact on the family. Reportedly, the family practiced Jewish religious ceremonies until their mother's death, and in an interview, Lispector says that she stopped believing in God when she died (Lowe 1979, 37; Marting 1993, xxiv).

Lispector also says that her mother's death provokes a mode of writing in her. "When I was nine, I composed a song, 'Lament,' for my mother, who had just died" (Lowe 1979, 36). And it is tempting to read her melancholy novel and her collection of short stories as written versions of a musical lament after the loss of the mother. Lispector herself describes the tone of "The Imitation of the Rose" as "monochromatic" and compares its deliberate use of repetition to "an insistent cantilena which has something to express" (1992, 313).[8] In *The Apple in the Dark*, Lispector describes a world of deadened affect, where love has been drained of its passion, a world "where father and mother have been denied and there is a thirst for love" (35). In "Preciousness," she describes a "bombarded city" without parents (107). In "The Buffalo," love is reduced to a resigned ritual: a monkey breast-feeding her young (148). And maternal paralysis and anger are of course the central tropes of the short story "Happy Birthday," whose catatonic protagonist is a figure of Lispector's grandmother according to her (1992, 311).

But Lispector's novel and short stories also go beyond the biographical dimension. They also suggest the symbolic nature of the death of the mother at the center of her melancholy works and at the origin of her call for a witness. Lispector's world is shot through with the impossible and monstrous fantasies of perfect and fertile Maternity, fantasies that haunt, possess, obsess, and destroy its inhabitants, including Anita in "Happy Birthday," Laura in "The Imitation of the Rose," and the narrator in "The Daydreams of a Drunk Woman." The women in Lispector's fiction are imprisoned in what Ruth Silviano Brandão calls a "suffocating imaginary," a "discourse of the impossible" that holds hostage the "feminine word" with its figures of virginal maternity and maternal plenitude (1991, 105, 109). Brandão also argues that the suffocating imaginary goes beyond the maternal figures of Lispector's fiction. It also provokes Lispector's style, her preference for certain tropes such as irony, exaggeration, and distortion, in her effort to escape by making strange what Brandão calls the "grandiose projections of the desire for plenitude" (1991, 109).

While Lispector's description of her tongue as imprisoned seems to confirm Brandão's analysis, her description of her tongue as sequestered by her mother tongue calls it into question. Lispector spoke Portuguese with an accent that made her sound foreign, even Russian, by her own admission, and she was notably defensive about it (Marting 1993, xxiv). When asked about her mother tongue, she would reply that her first language was Portuguese and she was emphatic that she didn't speak any Russian whatsoever (Gotlib 1995, 65). Asked about her accent, possibly a trace of her parent's language, she would compare it to a French style of speaking and would sometimes say that it was the result of a biological defect. She would insist that it could be corrected without difficulty (Gotlib 1995, 114). But she never corrected this so-called defect. Instead she said she was too lazy to do so or said it would be too painful to correct it. "Many people believe that I speak this way because of a Russian accent. But my tongue is imprisoned. It is possible to cut it [free], but my doctor told me that it would be very painful" ([My translation], Gotlib 1995, 65).

Lispector's description of her sequestered tongue suggests a dilemma that does not contradict Brandão's account of her symbolic prison and semiotic escape through a Feminine mode of writing. But it does suggest that Lispector's account of her problem mixes together the two aspects (symbolic and organic) that Brandão keeps separate. And it also suggests that Lispector feels profoundly ambivalent about a condition that she poignantly associates with her mother tongue. At first, Lispector denies her mother tongue. She compares it to a mistake and even to an abject organic defect. But Lispector is also unwilling to free herself from her mother tongue. She refers to her first language as Portuguese, to her accent as French, and, emphatically, not as Russian. She describes her accent as a sound and as a biological defect, as a mistake that can be corrected easily, and as a prison that can only be escaped through a painful cut that she is not willing to make. The description of the sequestered tongue suggests Lispector's identification with a complex trace on her tongue and on her language. This trace is a mark made of both linguistic and organic material. It is both a denial of, and identification with, her biographical mother. But it is also an expulsion and an incorporation of something beyond Marieta, of something that is both too painful to cut and too painful to keep. It is the remaining trace of a symbolic maternal body. Indeed, the description suggests an ambivalent movement between cutting or expelling and keeping or incorporating. In her writing, Lispector figures this ambivalence toward the maternal body as a movement between hunger or binging and nausea or vomiting. This ambivalence is the hallmark of Lispector's writing.

Melancholy Witnesses

Recent work on testimony and witnessing might offer a productive way to interpret the ambivalence that marks Lispector's early stories and novel as two modes of melancholy witnessing to a matricidal limit-event. Following Julia Kristeva, Shoshana Felman, and Dori Laub, Kelly Oliver, has suggested that limit-events of modernity such as the Holocaust, slavery, and the World Wars, may have at their source a symbolic matricide that overdetermines the violent, oppressive, conflict-prone, and also suicidal make up of the modern subject. She argues that at the source of our violence and self-violence there is a matricidal economy that expels, excludes, and abjects the maternal body from language, the mother figure from sociality, the Kristevan semiotic from the symbolic, and our affect from our words. In the introduction to this book, I argue that this event without a witness produces what Kristeva calls implosive and explosive melancholy subjects, and what Felman and Laub call the related traumas of the survivor and the culture that emerges in the shadow of the limit-experience. Felman and Laub describe these traumatic states with the image of a black sun sucking the life out of the survivor and with the image of a black hole erasing our cultural memory. Both states set the conditions of possibility for the return of the repressed.

The growing gap between the melancholy forms of witnessing to this limit-event makes it difficult to stop its evermore catastrophic and liquidating effects. For these forms of melancholy witnessing to be positively transformed, there must be room for a third position, a position that troubles Kristeva's exclusive definitions of melancholy witnessing as male and female, heterosexual and homosexual. This is the position of transformative witnessing. It is a position that, as Oliver suggestively puts it, opens up the possibility of a response to the witness by creating and nurturing an inner witness to the limit-event. It is also a position that must be announced or called for by the witness in ways to which the transformative agent must be ever so vigilant. It is a position that depends on listening for the faint pulse of the maternal speaking body. It is a position that calls for the work of interpretation or working through the insistence of the witness to the matricidal limit-event on the impossibility of bearing witness to it. This is the position developed by Lispector in her stories and in her novel.

"The Crime of the Mathematics Professor" is the second to last story of *Family Ties*. In this story, a mathematics professor laments the loss of a dog he once owned and then abandoned. His melancholia takes the strange form of burying an anonymous and substitute dog in the place of the dog he lost. As the professor digs the grave, he remembers his dog, and the mysterious lesson that led him to abandon it: "It was on this point of the resistant reality of our two natures that you hoped we might understand each other. My ferocity and yours must not exchange themselves for sweetness; it was this which you were teaching me little by little, and it was this, too, which was becoming unbearable" (143–144). Man and dog are forever separated by their different natures, but this radical separation also produces an identical ferocity in both. The professor finds the point of mutual ferocity unbearable and in a moment of weakness he abandons his dog.

The professor cannot forgive himself for having done this, and he tries to mourn the dog and expiate his crime by burying another dog, a substitute dog. The narrator, however, describes the mournful act as a self-deception. She compares the burial to giving alms in order "to eat at last a cake which deprived the beggar of bread" (146). To bury the substitute dog is to feel a guilty hunger, and this hunger in turn returns the professor to his unbearable animal ferocity, a symptom of incorporative melancholy. Thus, the professor can no more sustain the mournful act of self-deception than he can his hunger and so he decides to exhume the dog and leave its dark and nauseating form exposed. The story ends when the professor pleads for a witness in an attempt to stop the repeating cycle that leads him from abandoning the dog, burying a dog substitute, to feeling once again the unmitigated hunger or ferocity that accompanies his identification with the lost animal.

In *The Apple in the Dark*, unlike the professor who pleads for a witness, Vitória angrily demands a witness to her forgotten life. She is the owner of an Estate or a farm somewhere in Brazil, and she hires Martim (the protagonist of the novel) who is running away from the law. Martim believes he has killed his wife and this crime has transformed him. Martim abandons his past life as a husband, a father, and a statistician and wanders the countryside alone looking for work as a hired hand. During his wanderings Martim meets Vitória who undergoes a similar transformation after betraying him. Silent about her life for 50 years, at the end of the novel she demands that her victim, Martim, bear witness to her life in a melancholy scene.

Vitória loses her father at a young age and the loss leaves her "raw and exposed" (287). Unable to face her new life, she instead feigns a voracious appetite for life, pretending that everything is perfect (287). She binges, eating big and heavy meals, abandoning her earlier taste for dry and simple food—an old eating habit that she associates with her father. She realizes that ugliness, rot, and death surround her, and she comes to identify love with the nausea that follows binging.

> She stayed there for a moment with an unraveled look, reduced to remembering herself alone as in the restaurant and how her mouth glowed at the sauce as it poured out, giving her a touch of repugnance; how in those days it had seemed to her that one had to exult in what was ugly; and then, with a feeling of nausea that she suddenly had not been able to separate from love, she had admitted that things are ugly. (294)

Vitória metaphorically binges for 50 years, until she confesses to Martim. On that day, something hidden in her reveals itself to her senses, something she compares to the smell of ripe fruit and old wine (303). Her body revolts and she abjects that internal rotting core, confessing to her life "as if she were regurgitating her soul" (285). After the confession, she comes to feel herself to be queen of a world where, in her own words, she can look into her entrails and no longer be surprised (303).

Despite her melancholy triumphalism, Vitória's confession is not as liberating as it might otherwise seem. Martim, for one, is both fascinated and repelled by the abject confession. On the one hand, Martim is fascinated by the darkness Vitória reveals and the abject core of her melancholy subjectivity. "The man looked with speculating eyes at the blouse of the woman which was wet around the armpits. He tried to turn his eyes away, but something in that dark dampness held his fascinated eye" (309). But Martim is also repulsed by her confession for, as the narrator puts it, "no one could live on the basis of having vomited or of having seen someone vomit" (289). Martim even feels threatened by the confession that consumes something inside him. "With the mouth of a leech, she was sucking something out of him, something that was not valuable, but which after all still belonged to him" (292). Thus, Martim experiences Vitória's confession not only as a cathartic abjection of traumatic material, but also as a repetition of the uncontrollable hunger produced by the original loss. Sadly, Martim's insight into the melancholy nature of Vitória's contradictory and dynamic confession remains beyond both their understandings, and he ends the chapter by describing Vitória as an "uncertain and menstruous woman" (308).

The novel then describes a repeating cycle that differs from the separations and reduplications of the short story, but which describes a similar act of melancholy witnessing. The novel describes a melancholy pattern of incorporation and identification that supplements (and perhaps complicates) the voracious hunger described in the short story with an equally reflexive and corporeal regurgitation. In a melancholy gesture, Vitória incorporates the loss that surrounds her after the death of her father. Martim experiences her confession as a repetition of the symptomatic incorporation. Similar to the mathematics professor, Vitória calls for another kind of witness that will end her melancholy cycle of suicidal incorporation and regurgitation. But while the witness is absent in her short story, here Martim, though present, is unequal to the task.

Explosive Rage

In the last story of *Family Ties*, we meet a character that resists a deadening instinct that has turned love into pacified and domestic ritual. Instead, the anonymous woman of "The Buffalo" looks for passion, for hatred, for an explosive sign of life in the incarcerated animals of a zoo, and in herself. She is alone, and faces a profound loss, but she is also unrelenting in her drive to expose the murderous prohibitions that surround her. As she walks through the zoo, the woman is dismayed to realize that she still feels love after her loss, that she wants to pardon, and like the imprisoned animals she also wants to resign herself to this feeling. Love becomes a cipher in this story for a deeper loss. Love covers over the loss of hate, of explosive rage in this woman. The unwanted love she feels, the love that spring brings to the story, and the love in the animals' eyes, covers over a violence that is prohibited to her, but, which she is intent on feeling nevertheless.

Exhausted by her frustrated search, she rests her head on the bars of the buffalo's cage and she finally feels an impersonal, objective, and cold resistance. She raises her eyes to see a black buffalo in the distance that either sees her or feels her presence. As she watches the buffalo, its "blackened shape of tranquil fury," she feels something white inside her, "white as paper, fragile as paper, intense as whiteness" (155). This "white thing," "viscous like saliva," then turns into "black blood," a "bitter oil" (155), and she is caught "in mutual assassination" with the buffalo (156). In "Dies Irae," one of her biweekly columns, Lispector describes her writing as a similar explosive rage, a growling organ language set against a world of semi-paralyzed humanity, and an angry and sad sound rooted in loss (1992, 53). In that essay, she also says a paradoxical "yes to life" against a world haunted by repeating, contaminating "no's," a world deaf to the "other non-existent life" that nevertheless wakes her up in the middle of the night.

The action of *Apple* is motivated by a similar explosive reaction against a deadened existence. In the second chapter of the novel, the narrator uses the image of growing dead organic matter to describe the effect of the world on its inhabitants. The people of the "luminous world," now set apart from the darkness of Martim's existence, are compared to the deadened fingernail that covers over sensitive fingers, protecting them from touching organic, corrupting matter. The impermeable nails are metaphors for an anaesthetized life that Martim wants to interrupt. They are covers against the mortal, material, and impure aspect of the body. But the nails also cut the link to the necessary life of the body, turning the inhabitants of Martim's world into insensitive and even dead beings giving handouts to beggars outside movie theatres, saying no to life, imitating life rather than living it.

And yet, the rage these characters feel against, and aim at, their anaesthetized world brings them back to an abject body: the dubious reward of their explosive and murderous rage. Martim's rage turns into a crime and crime sends him away from the light into darkness. It sends him traveling back to an earlier, to an archaic murder scene, an irreducible place before order, before names, and before the number one (335). He travels to a solitary land. His arms extended outward, he takes a great blind leap. He falls into an impossible place: a place "where the innards of a woman are a future child" (346). It is a place of horror: the place where identity threatens with collapse. It is the body in the grips of the maternal experience.

The setting of *The Apple in the Dark* is an allegorical space that suggests an archaic pregnant body. "The same wind sometimes carried the heavy, fertile smell of ripeness—which Martim, . . . recognized from the depth of centuries [as] the smell of fertility. The world had never been so large" (311). Martim undergoes an education of the body in this world. Inside this place, he becomes both a hunted and a hungry animal. In the dark, he blindly reaches out for nourishment to satisfy his hunger. He unlearns to think. He returns to a bodily way of knowing, of understanding. He gradually comes to know by heart, and to know in the skin. He slowly learns to touch what he wants with his clumsy hands. Without grasping, he learns to recognize with his sensitive fingers. By the end of the novel, he no longer asks for things by their name. His hands turn into the knowing hands of a blind man. In the mysterious central metaphor of the novel, Martim comes to understand like a hand that feels a pulsing vein (343).[9]

Knowledge of the body gives Martim access to a pulse at the center of the great lack within him; an impossibility that nevertheless asks to be felt (343). Martim says in calm despair "Our parents are now dead and it is useless to ask them 'What's that light?' It is no longer they, it is ourselves. Our parents are dead. When will we finally face up to that? Oh God!" (237). But the narrator tells us that to touch this lack is also to touch a pulsing and sustaining vein (356). By touching this lack, Martim appears to recover the pulse of his heart and the source of his life. If he is afraid of "a world without father or mother," he ends by facing "the fact that our parents are not dead. At least not completely dead" (35, 338). *The Apple in the Dark* challenges its readers to approximate and find life within an archaic loss, in Martim's catastrophe of identity after his explosive rage. The novel bears witness to what Kristeva has called the semiotic.

Implosive Paralysis

Sometimes, Lispector writes, she wakes up in a rage and is tempted to "do something once for all to burst this straining tendon which sustains my heart," but a "sadness" stops her from cutting this dark tie to her body (1992, 52, 53). Many characters of Lispector's fiction are possessed by a different melancholy from the explosive rage of Martim, the mathematics professor, and the female protagonist of "The Buffalo." Anita in "Happy Birthday" and Laura in "The Imitation of the Rose," instead suffer from a melancholy paralysis. Anita seems to be paralyzed by her anger, while Laura is paralyzed by her perfection. Despite their differences, both characters embody fantasies that are similar forms of containment of the abject maternal body. Like the courtesan–virgin of Pietro de la Francesca, or the virginal mothers of the Counter-Reformation, Anita and Laura become figures from a maternal imaginary that screens the troubling nature of the maternal speaking body.

Laura is the daughter of a clergyman. Educated at the Sacred Heart Convent, she fights the temptation to imitate Christ.[10] In fact, we meet Laura as she is recovering from a nervous collapse, after she unsuccessfully attempted to remove herself completely from her world and her family. But Laura's obsession with the exuberant happiness of a perfect existence is not only a side effect of a zealous religious education. The tranquil impassivity that Laura so desires is also a defensive reaction to her aging and imperfect body, a reaction to the "offenses" her body gives her. Her well-meaning husband, nevertheless unwittingly supports Laura's lethal fantasies by treating her like a child, by making light of her complaints, and by ignoring Laura's vexed relationship to her body. Laura confesses to finding herself slightly nauseating, and she is embarrassed by an "ovarian insufficiency" (58). The narrator sees a deeply offended spot produced by her lack of children in her eyes (54). But her husband simply shrugs away Laura's complaints about her imperfect body, dismissing them with jokes. To her complaints about her wide hips, he answers, "what good would it do me to be married to a ballerina" (60)?

One day, as Laura is preparing to go out to dinner with Armando (her husband) a bouquet of roses captures her imagination. She is overtaken by their translucent, minute, and tranquil existence where "one could sense the redness circulate inside . . . as in the lobe of the ear" (62). She is both afraid of, and tempted by, the perfect existence of the roses; and she struggles to send them away. But she cannot bring herself to let go of the roses completely. Giving in to their temptation, she gives the bouquet away but imitates "the roses deep down inside herself," becoming absolutely independent, detached, serene, remote, and luminous (69). By imitating the roses, Laura mysteriously creates within her imperfect body (marked by a profound lack or "insufficiency") an imitation of eternal life. If early in the story she had felt that "anyone who imitated Christ would be lost—lost in the light, but dangerously lost," by the end of the story Laura is indeed dangerously lost (55). She becomes a modern image of the crying Madonna. Her husband watches Laura as she leaves him, eerily transported by her fantasy of perfection into another world. "From the open door he saw his wife sitting upright on the couch, once more alert and tranquil as if on a train. A train that had already departed" (72).

Similar to Anita in "Happy Birthday," to the nameless protagonists of "The Daydreams of a Drunk Woman" and "Preciousness," to Anna of "Love," and to Catherine in "Family Ties," Laura is a master of self-abstraction. Inward-looking like many protagonists of Lispector's fiction, and identifying with a dark secret inner core, Laura abandons her body and her family. Similar to the maternal figures of Christianity, these women reify absence, and it is no surprise that the stories have been read as struggles with an existentialist void.[11] But it would be a mistake to ignore the distinct nature of this void, mystery, or core and to assume instead that it is the undifferentiated Nothingness at the center of the condition of Being that Existentialism would have us believe. Instead, many of Lispector's characters return to a living core that interpellates them and draws them in. Lispector calls this interpellation an annunciation, and refers to the core as a state of grace. "With pregnant souls we raise our hands to our throats with surprise and anguish" (1992, 210). She also compares this core to a pregnancy in *Family Ties* (31, 94), to a mysterious heartbeat (103–104), and to a murder (43).

The characters that pay heed to this call in Lispector's fiction suffer paralyzing, implosive, and depressive consequences. If only for this reason, it is difficult to accept Cixous's or Negrón-Marrero's categorical interpretation of this response as a necessary or an ethical aesthetic opened to otherness.[12] The characters are surprised by this call and are anguished by it (1992, 210). It is a call and an annunciation to a state of grace, and to a mode of knowledge that is both pleasurable and addictive to the point of forgetting life itself. Lori, the main character of Lispector's 1969 novel *An Apprenticeship or The Book of Delights* poignantly describes its pleasurable traps. "No, not even if it depended on her would she want to experience grace very often. . . . She would start wanting to live in a state of grace permanently. And this would represent an unpardonable escape from human destiny which was made of struggle, suffering, perplexity and joy" (1986, 99).

Lispector illustrates the defensive impulse that follows the annunciation with a gesture that repeats throughout her work. "And the Virgin, as if overwhelmed by the archangel's message, prophesying her destiny and that of future generations, raises her hand to her throat with surprise and anguish" (1992, 210). Anna in "Love" is similarly gripped by a convulsion (nausea in her case) when she realizes that her love must incorporate the richness and decay, the horror of the material world. Anna significantly compares this horror to being both "pregnant and abandoned" (43). In *The Apple in the Dark*, Vitória responds with a similar irrepressible movement to Martim's request for maternal forgiveness. She "clasped her stomach with her hands, there where a woman pains" and later looks at him "with the taste of blood filling her whole mouth" (352–353). The convulsions and anguish of these characters suggest their desire to expel the maternal position they are expected to occupy. "Oh, it was something impossible to escape from—sculptors had already done images of women and kneeling men, there was a whole long past of forgiveness and love and sacrifice, it was something from which it was impossible to escape" (1995, 353). The characters of Lispector's fiction resist the paralysis that follows from the lethal fantasy of maternal perfection and virginal plenitude.

Transformative Witness

In her column, Lispector writes "Today I am paralyzed and mute. And I try to speak, all that comes out is a mournful growl" (1992, 53). Lispector writes about an accident she suffered, that almost killed her, and landed her in the hospital with severe burns for three months.[13] She writes that a stranger would visit her in the hospital when she was bandaged up and immobilized. The stranger would sit down at her bedside, saying little or nothing. From Lispector's account, it appears she merely watched her, kept her company, and sustained her with her caring and loving presence. Later the mysterious stranger made herself known to Lispector as Teresa during a telephone call where she asked Lispector to stop writing for the newspaper so that she could develop the topics of her weekly columns into full-length books. Lispector continues to write as a response to Teresa's request. Lispector says that she wants to write in order to show Teresa that she is "not semi-paralyzed and can still say yes" (1992, 53).

Teresa's position is similar to the position of Cordelia in the short story "Happy Birthday." That story centers on a party that "celebrates" Anita's eighty-ninth birthday. Curiously, however, the birthday party rather resembles a wake. Indeed, Anita's family almost appears to celebrate her death.[14] She is barely alive to them, and they substitute her anticipated absence with an idealized image of motherhood. The idealization is defensive. It creates a safe space for the family, an unbridgeable gap that separates their future from her decaying body. "Each year the old woman survived vaguely represented another stage in the whole family's progress" (76). This gap also condemns the living Anita to a premature death. She is turned into a horrific and angry ghost by her family. And she returns to haunt them. She punctuates the story with raging and sudden awakenings, first when she aggressively cuts the cake with a knife, then when she suddenly spits on the floor, and finally when she angrily demands a glass of wine.

The narrator suggests that the old woman directs her anger at her family but also at life itself. Ana embraces her maternal role with a vengeance, and the premature death of her favorite first born son (Jonga) produces an implosive paralysis in her, turning her into a large, gaunt, and "almost hollow" woman (75). Curiously, her angry outbursts have the effect of bringing the family together. "The first cut [of the cake] having been made, as if the first shovel of earth had been thrown, they all gathered round with their plates in their hands . . . each reaching out for a slice" (79). Her angry outbursts are the dark ties that bind the family together. "The daughter-in-law from Olaria . . . had enjoyed her first moment of unison with the others when tragedy had triumphantly seemed about to unleash itself" (82). Together they turn the family into an impassive blind, deaf, and mute group: a family incapable of testifying to the matricidal violence that binds them.

One character, however, remains at the periphery of this deadly entrapment. Cordelia is Anita's youngest daughter-in-law. She is the mother of Rodrigo, Anita's favorite grandson, "the flesh of her heart" and possibly the wife of the dead Jonga (80). Unlike the other characters in the story, Cordelia never speaks. Instead, she sits and watches from the sidelines. She is a privileged witness in the story. The narrator turns to her several times with the question "And Cordelia?" as if she were a gauge to measure the events at the party. The character appears to be named after the third daughter of King Lear, a king who retires from the stewardship of his kingdom in a well-known suicidal gesture steeped in self-pity. In that play, Cordelia famously remains silent when Lear asks her to tell him that she loves him the most of his three daughters. Like her namesake, Cordelia is the only guest that appears to love Anita, and at the end of the party, just as the guests are taking their leave (deliberately and effusively garbling their words on their way out) Cordelia senses that this might be Anita's last birthday. Indeed, Anita appears to the rest of the family as a lifeless monument to powerful death: seated at the head of the table, she holds on to the tablecloth as if she were a queen at her throne, holding her scepter. But the loving Cordelia resists the temptation of Anita's implosive paralysis and explosive anger. Instead, she interprets Anita's angry outbursts as signs of life. Thus, Cordelia works through the phantasmagoria built around her mother-in-law. She is also able to demystify Anita's mute and severe anger in order to reach the meaning of Anita's closed fist. For a brief moment, the clenched hand opens to reveal faint and painful pulse, "a lacerating impulse." Cordelia holds on to this pulsation as a "last chance to live" (84).

For Cordelia, Anita's silent, ghostly, and haunting gesture comes from the very edge of life. It is an injunction to hold on to the edge, to the last chance, to the moment before succumbing to radical unintelligibility. It is not the triumphalist promise of an idealized existence. Instead, it is a call to life based on the lacerating impulse of that edge. For Cordelia, it is a call to witness a truth that cannot be seen directly. "Truth came in a glance," says the narrator (84). Cordelia briefly bears witness to the complex process that inters Anita, turning her into a living-corpse; "making death her mystery" as the closing line of the story reads (84). More importantly, she bears witness to a lacerating edge, to Anita's place between life and death. Cordelia cannot hold this position for long, and she leaves the party in terror, but she comes closer to that place than any other character in this book of short stories or in the novel. Without succumbing either to an implosive or an explosive form of melancholy, Cordelia briefly enters the space of transformative witnessing to matricide. "My tongue is imprisoned," says Lispector. Lispector's two works are painful attempts to find life within this prison, to inhabit the position of the transformative witness. In them, she leaves her mother tongue intact while translating its abject sound.

2

Maternal *Jouissance*: Elena Garro's *Recuerdos*

"And what about you, Nachita, are you a traitor?" She looked at her hopefully. If only Nacha shared her treason it would mean that she understood Laura, and that night Laura needed someone to understand her. Nacha thought for a moment, turned to watch the water that was just beginning to bubble noisily, and poured it over the coffee. The warm smell made her feel comfortable with her mistress. "Yes Señora Laura, I am also treacherous."

—Elena Garro, It's the Fault of the Tlaxcaltecans

In a letter to Emmanuel Carballo, Elena Garro reveals an intense ambivalence toward her first novel, *Recollections of Things to Come* (originally published in 1963). After she finished writing it in 1953, she first tried to burn it, and then hid it in a trunk for many years. The letter suggests that even after the novel was recovered and published, Garro still invested it with negative associations. Garro claims that others were responsible for its rescue. She writes that the novel was published only after the intervention of Octavio Paz, who also gets credit for finding it (Muncy 1990, 23–37). She resists remembering the prize awarded to the novel, as if denying any involvement in its recognition by its readers, and she insists that "nobody wanted it" (Carballo 1986, 505).[1] And yet, the fact that she hid the three hundred pages of abject text also contradicts her apparent wish to destroy the novel. Her ambivalence is further evidenced by her admission that she was not only responsible for burning parts of it, but also for rewriting it. "The novel was half burnt. I put it in a stove in Mexico and Helenita Paz and my nephew Paco rescued it from the fire. So I had to mend it" (Carballo 1986, 504).

Garro hints at the cause of her ambivalence when she says that she hid the novel together with poems to a love that almost killed her. "I put away the novel in a trunk, together with some poems that I wrote to Adolfo Bioy Casares, the insane love of my life that almost killed me, even though today I realize that it was all a bad dream that lasted many years" (Carballo 1986, 504). By hiding the novel together with love poems to the famous Argentinean author of *The Invention of Morel* (*La invención de Morel*, 1953), she suggests that at some level *Recollections of Things to Come* was an attempt to celebrate the love of her life. But Garro suggests that her novel and poems also might contain a love that almost killed her; and that by hiding the novel she was trying to protect herself from it: "a bad dream that lasted many years."

Indeed, Garro associates *Recollections of Things to Come* with a first love. She describes the novel as "an homage to Iguala, [and] to her childhood" (Carballo 1986, 504). Garro was born in the city of Puebla, in the Mexican state by the same name, but she grew up in Iguala, Guerrero, a village she describes as her hometown: "My home was in Iguala, Guerrero" (Carballo 1986, 496). So, the love that troubles Garro is also a love that one might call archaic. It is both the "love of her life," her love for Bioy Casares, and a love for her place of origin, the town of her family home, Iguala. Moreover, it is her first love in at least two contradictory ways. On the one hand, it is her first love in so far as it is now lost. But on the other hand, it is also her first love in so far as it is primordial and as such recurs insistently, surviving as it does in the shape of a bad dream that lasts many years. Could it be that this archaic love takes the shape of the half-burnt novel that Garro compares to "old" torn clothing? Is it a feeling that Garro cannot dispense with, but is also a feeling that returns as a "treacherous memory" that threatens to lead her and her characters to "a dark inlet where nothing happens" (1991, 192).[2]

Garro's writing is similar to this troubling memory in that she also "inverts the order of events" (192). In fact, her novel tampers not only with the chronological line but also with our sense of a stable place. But Garro also manages to transform and change this troubling memory of a first love. After trying to destroy the novel, she patches it together again, emphasizing that she has to mend it.[3] On the one hand, the image of mending the novel suggests that the result is imperfect. The image suggests that the novel reveals its imperfections through the patches that cover the places where it was burned or destroyed. But on the other hand, the image also conveys the need to revisit and repair the love at the center of the novel. In the end, the writer of *Recollections of Things to Come* emerges as a thrifty seamstress, a servant, who mends the rips and gaps of a long lost love, remembering it, and transforming it.

Matricide and Maternal *Jouissance*

What is this first, lost and haunting love?[4] The novel begins with the voice of memory describing the death of the mother, a figure who occupies the center of the narrative. Ana Cuétara de Moncada, the matriarch of the Moncada family, is the last family member to die, and the novel begins on the day they take her body away.[5] "The day they came to take away Señora Moncada's body, someone—I do not remember who—closed the front door and dismissed the servants. Since then the magnolias have bloomed with no one to see them, and weeds have covered the stones of the patio; spiders take long walks across the pictures and the piano" (5). The loss of the mother in the narrative has both creative and catastrophic consequences. The death of Ana Moncada marks the beginning of the novel, but it also signals the end of the Moncada family home and the end of chronological time. "Time does not pass there: the air stood still after so many tears were shed" (5).

The death of Ana Moncada brings about the loss of an archaic joy, a troubling pleasure that drives the social dynamics of the town and the psychic economies of the characters at the center of *Recollections of Things to Come*. (Indeed, this troubling and troubled association with the maternal figure could be said to drive the narrative itself.) Moreover, the death of Ana Moncada brings about the end of two different approximations to the troubling maternal pleasure at the center of the narrative, a pleasure that I associate with maternal *jouissance* following the work of Kristeva.[6] Ana's death brings about the end of both a feminine and a masculine mode of identification with this maternal pleasure.[7] In this chapter, I argue that these identifications either remember and repeat this troubling pleasure or else struggle obsessively to master it.[8] I also claim that Garro represents these identifications in her novel as processes of subject formation that are particularly insufficient and even dangerous for women.

From a psychoanalytic perspective, these two approximations to maternal pleasure result in distinct collective fantasies and social organizations that are limited and dangerous in different ways. On the one hand, Garro suggests that the obsessive mastery of maternal joy produces phallic mothers, fetishes, and cults in her novel. But she also suggests that something is lost as maternal *jouissance* recedes into the background. Patriarchal subjects emerge handicapped by a melancholia that eventually consumes them. On the other hand, Garro also suggests that these fantasies and social organizations are particularly catastrophic to women. Indeed, she suggests in her novel that the defensive mastery of maternal joy through the fetish and the cult is relatively more effective than the repetition of unmediated maternal pleasure. The fetish and the cult produce the figures of Universal Motherhood, which can phantasmatically contain maternal joy, and isolate the male ego from its catastrophic effects if only temporarily; but the daughter enjoys no such haven. Instead, she is forced to identify with a maternal figure that puts the emerging female subject in an impossible situation. She is either socially reduced to play a maternal role, or she is branded a sexual outlaw, a traitor.[9] In short, no matter the mode of identification, the choice is always catastrophic both to the daughter's identity and to the identity of the mother. Either they take on the mythical role of the phallic mother, which erases their individuality, or they become incestuous figures without identity.

The death of the mother at the beginning of the narrative interrupts both of these modes of identification, and sets the stage for a different approximation to maternal *jouissance*. The interruption would seem to allow Garro to offer examples of both types of maternal identification in her novel, and sets the stage for a figurative antidote to the plight of female subjectivity. Other Latin American and Latina writers studied in this book pick up this suggestion. But Garro also struggles to move beyond the matricide that marks the beginning of her novel, and the descriptions of lethal maternal identifications that immediately follow. Garro also tries to remember the archaic love that is maternal joy and pleasure through the figure of Gregoria Juárez, an alternative to the lethal choice faced by the female characters in the novel. Gregoria is the racialized maternal figure that ends the novel on a disturbing note; and her writing on the stone at the end of the novel can be interpreted as interrupting the violence with which the protagonist abandons herself to her troubling pleasure. From this perspective, it seems significant that Gregoria (along with the other servants of the household) survives the death of the mother at the beginning of the novel. Indeed, she might even be the nameless character who closes the door and dismisses the rest of the Moncada's servants. Be that as it may, one thing seems fairly clear: Gregoria begins the process of disinterring and transforming the maternal corpse that starts the novel and startles the reader from the beginning of the novel.

Ixtepec as Allegory

Recollections of Things to Come tells the story of a terrorized town in the south of Mexico and of the desperate efforts of its loving sons and daughters first to save it and then to leave it. Francisco Rosas rules Ixtepec. He is a *caudillo* (the preternatural strongman of Mexican political life) set in the mold described by Octavio Paz.[10] He is also a lovesick *caudillo* who is haunted by an invisible reality and by an archaic lost love. Rosas projects this impossible love on to Julia Andrade, his increasingly unhappy and alienated lover. As Julia becomes more distant, Rosas's hold over the town becomes increasingly violent. By the time Julia finally betrays him and runs away with an out-of-towner half-way through the novel, Rosas has become an unbearable and arbitrary tyrant.

Rosas exacts his revenge on the town during the second half of the novel, and his revenge coincides with the moment in Mexican history when the state imposed a ban on religious worship.[11] Rosas is implacable and he carries out his orders by closing down the town church and by persecuting and trying to kill its sexton and priest. Ana Moncada, her two sons (Nicolás and Juan) and her daughter (Isabel), together with other pious women of Ixtepec, organize a town celebration to distract Rosas and rescue the endangered men. But the Indian lover of one of Rosas's lieutenants betrays the plan and the whole town suffers the deadly consequences.

Faced with the failure of the plan and with the inability of Ixtepec to protect itself or to protect them, both siblings choose a radical escape route. Though Rosas gives Nicolás the opportunity to escape, the young Moncada insists on being executed. Isabel betrays her family in turn and becomes Rosas's lover. At the end of the novel, she magically turns to stone just outside of town, staying away but close by. Self-violence, death, or a suicidal love is the siblings' ambivalent way out of Ixtepec. There are both social and intimate reasons for their desire to escape their hometown, or their place of origin.

Ixtepec is a thinly veiled allegory for Mexico after its revolution (1910–1917). The novel suggests that the violence of the Mexican Revolution fragments and destroys both the country and the town. Francisco Rosas's murderous tyranny echoes Mexico's postrevolutionary upheaval. Town and country live through a civil war in which prominent figures including Francisco Madero, Emiliano Zapata, Venustiano Carranza, Pancho Villa, and Alvaro Obregón are assassinated, while several thousand Indian peasants are murdered at the hands of antiagrarian reform forces. Mexico also lives through a fragmenting power struggle between religious and secular groups. A revolutionary government competes for power with a class of Creole landlords and with powerful church officials.

This struggle for power similarly splits Ixtepec and turns it into a war zone. It leads Rosas to close down the church, to burn the statue of the Virgin of Guadalupe, and to install government offices in the town's sanctuary. It turns the Moncada children against him with fatal consequences. They join forces with their mother, who is part of the counterrevolutionary matriarchs of Ixtepec. The strong-willed and daring trio of *Doñas* (Ana Moncada, Carmen Arrieta, and Elvira Montúfar) plans and executes an audacious but ineffective conspiracy against the tyrant. Finally, the struggle isolates and benefits the incestuous landowning Goribar family. Lola and her son Rodolfo Goribar consolidate their power as they watch the destruction safely from the sidelines (249).

The Labyrinth of Solitude

This allegorical interpretation of the novel also suggests an intimate explanation for the stifling nature of the town, and points to a different dimension of the struggles that surround, constitute, and destroy Ixtepec. Garro wrote her novel only three years after Paz's first edition of the highly influential *The Labyrinth of Solitude*. She finished it while still married to the famous Mexican poet and essayist. Not surprisingly, *Recollections of Things to Come* is a similar study of the familiar patterns and of the psychic economy responsible for the Mexican psyche. Like that famous essay, the novel diagnoses the ills of Mexican society by simultaneously focusing on history and on what Paz calls myth. Like Paz in his essay, Garro brings to light an invisible, buried, and intimate reality, a family history or drama that both affects and is affected by historical events.

Briefly, Paz wrote that the troubled Mexican psyche and the vexed nature of his history are both the cause and effect of an original wound, expulsion, or separation. For Paz, this original wound is the universal condition of man that affects the Mexican psyche in a particular way. It leads him to engage in a violent servant mentality or psychology whose axis of power and main symptom is an insistent and nihilistic negation of his origins and future. A "fear of being" makes the Mexican engage in what Paz calls stubborn negativity. This negativity is the solitude that defines him and leads him to unwittingly repeat the original wound.

The wound is the result of the split of a mythical and divine pair for Paz. It is not a biological mother–child dyad. It is, instead, a fusion of abstract opposites that together make up the radical heterogeneity that Paz calls "pure life." For him, the constitutively passive and open mythical body of the Eternal Feminine and of the Archaic Mother allows the violent penetration by a similarly archaic and eternal but active and aggressive Father. This passive, eternal, and open Mother also allows the separation from a now humiliated and resentful child. The child then avenges himself by denying his mother, calling her La Chingada or La Malinche of Mexican myth, by adoring a violent and murderous Father through figures like the mythical *caudillo*, and by identifying with the figure of the humiliated Son: Jesus Christ or Cuahutémoc.[12]

But the Mexican that Paz imagines also hurts from this wound and cannot help himself as he pines nostalgically for a return to idealized origins. Such nostalgia is for Paz a defensive return to the protective maternal womb, figured by the passive Virgin of Guadalupe. According to Paz, Mexicans find themselves caught in between these two contradictory movements, the movement away and toward their incestuous origin, a departure from and a reunion with a mythical time. For Paz, the Mexican labyrinth of solitude is the constant movement between the separation from, and the return to, a mythical incestuous state of pleasure.

Informed by careful readings of Freudian psychoanalysis, Paz traces the Mexican's servant mentality, his cult to the Virgin of Guadalupe, and his obsession with La Malinche to the same origin: an archaic lack or wound through which plenitude has escaped. La Malinche is an attractive and repellant fetish that disavows or represses this lack or wound. It is similar to Freud's fantasy of the maternal phallus.[13] The Cult of the Virgin of Guadalupe, on the other hand, sublimates the threat and idealizes the lack. Paz argues that both La Malinche and the Virgin of Guadalupe allow the necessary separation from that original maternal enigma and the entrance of the Mexican subject into language, representation, and solitude.

According to Paz, however, these psychic operations are not only insufficient but they are also potentially dangerous. In a later essay, Paz suggests that left unexamined these operations are unable to stop the return of the repressed void or wound at the origins of the subject. Written as a response to the infamous violence of October 1968 in

Mexico City's central square, "The Other Mexico" suggests that the archaic forces of that wound flow right back into history. The essay is a postscript to *The Labyrinth of Solitude*, and it posits that these forces can be and must be "dissolved" by critical or aesthetic practice. "Criticism is the imagination's apprenticeship in its second turn, the imagination cured of fantasies and determined to face the world's realities. Criticism tells us that we should learn to dissolve the idols, should learn to dissolve them within our own selves" (1985, 325). Like psychoanalysis, this practice should expose and suture the psychic wound. Paz aims to close the constitutively open and mythical maternal body through criticism and poetry.

Body and Agency

Much of Garro's novel echoes Paz's account of this "invisible reality" at the origins of the Mexican psyche: the separation from, and reunion with, an incestuous maternal experience. The enigmatic experience is also at the origins of Garro's deployment of mythical figures such as La Malinche and the Virgin of Guadalupe. Moreover, Garro remembers the maternal experience in her novel in a way that reminds us of the therapeutic function of the aesthetic practice according to Paz. And yet, Garro's account of these figures in her novel also differs from Paz's in at least three significant way. First, Garro suggests that the origin of the threat repressed by the treacherous Malinche (and sublimated by Guadalupe) is not the constitutive lack of Freudian psychoanalysis. Instead, she suggests that this archaic danger is the overflowing plenitude and archaic state of pleasure that might precede this so-called lack or maternal *jouissance*. Moreover, Garro suggests that far from being a passive and mythical state of union, this state of fusion has an organic aspect that invests the maternal body with a powerful agency. Finally, Garro suggests that her aim is not so much to dissolve the dangerous force of maternal agency but to enable it by transforming it.

Alberto Manguel tells a funny anecdote that highlights Garro's emphasis on the powerful effect or agency of the female body in this archaic state. "The Cuban novelist Severo Sarduy told me of a visit to Elena Garro when she was still married to Octavio Paz. Paz was working on the theory that the theme of incest, one of the ground themes of Mexican literature, was inherited from the Indians. He had been talking about this for several hours when at last Garro stopped him. 'Instead of all this theory,' she said, 'why don't you try it out for once?

I'll call your sister, and we'll all three head for the bedroom.' With a hurt look on his face, Paz got up and left. 'Now he'll never know if it's in his blood, will he?' Elena Garro asked Sarduy" (Manguel, 159).

The anecdote describes Garro cruelly humiliating Paz in front of a fellow writer by irreverently challenging him to put his conceptual abstractions to the test. The story is both a successful joke and an interesting criticism of Paz because it anticipates his visceral response to incest. Paz can theorize all he wants about the incestuous relationship of the Mexican with his archaic Mother but when it comes to imagining incestuous physical contact with his sister he cannot bear the idea. He leaves the room looking hurt. Garro follows his exit by ironically insisting on the importance of knowing the body, and by sarcastically pointing out the material limits of Paz's knowledge. "Now he'll never know if it's in his blood, will he?" Garro's emphasis on blood and on the female body contradicts Paz's abstract ideas about the Feminine. Her cruel and provocative evocation of the naked body of Paz's sister (and its obviously powerful effect on him) contradicts his insistence on the passive nature of the Feminine and his idealization of incest.

Significantly, Manguel's account of Sarduy's anecdote also reduces the maternal agency back into a castrating force by turning Garro into a phallic mother who infantilizes Paz. Indeed, his account of Garro's perverse cruelty and treachery should give us pause. Garro's treachery was the object of popular lore and her fetishization had a terrible effect on her private and public life.[14] But *Recollections of Things to Come* bears the story's humorous emphasis on the female body and on its powerful agency. Indeed, this emphasis on the maternal body's agency constitutes the basis of Garro's account of the intimate history or drama that shapes Ixtepec (and by extension, Mexico's collective consciousness.) This history is the conflict between a matricidal and a catastrophic identification with the maternal body.

The Maternal Outlaw

The related tragic stories of Ixtepec and Isabel Moncada (Ana Moncada's rebellious daughter who turns into stone at the end of the novel) remind the reader of the biblical tale of Sodom and Gomorrah.[15] In that story, the divinity famously strikes down the two sinful towns with fire and brimstone while sparing Lot, his wife, and two daughters. Yaweh warns Lot and his family not to look back as they escape from the town. Lot's wife, however, ignores His warning.

She looks back and is severely punished for breaking His law. He famously turns her into a pillar of salt. The destruction of the towns and of the maternal outlaw leads to a new order. Without the mother, the daughters take advantage of Lot, make him drunk, and have sexual relations with him. Two new tribes are born from the incestuous union between Lot and his daughters.

Recollections of Things to Come tells a similar cautionary tale but to a very different effect. Rather than associate women in general, and the maternal in particular, with sin, the novel instead emphasizes the historical, social, and biological dynamics that combine to turn the maternal into an outlaw: a phallic phantasm and an irresistible force outside the phallic economy. The Mexican Revolution plays an important part in this transformation. On the one hand, it is a terrific force responsible for the death of the men in the novel, and for the apparent empowerment of a matriarchy that nevertheless still abides by the patriarchal law. On the other hand, the Revolution is also a liberating force that offers the women of Ixtepec a historic way out of that law and its traditional roles for women. And Garro also suggests in her novel that the Mexican Revolution also screens the revolutions of a body. More specifically, the haunted characters of Ana and Martín Moncada suggest that behind the Mexican Revolution there is also the memory of an archaic and maternal cycle of creation and destruction.

Ixtepec is a matriarchal town under the oppressive rule and watchful eye of a patriarch who is also haunted by the memory of an impossible incestuous reunion (as we will see shortly). All the mature men of Ixtepec are dead, insane, or weak and under the influence of their wives and mothers. Not only are the three the matriarchs of the town who plan and carry out the single rebellion against the tyrant Rosas, but the traitor who betrays their plan is also a woman, a treacherous Indian woman, who is in love with a soldier. In short, it is a town where women appear to be in charge of all three of its battling social groups.[16] But Ixtepec is also a town under patriarchal law, and the powerful mothers that step outside of this Law are severely punished or destroyed, not unlike Lot's wife in the biblical tale of Sodom and Gomorrah.

Revolutionary violence in the novel substitutes the wrath of the divinity in the biblical story, with Rosas and his henchmen in the role of the avenging angels. Similarly, the Mexican Revolution is an overwhelming force that strikes twice in the narrative. First it "finishes" the northern town of Francisca Cuétara, Ana Moncada's mother; and then it destroys the Moncada-identified southern town of Ixtepec.

The revolution imprints forever its haunting destructive force on the memory of the inhabitants. The destruction of her mother's house in the North is forever fixed in Ana Moncada's memory. "A smell of burning firewood and a frigid wind coming in through the cracks of the window mingled in her memory with the room where a candle blinked. The Revolution had finished her house in the north. And now, who was finishing her house in the south?" (232).

But the Mexican Revolution is also figured in this novel as a force that is both maternal and liberating to women. Ana is clearly haunted by its violence, but she also identifies with its music and natural rhythms to the point of waxing nostalgic about them. At one point she wishes for a similar catastrophe to hit the town of Ixtepec. " 'Oh, if only we could sing "La Adelita" again!' the señora said to herself, and was glad that they had blown up the train from Mexico City . . . 'If we just had a good earthquake!' doña Ana exclaimed, angrily jabbing her needle into her embroidery" (31). Ana desires the return of its violent force. Moreover, she nostalgically associates the revolution with her lost mother, with a natural violence (the earthquake), and with the rhythmic sounds of "La Adelita," a famous revolutionary song about a lost woman who must be found again. To her dismay, Ana gets her wish, and the lost mother, the revolutionary rhythm, and the lost woman of the song combine into a force that returns to destroy her and her town. By the end of the novel Ana also becomes the object of its complex violence. She becomes the unwitting instrument that brings about Rosas's implacable revenge and she dies a victim of its violence.

The Other's Heartbeat

Recollections of Things to Come also describes the incestuous identification that results when the power of the maternal outlaw is left unchecked. The pleasure from the maternal experience outside the law of the Father, outside of social and symbolic restraints, is both a promise and a threat in this novel. It promises an intact moment of plenitude and it threatens individuality and speaking subjectivity. Its promise, however, can prove to be catastrophic. Martín's nostalgia, or his lingering memory of a close and unmediated relation to his mother is an example of an incestuous type of identification that allows a hysterical return to a paradise of petrified time. It promotes the return of a monstrous first love that protects him even as it frustrates his entrance into society and language.

Martín Moncada (Ana's husband) suffers from a profound and debilitating sadness that makes him "careful with his fellow men, and [takes] from him the last vestige of efficiency" (16). More specifically, Martín's moral weakness leaves him unable to decide what to do with his children during a time of family and national crisis. He wavers between sending his sons to work in the mines far from town and marrying off his daughter and sending away all the children as Félix (the family's Indian servant) wisely recommends. While Martín wonders what to do with his children, Félix performs a strange ritual, an "old custom of the house" (13–14). At nine o'clock every evening, he gets up from his stool, goes to the clock, and unhooks the pendulum. Martín and his family then undergo a mysterious transformation. "Without the ticking, the room and its occupants entered a new and melancholy time where gestures and voices moved in the past" (14). The defensive ritual separates Martín from "calendar" time and from the uncertain future.

The ritual also triggers a series of memories in Martín, memories of his mother that appear to suspend (or cover over) his painful decision to separate from his children. "Sitting under the bougainvillea he felt possessed by a white mystery, as certain to his dark eyes as the roof of his house. 'What are you thinking about, Martín?' his mother asked" (14). The memories have an uncanny effect on Martín. They remind him of his terror when he was five years old and "feeling that he was lost in an unfamiliar place" (15). Indeed, Martín's memories are radically nostalgic, and the narrator describes them as "unlived" experiences.[17] The description suggests that Martín never had these experiences but yet their memory still petrifies him. In fact, these unlived memories appear to be both sensory and a challenge to the senses. They are described indirectly, in metaphor, and dream-like images similar to those used to describe Ana Moncada's memories. Martín "hears" them as a "form of silence," "smells" them as "unknown odors" such as "the aroma of burning torch pine," or the "smell of a cold, resinous wind" (14–15). He "sees" them as the consoling "white mystery" and the petrifying "violence" of a bougainvillea bush. Finally, the experiences are "unlived" in that they appear to be anterior to life itself. They remind Martín of the experience of death, which the narrator describes as listening to the body of the other. "When he was very small, when his father bounced him on his knee, it made him uneasy to hear the other's heartbeat, and the memory of an infinite sadness, the stubborn memory of man's fragility, even before they had told him of death, left him overcome with grief, unable to speak" (16).

Martín's unlived memory of man's fragility blends with the certainty of his future death, making for the temporal paradox suggested by the novel's title: *Recollections of Things to Come*. The future holds the promise, and the threat, of man's fragility, the death at the center of these unlived memories for Martín. "As he grew older, his memory reflected shadows and colors of the unlived past, which blended with future images and acts, and Martín Moncada always lived between those two lights, which in him became one" (15). Living between the past and the future is also to live unlived memories for Martín. By living so, he opens a multitude of spaces and times between himself and the future, a multitude of displacements that consoles Martín by appearing to stop time. "He never said to himself, 'Monday I shall do such-and-such a thing,' because between that Monday and him was a multitude of unlived memories" (14). But to live unlived memories is also to inhabit the very death those unlived memories are meant to postpone. Martín's defensive memories suspend time and the future, shield and protect him from deciding what to do about his children, but they are also made of the same deadly stuff from which he is shielding himself: a form of silence, an unknown odor, the bougainvillea, or the other's heartbeat.

The novel's paradoxical temporal scheme and Martín's entrance into this paradoxical time have been the objects of some critical attention (Kaminsky 1993, Méndez Rodenas 1985, Messinger Cypess 1990). Critics have emphasized the problem of sexual difference at the core of the novel's temporal paradox but they have missed the ambiguous role that the maternal rhythms and cycles seem to play in this temporal paradox and in the disturbing memories that seem to trigger the paradox.[18] Martín's entrance into this time has an ambiguous effect on him that is identical to the simultaneous terror and consolation associated with the memory of the mother under the bougainvillea tree. His eerie memory combined with the sound of the other's heartbeat, suggest the rhythms and cycles and the shocks and joys of the maternal experience that Ana Moncada compares to a violent earthquake and revolution. These combined memories suggest Ana and Martín's entrance into the aporia of the maternal experience: the simultaneous identity and loss of identity at the core of what Kristeva calls "Motherhood's impossible syllogism" (1980, 237). As such, Martín's "infinite sadness" would be the effect of a nostalgic and problematic embrace of this terrifying state: the incestuous identification with a solid temporality or monumental time.[19]

Martín's identification with monumental time reminds the reader of Paz's similar idealization of the incestuous primal scene in *The Labyrinth of Solitude*. By presenting Martín as a weak and emasculated patrician, Garro seems to criticize such idealizations. Through his jumbled and disconnected visions, Garro points to the catastrophic effect of an unmediated identification with the maternal. At the end of the novel, Martín not only loses his family but also his hold on reality. Garro sounds a similar warning against abandoning oneself to fantasies of violent maternal revenge. Ana Moncada also dies a victim of the revolutions she herself desires and perhaps unwittingly unleashes on her town. Thus, through the characters of Martín and Ana Moncada, Garro suggests that an unmediated identification with the maternal can lead to a deadly self-violence.

A Closed Mouth

The incestuous dyad of Elvira Montúfar and her daughter Conchita is a similar study of the tragic consequences of an unmediated identification with the maternal. But in their case, Martín's fear of the present and nostalgic idealization of the past are compounded by an identification imposed from the outside, by an oppressive patriarchy that levels all women into the same inferior category and reduces their language to worthless speech. *Recollections of Things to Come* suggests that this added social component intensifies the incestuous identification and leads to radical female societies that nevertheless have the opposite effect to the one they intend. Hoping to free women from the oppressive social system that excludes and silences them, these secret and anti-symbolic societies paradoxically result in a more radical internalization of the very same effects they seek to contain. Like Conchita, their members are haunted by an intense silencing melancholia.

Elvira is the widow of Justino Montúfar. While he was alive, she was the object of his violent oppression. She endured a silence imposed on her by her husband and his father who believed in the inferiority of women and found women unbearable "because they talk too much" (169). The men repeat the popular Spanish dictum "A closed mouth gathers no flies!" (*"En boca cerrada no entran moscas"*) until it silences and almost obliterates Elvira, turning her into a "blind woman" (23). Similarly, Conchita grows up to be stoically quiet. During a heated conversation about the Indians of Ixtepec, Nicolás Moncada defends them and earns the admiration of Conchita who says melancholically to herself, "How wonderful to be a man and to be able to say what one thinks!" (22).

After Justino dies, Elvira becomes a quiet but formidable (even monstrous) force in the town. Compared to a black widow spider at the head of an army of insects, she weaves a powerful web of gossip around Julia Andrade. In public, she murmurs lethal and categorical (if choked) statements against the town's Indian population. "I don't have a single drop of Indian blood!" (22). She becomes (with her daughter) the head of a secret female counter-society responsible for masterminding and executing the ill-fated plan to distract Rosas, and free the church officials, keeping stubbornly silent when the military search her house looking for the missing sexton and priest. Elvira never remarries and wishes her daughter would never marry either, saying to herself "Not all women can enjoy the decency of being widows" (24).

In private, Elvira speaks "for the simple pleasure of speaking" as if to compensate for the years of silence to which her husband condemned her (23). But the idleness of her chatter takes her to uncharted and dangerous territory that upsets her daughter and has fatal consequences. A master of doublespeak, Elvira urges her daughter to marry Tomás Segovia even as she symbolically emasculates him. On one occasion, Elvira's excessive chatter and double-talk allows her daughter (and the reader) a glimpse of the sexual current underlying Elvira's close relationship with her daughter, and Conchita is clearly taken aback. " 'The flesh of blondes must be very sugary. I think it must taste rather like custard . . .' 'Mamá!' 'What does Tomás Segovia taste like? He's a brunette, you know' " (116).

Conchita resents her mother's strong influence over her but she cannot bring herself to openly challenge her or leave the household. But when Elvira's relish for scabrous jokes, gossip, and idle chatter, finally betrays her, Conchita is virulent enough to get her revenge against her mother by silently echoing the words of her father. Elvira's metaphorical blindness is not only the result of sexual oppression. Racism also prevents her from seeing her Indian servants as human beings, and she invents and details the plan against Rosas in the presence of Inés, her Indian servant. Unbeknownst to her, Inés is in love with one of Rosas' henchmen and she betrays the plan. When Conchita discovers the betrayal, she releases her accumulated fury on her mother. " 'Do you know what that means?' the girl asked, looking sternly at her mother" (252). By the end of the novel Elvira chastises herself, violently echoing her husband's words against her and against all women. " 'How right your father was. How very right! A closed mouth gathers no flies.' And Elvira, exhausted, retired to her room" (253).

The Fetish and the Cult

Ana's death, Martín's insanity, and Conchita's melancholia are all catastrophic effects of an incestuous type of identification with the maternal that Western culture has traditionally associated with femininity or with a feminine type of subjectivity.[20] As we have seen so far, this identification is based on an unmediated proximity or overwhelming sense of debt to the mother, it repeats the maternal experience, and it can take the form of an idealized plenitude, or of a silencing form of hell.[21] The cult to the Virgin of Guadalupe and the myth of La Malinche are also effects of identification with maternal joy or pleasure, but it is a mode of identification traditionally associated with masculinity.[22] The cult and the fetish do not so much repeat the maternal experience as they repress or idealize its shock and pleasures. Briefly put, the cult and the fetish are the effect of the attempt to master the maternal experience by metaphorically erasing or killing the mother figure and by replacing her with idols or goddesses.

Fetishes and cult figures are coherent events. This coherence is explained by the fact that fetishes and cult figures either repress or idealize the anti-symbolic aspect of the maternal experience. They contain the force that Kristeva sometimes calls the semiotic. They contain it in the double sense of that word. They either push the semiotic back into the unconscious or they push the semiotic out into objects clearly separated from the self. A living and speaking subject emerges as the incestuous reunion of mother and child recedes into the background or is displaced into an object. But the subject often emerges from these psychic operations seriously handicapped by a virulent melancholy. Ultimately, these phantasmatic masculine fetishes and cults are just as insufficient and dangerous as the dreams and returning memories of feminine incestuous identification, as Garro suggests in her novel.

Although Ixtepec appears to be under the brutal government of Francisco Rosas, the town's inhabitants rightly suspect that the tyrant is actually under the spell and power of Julia Andrade, his lover during the first half of the novel. The nature of Julia's power over the General is the object of many discussions throughout the novel but remains a mystery to the people of the town. They can see, though, that she leaves him irremediably sad (73). Rosas' sadness appears to be the result of a curious amnesia. He seems to have no memory and no past. He is a revolutionary without a cause, rejecting the ideals and power of the Mexican Revolution. Instead, he longs for something he can't remember, something that the narrator describes as "ardent and perfect" (73). But Rosas is also cursed and haunted by the past of the other. He does not own this past, and is instead possessed but it. He is haunted by Julia's past, by her memory of her past, and this memory has great power over him. "That shining past in which the luminous Julia floated in mis-shapen rooms, jumbled beds, and nameless cities" (73). Rosas feels "in the presence of a besieged city with its invisible inhabitants eating, fornicating, thinking, remembering" when he is with Julia (73). This lost and haunting past, the powerful memory of the other, its "ardent perfection," its nightmarish loss of self in a fantasy of erotic excess, all combine to suggest to the reader that Rosas, like Ana, Martín, and Conchita, also faces the impossible syllogism of motherhood or maternal *jouissance*.

Rosas turns Julia into the fetish that contains this perfection: her repulsive and attractive, erotic and embodied memory. She becomes the external object of Rosas's obsessive love and hate. Julia, as the fetish of Rosas, contains erotic excess in two related ways. She helps Rosas to disavow, deny, and push back the memory of an original and archaic wound or lack of self. She also pushes this memory out of his body and into hers. She becomes what Kristeva has called an "internal seal" that keeps Rosas safe from the vexed memory that haunts him. This is the mysterious power of the fetish, and its mystery results in an intensely ambiguous feeling. It is no surprise that Rosas is as afraid of Julia as he is afraid to lose her.

The novel, however, also suggests that the solution provided by the fetish is only temporary. Ultimately, the fetish leaves Rosas on unstable ground. It produces an intense feeling of jealousy in him, which turns him into the melancholy and violent butcher of Ixtepec. Just as he displaces the troubling memory into a fetish, he also displaces the effect that Julia has on him onto the inhabitants of the town. But this displacement also proves to be only a temporary solution, and the insistent jealousy leads him to kill Julia and to destroy the fetish, all of which only succeeds in intensifying his melancholy. If incestuous identification repeats the maternal experience, fetishistic identification returns to its hidden goddess. After killing Julia, Rosas substitutes her with another love object in the novel's second half. Isabel Moncada, however, also turns out to be a temporary and insufficient fetish.

Lola Goribar's self-sacrificing motherhood is another version of a fetishistic identification. But if Rosas displaces the memory of "ardent perfection" or maternal *jouissance* onto a fetish, Lola instead displaces it into a matricidal cult of the Son. Lola and her son enjoy a life of plenitude and material excess in the novel, but Lola also lives in constant fear of divine punishment, perhaps because her incestuous relationship with her son appears to be intact. " 'We never know what God has in store for us,' and this thought terrified her. There was a chance that God might want to make her poor; and to guard against the divine will, she accumulated more and more wealth" (60). She defends herself against the punishment of poverty by combining fanatical piety with feverish accumulation of capital. Afraid of a radical kind of poverty, she becomes a strict self-denying Christian. "She was a very good Catholic; she had a chapel in her house and heard mass there. She always spoke of the 'holy fear of God,' and we all knew that the 'holy fear' referred only to money" (60). She piously worships the divine Son of God, and accumulates wealth, all in the name of her son. But Lola's love for her son also includes self-denial and sacrifice. She denies herself pleasures, even as she accumulates wealth for Rodolfo. "We admired the young man's gabardine suit and the diamond brooch that sparkled on doña Lola's bosom. He bought his clothes in Mexico City and the servants said he had more than a thousand ties. On the other hand, his mother always wore the same black dress, which was beginning to turn green at the seams" (60).

La Malinche and the cult to the self-sacrificing Virgin of Guadalupe are the counterparts of Rosas' fetish and Lola's motherhood and cult to her son. One way of reading the novel is as a struggle between these two phantasms that are collectively hated and loved. The "good" people of Ixtepec hate Malinche and worship the Virgin of Guadalupe, while the "evil" soldiers desire the first and destroy the images of the second. Either way one looks at the struggle, both figures repress or idealize the ambiguous love for, and love of, the mother. The phantasmatic battle between good and evil also excludes the possibility of a sexualized maternal body. The conflict reduces motherhood to one of two exclusive options: either it idealizes the sexual body of the mother into a de-corporealized divinity, or it represses maternal desire in the figure of a demonized, mythical female outlaw. The combined operations that result in the fetish and the cult exile motherhood from the ambiguous ground of desire.

Between a Rock and a Hard Place

The fetish and the cult complement one another, and their interdependence is best represented in the novel by Ana, and by her reaction to the betrayal of her daughter, Isabel. Ana chastises her daughter's treacherous desire for Rosas, even as the narrator points out her own disturbing pleasure. The reader wonders whether Ana might in fact chastise her daughter in order to cover-up her own troubling desires. Does she worship the Virgin of Guadalupe in order to separate herself from the troubling desire represented by the mythical Malinche? This possibility does not seem lost to her daughter, who rebelliously and tragically embraces the troubling pleasure that her mother seems to contain.

Isabel's response suggests that the very repetition of these self-sacrificing operations have the opposite effect to the one intended on the daughters. On the one hand, Isabel's mastery over her own troubling desires and pleasures requires revisiting them, and this repetition only intensifies them as we see later. On the other hand, Isabel reacts defensively against her mother's attack on her individuality (represented by her desire for Rosas). And her defensiveness comes as no surprise, since Isabel stands to win nothing by following her mother's self-sacrificing example, unlike Rodolfo, for example. Instead, Isabel stands to lose her own voice and her self (similar to Conchita) if she becomes an acolyte of her mother's cult of Universal Motherhood. Damned if she joins maternal power, and damned if she doesn't, Isabel is caught between a rock and a hard place. Like the mother, the daughter is prevented from occupying the vexed place of pleasure and desire.

The love that Isabel feels for Rosas reminds her mother of her own "shameful" love for Martín. In fact, Ana's shame results from the maternal nature of her pleasure, a source, she fears to be the origin of her daughter's own desires. " 'She's bad! She's bad!' Ana Moncada shouted, feeling that she herself was guilty for her daughter's evil conduct. She looked apprehensively at her bed and heard herself saying, 'Coming?' that was the word Rosas had used when he called Isabel, and her daughter went away with him in the darkness" (233). Ana suspects that her daughter's liveliness, beauty, and "evil conduct" are but forms of her desire in conceiving Isabel. Ana is reminded of the prescient words of her midwife, which confront her with her own pleasure. " 'You can see that she was conceived with pleasure!' she heard the midwife say as she bathed the newborn Isabel" (233).[23] Ana's shame of her pleasure leads her to punish her "unknown and unrecognizable" desire by angrily silencing herself. "From her bed, Ana blushed. Martín looked at her with desire . . . She bit her lip with anger . . . She swore to amend her ways, and did" (233).

The death of the male members of her family at the hands of revolutionary violence compounds this act of self-discipline. Together, revolution and self-discipline transform Ana into one of Ixtepec's powerful trio of matriarchs. But if they are all powerful mothers, they are also mothers who unwittingly destroy their own brood. Ana is indirectly responsible for the death of Nicolás, and she also manages to turn Isabel against her and her town.[24] Ana expects Isabel to stay at home, while her brother is encouraged to leave and work in the mines of Tetela.[25] Isabel is similarly expected to be the faithful guardian of the interests of the town, and she must remain close to the values of the Moncada family. Above all, she should not express a desire for Francisco Rosas, the judge and executioner of her town and her family. But the attempts to turn Isabel into a pious, self-denying, and faithful daughter backfire, perhaps because they approximate Isabel to a troubling desire manifested by all the children at the beginning of the novel. " 'We want to see the Virgin naked!' Isabel and her brothers shouted as they came running into the church. Taken by surprise, the women quickly covered the statues. 'Why, children, your eyes must not see these things!' " (9).[26] Curiously, when Ana urges Isabel to pray to the Virgin Mary as a way to silence her desires, the prayer also seems to put Isabel in a vexed state of meaningless ecstasy with her mother. " 'Pray, be virtuous!' they said, and she repeated the magic formulas of prayer until they broke up into words, with no meaning" (25).

Given the threats that accompany the daughter's proximity to the mother in this novel, it is not surprising that the parental decision to keep their daughter at home has a strong and paradoxical effect on Isabel. She responds to being circumscribed to the domestic space, and to the bonds imposed on her and her mother with an embrace that is violent in its intensity and in its effect. Unlike Martín, who nostalgically enters the split and paradoxical time of maternal *jouissance* looking for a haven of security and safety, Isabel splits herself in two as a way of detaching herself from her parents. "She detached herself from them, moved backward to change herself into a point lost in space, and was filled with fear. There were two Isabels, one who wandered through the rooms and the patios, and the other who lived in a distant sphere, fixed in space" (25). Similar to Martín, Isabel enters the aporetic flux between unlived memories, between the memory of past and future death. Also similar to Martín, Isabel's entrance into this temporal flux both consoles and fills her with fear. But unlike Martín, Isabel enters this paradoxical temporality in a self-consuming anger. Martín compares her anger to a furious meteor that leaves Isabel trapped in a living hell. " 'A meteor is the furious will to flee,' [Martín] said to himself, and remembered the strangeness of those burned-out masses, flaming in their own anger and doomed to a more dismal prison than the one they had escaped from. 'The will to separate oneself from the Absolute is hell' " (26).

Isabel's spiteful abandon to the temporal fantasies of incestuous identification also leads her away from her mother and her family. Her love for Rosas not only affirms her will to escape from her town and from her family, but also from her mother. Her love affirms her individuality, her separate identity from all of them; and she assumes her love also with a similar vengeance. From this perspective, the love of Isabel for the tyrant of Ixtepec is an aggressive alternative to self-erasure. From this perspective, she falls in love with him because Rosas makes war on the matriarchal and incestuous town, because he destroys the home that is a prison to Isabel. Indeed, her love for Rosas radically demystifies the mother's law. Her forbidden love brings down the protective walls of Martín's imaginary shelter, and reveals the true farcical nature of the plans of the matriarchs against Rosas. Isabel's words after the failure of the maternal plot suggest as much. " 'I always knew what was going on. Nicolás knew too. Since we were children we have been dancing on this day.' Isabel's words caused landslides; layers of silent earth erased the subterranean world where Martín Moncada went in pursuit of his memory" (201). Her words are similar to an apocalyptic meteor that levels all the compensatory fictions within her reach. Given this interpretation, it is not surprising that Isabel should escape when the plan to fool Rosas backfires.

The daughters of Ixtepec are unlike their mothers in that they suffer the limiting consequences of maternal identification, but do not enjoy the benefits (neither in prestige, power, nor position) of the disciplinary (or phallic, if you will) role of their mothers. So, Isabel is caught between two alternatives, both of which are lethal to her individuality, and neither of which carries with it any compensating benefits. She is caught between Universal Motherhood and her troubling desire. Instead of moving between these extremes, Isabel seems petrified by them. "Here I shall be, alone with my love, as a memory of the future, forever and ever" (288–289). In this sense, Isabel and Lot's wife share the same fatal destiny. They are both examples of the Patriarchal Law that fixes women to the boundary of the social. They are the tombstones just outside town from which (and against which) emerges the new social order.

But Isabel is also very different from the nameless wife of Lot. She rebelliously affirms her identity. "I always knew [she thunders] what was going on" (201). She signs her own death sentence, but also brings the town down with her in a final willful act of self-definition. Her tombstone defiantly reads "I am Isabel Moncada, the daughter of Martín Moncada and Ana Cuétara de Moncada, born in the town of Ixtepec on December 1, 1907. I turned into stone on October 5, 1927, before the startled eyes of Gregoria Juárez. I caused the unhappiness of my parents and the death of my brothers Juan and Nicolás. When I came to ask the Virgin to cure me of my love for Francisco Rosas, who killed my brothers, I repented and preferred the love of the man who ruined me and ruined my family" (288).

Gregoria's Lesson

Recent accounts of the ending of the novel interpret Isabel's rebellious petrifaction as the slave's reaction to oppression. According to these critics, Garro's Isabel Moncada, and Isabel's servant Gregoria Juárez, can only protest the injustice done to them by inscribing in stone the exclusion of women from history (Franco 1989, 138), or by "[gouging] the familiar woman's story of sexual crime and punishment into Isabel's flesh-made-stone" (Kaminsky 1993, 93). I would like, however, to highlight another dimension to the novel's ending by giving Gregoria's role a more hopeful interpretation. Isabel may be turned into a stone, but the complex meaning of the words inscribed on this stone has escaped many readers.

On the one hand, the words are clearly an ethical epitaph. Like these critics suggest, the words stand as a testimony to the impossibility of the lives of the women of Ixtepec, and by extension of Mexico. As I suggest above, the stone is a monument to the impossible choice between a desire outside the law and Universal Motherhood, a choice between equally deadly modes of identifications with the mother: either incestuous or fetishistic. From this perspective, the monument stands as a memory to Isabel, a victim to an impossible choice.

But Gregoria Juárez's writing on the stone also opens a metaphorical space that is different from either the stifling prisons, or the erotic cities, of incestuous, or fetishistic, identification. "The stone, the memory of my suffering, and the end of the fiesta of Carmen B. de Arrieta are here. Gregoria put this inscription on it. Her words are burned-out fire-works" (288). Gregoria's writing ends the novel, and the narrator compares it to burned-out fireworks, which comparison suggests the remaining trace of both suffering and joy. And Gregoria's writing is a troubling note indeed. It is neither the melancholy silence of incestuous identification, nor the mournful prayers of fetishistic identification.

It is neither a mode of repression nor idealization. Instead, it is something between words and stone, and as such it transforms words and stone, joy and suffering. On the one hand, Gregoria composes her words out of the petrified material of Isabel's body, transforming the stone into symbols. On the other hand, her inscription adds symbolic depth to the otherwise hermetic surface of Isabel's petrified body, giving a reading, an interpretation, to Isabel's petrifaction. Gregoria's inscription troubles Isabel's petrifaction. It interrupts the effect of her impossible choice. From this perspective, Gregoria is also a figure that stands in between remembering and forgetting, embodying their combined promise. She both brings news of Ixtepec to Isabel, and later will tell the story of what happened to Isabel to the town. But she also knows how to induce forgetfulness to "escape from anger or from an enemy" (121). If only for a second, Gregoria's prayers and chewing allows Isabel to forget both Rosas and her past (286).

When asked about characters like Gregoria in her works (characters who are women of an age, a race, and a social class different from her female protagonists, characters who appear to be old, Indian, and are also servants in Garro's fiction) Garro emphasizes the lesson they teach. "I was raised among them. I believe that they are all inspired in women that I knew. And yes, I do believe that there is much fatality in them, that Mexican women are deeply marked by fatalism. But they educated me. Parents give us a traditional education. But servants teach us a more profound lesson" (Ramírez 2000, 56). Gregoria's inscription at the end of the novel perhaps can be interpreted as one of these lessons. As such, Gregoria's inscription changes the voice that begins the novel. It promises to transform the haunting memory that makes this novel so difficult to read, and that often obscures the voice of its narrator.

Gregoria is like Nacha, the old Indian servant in Garro's story "It's the Fault of the Tlaxcaltecans."[27] In that story, Nacha is the only character who understands Laura, its suffering protagonist. Similar to Julia and Isabel, Laura is fetishized and turned into a version of La Malinche. Similar to Julia and Isabel, Laura embraces and is disturbed by an incestuous desire. Laura looks to her Indian servant for a way out of her impasse, and like Gregoria, Nacha doesn't let her mistress down. When asked if she is a traitor (*"traidora"*) like her, Nacha answers affirmatively but also ironically. While agreeing with Laura, Nacha nevertheless changes the meaning of her mistress's melancholy and self-hating words. *"Traicionera"* also means to be a traitor, but it carries an added meaning in Spanish. The adjective "*traicionero*" is often found as part of the stereotype for the indigenous subject, who is said to be sly, lying, a back-stabber, and untrustworthy. "They are such traitors" Elvira Montúfar says at one point of Garro's novel when she refers to the Indians of Ixtepec. In this context, the word "*traicionera*" would seem to be a conscious deployment of a racial slur, which emphasizes that the position of Nacha is singularly vexed. It is both different and similar from that of her mistress "Doña" Laura. But this does not prevent her from helping Laura. Instead, Nacha offers Laura the support she needs, while subtly reminding her of their incommensurable positions.

The scene dramatizes an ethical, respectful, and disturbing act of linguistic displacement and translation. While preserving the general meaning of the word "traitor" in Spanish, the translation by Nacha also displaces its signifier from a political to a moral and racial register. By revealing the racial slur contained within the original term, the translation makes visible the unsettling and promising perviousness of language. By substituting the word "*traicionera*" for "*traidora*," Nacha troubles the identification that Laura seems to calls for, while acknowledging her familiarity with Laura's feminine position. Nacha's translation screens (hides and reveals) the uncanny language of women in Garro's fiction.

Recollections of Things to Come ends on a similar uncanny note. Gregoria's inscription interrupts the simultaneously catastrophic and matricidal tone of the novel's melancholy words, and brings a will-to-meaning back to this difficult novel. Like Nacha's translation, Gregoria's inscription is an enabling and supporting space not only between fetishistic and incestuous maternal identification, but also between idealization and repression, between matricide and catastrophe. This space is not the traditional home of the m/other—it is not a dystopic enigma (unintelligible, pure noise) or a utopic ideal (Universal Motherhood, the Good Savage). Neither is it the traditional residence of the fortified self. Instead, it is a troubling space of distance from both. It is an epitaph and an enigma that calls for analysis and interpretation.

The Mother Tongue: Rosario Ferré's Ec-centric Writing

Speaking an other language is quite simply the minimum and primary condition for being alive.

—*Julia Kristeva,* Intimate Revolt

In an interview with *The New York Times*, Rosario Ferré says that she felt detached enough to explore the death of her mother in her writing only when she began to write in English and could distance herself from the event. Before that, she says she found it impossible to deal with the subject because it was taboo in her native Spanish (Navarro 1998, 2). A year later, she describes her novel *Eccentric Neighborhoods*, written in English, in the same terms. The novel is "an attempt to lay bare the relationships between mothers and daughters," an attempt, she says, to come to terms with the death of her mother in 1969 (Burch 1999, 31). In both interviews, Rosario says that writing in English gives her a psychological distance that allows her to write about that loss. She describes writing in English "as if another person were writing" (Navarro 1998, 2). Writing in that other language makes her feel like a spectator, less vulnerable. She suggests that language is a contradictory boundary. On the one hand, it can be a distance between the writer and its subject and here she compares English to a brush that mediates between the painter and the canvas. But on the other hand, language can also be a porous space of passage. Language, she says meaning Spanish (her mother tongue), "is like your skin" (Navarro 1998, 2).

Rosario's reflections on writing, language, and maternal loss are provocative and paradoxical. In the interviews, she emphasizes the liberating effect of changing the language with which she writes. She compares changing language to shedding one's own skin. She describes the facilitating psychological distance gained by writing either in English or by substituting her mother tongue for another language. This language is not immediate and natural like one's own skin, but artificial like a brush, a tool, and an instrument of mediation, and representation. But she also claims that English allows her to come closer to a prohibited subject: the death of her mother. Paradoxically, she can write about her mother's death only by shedding (or losing) her mother tongue and substituting it with another language. She can write about the loss of her mother only by changing skins.

Rosario's reflections on writing, language, and loss raise three important questions. First, what makes writing about the loss of Lorenza Ramirez de Arellano difficult and even impossible for her? (In other words, why is writing about the death of her mother a taboo? And, who or what makes it a taboo?) Second, why is it so important and even necessary to write about that loss, to challenge that taboo? And third, what are the implications of challenging that taboo in another language? In other words, what does it signify that Rosario can write about the loss of her mother only by displacing her mother tongue, by losing her collective language, or by shedding her own skin?

Dies Irae

In her book of essays *Room for Eros (Sitio a Eros)* published in 1980, Rosario listens for an echo of the wrath that haunts her own writing. It is a sound, a ferocity, a furious tone also found in the writings of other women writers; an irascible sound that recalls the Wrath of the Lord in Mozart's *Requiem*. She appears to follow Walter Benjamin who aims "at the single spot where the echo is able to give, in its own language, the reverberation of the work in the alien one" (Benjamin 1968, 76). Rosario translates into Spanish the wrath, the fury, and the irascibility of Mary Shelley and George Sand, Virginia Woolf and Sylvia Plath, and Anais Nin and Erica Jong. She describes wrath both as a timeless negative light and as a spectrum of energies and wavelengths. She compares it to a constant radiation from an indefinite place that she sometimes locates outside, in the heavens, and at other times finds inside the body. She compares the radiation to both an ancestral universal force that gives birth to the stars and to a fever that turns the body livid and eventually kills it.

The book is a collection of thirteen essays. They are for the most part brief pieces, which Rosario has described as a series of *exempla* meant for young women (1992, 108). The longest essay in the book, however, is an ambitious piece that reaches far beyond the "example." Entitled "The Kindness of Wrath" (*"Las bondades de la ira"*), it is part literary analysis, part literary history and biography, part psychological study, part social criticism, but most importantly it contains within it a poetics of anger. In this polemical and unapologetic essay, Rosario demystifies women's writing, shattering the myths surrounding, imprisoning, and silencing its voice. She traces back the laws governing the irascible artistic creation of women writers like Sylvia Plath, Alfonsina Storni, and Delmira Agustini to an opaque acoustic and visual source: a phonographic negative, the inverse, the opposite, the other side of their own voice and light.

> A modern evaluation of literature must admit that the feminine writer does not exist: the feminine voice, the feminine style, traditionally identified with intuition, with sensitivity, with delicacy, with subtlety, is but another myth created by men. If we had to call anything at all feminine, it would have to be the voice of those terrifying works by women that we place over our recollections; the negatives of our own voice. And if [women] identify with these terrifying works it is because they are the exact and faithful transcripts of the truth. This is so because the experience of women is cumulative, and it travels through time in constant radiation, like the bands of light of the spectrum, which we read to uncover the composition of the heavens. (1980, 99) (All translations are mine unless otherwise noted.)

A negative placed on a positive, a silence imposed on a voice—these are Rosario's opaque and jarring images for the principle of writing. The origin and source of writing is an essential prohibition, a fundamental censorship, a primary exclusion, a terrifying negativity through which and against which voice, presence, light, and even joy express themselves. In her feminist essay, she identifies this primary censorship with the patriarchal order. She argues that the patriarchy builds myths around women writers like Sylvia Plath that are meant to tame and repress the threat contained in their writing. They are fortifications of the male self against the perceived threat of an other displaced outside its boundaries, and perhaps outside all boundaries. But male critics unwittingly unleash upon themselves the very forces they seek to keep outside their fortified egos by calling the work of women writers like Plath a hallucination, a hypnotic trance. By turning the irascible nature of their writing into the myth of the eternal feminine, male critics turn into monsters the very same forces they seek to silence and contain. Rosario reads Mary Godwin Shelley's novel *Frankenstein* (originally published in 1818) as one example of this return of the repressed as a repugnant, mutilated monster, a living cadaver that explosively incorporates the homicidal wrath produced by the prohibition, repression, and exclusion of women and their experiences from the patriarchal social order.

And yet this repression is but a more manageable form of a deeper, far more troubling experience. In the first essay of her collection ("The Authenticity of Women in Art," "*La autenticidad de la mujer en el arte*"), Rosario distinguishes between two fundamental problems that affect women: the problem of her external, material freedom, and the problem of her internal, psychological freedom. Of the two, Rosario finds that the second is by far the most difficult and dangerous. The internal problem is in turn divided into two parts: the psychological penalties or sanctions imposed by society on women through tradition and customs and the penalties or sanctions women impose on themselves in the form of an anger turned inward: a terrifying guilt.

> But the problem of the internal liberty of women has a second dimension, much more painful than the first. The law or social mechanisms need not punish the woman who tries to break the conventional patterns of behavior. More efficiently than any tribunal, she herself exacts her own punishment: she feels terrifyingly guilty. (1980, 14)

In her book, Rosario argues that guilt is anger turned inward. The anger turned against the external forces that threaten material freedom produces cathartic works like *Frankenstein*, works that sublimate the prohibitions into vociferous symbols of struggle aimed at unjust social forces. But the inwardly turned anger also produces irascible works aimed at the self, which could even lead to suicide. Paradoxically, this anger turned inward can also be a form of liberation for Rosario, even if it doubles as an extreme form of self-repression. Similar to Sigmund Freud, Rosario's reading of Shelley and Plath suggests two different modes of a psychological drive in language, two modes that are analogous to Freudian sublimation and repression. According to Freud, sublimation is a dynamic process that redirects sexual energy to a new nonsexual aim such as sublime artistic production. Repression, on the other hand, is an operation of the psyche that does not so much divert as it repels sexual energy, confining it to the unconscious, which it helps create together with thoughts, images, and memories. While Rosario's description of *Frankenstein* suggests the work of sublimation, her account of Plath's poetry suggests a mode of repression that aims the wrath at the psyche. According to Rosario, Plath's poetry seems to be the more lethal of the two. It exposes and creates a psychic depth that can either shelter dreams and memories, or can lead to suicide.

Rosario describes Plath's poems as photographs of the absence of light, comparing them to a projection, an x-ray, or a negative of Plath's feelings. These negatives reveal a composite force both developing and already inside of her. The negatives reveal this force with a paradoxical "meridian clarity," perfect poetic pitch, mastery of technique, and blinding Phoenix-like light. This composite of negative and positive forces is the complex and profound origins of a tyranny, echoed and doubled by the patriarchal order. This tyranny is at times described as a vampire of light gradually substituting and sucking the light out of Plath. Indeed, Rosario explicitly compares it to the maternal experience and more specifically to the newborn's involuntary end of the mother's private experience and internal freedom. At other times, this composite of light and darkness, of shelter and self-destruction, is compared to an ancestral force: the tyranny of the mother and of her maternal forebears—the cumulative experience of women.

Both timeless and historical, existing inside and outside the body, Rosario translates and metamorphoses this ancestral impulse (a composite force, sound, rhythm, music, that is both timeless and historical, and is located both inside and outside the body) into her own writing. This sound reverberates in every poem and short story of her first book, *Pandora's Papers* (*Papeles de Pandora*) published in 1976. An angry, rebellious, and irascible book, it explicitly locates itself within a feminist discourse and outside patriarchal order. Sometimes imprisoned, sometimes excluded by patriarchal fortifications, the sound of this book assaults its walls. Indeed, it is an eccentric and wandering voice, traditionally embodied in male figures similar to the despondent and melancholy Achilles of *The Iliad*. Achilles is a character consumed by his anger at the loss of his beloved Patroklos and a faithful servant of the angry will of the Gods, fuming and pacing outside the walls of Troy, biding his time, wandering through eccentric neighborhoods before his final penetrating assault.[1] A similarly melancholy figure but turned monstrous, and transformed into an infiltrator, the voice of

Pandora's Papers seeks to reappropriate an authenticity, a sincerity, a truth taken from her, a truth hidden behind the masks and walls built by forces including but not limited to the patriarchal social order.

> you leave throwing absinthe through your turpentine eyes
> forever drinking the sap of the Frangipani
> circling the walls
> dragging your hair grown of indifference through the dust
> while spears pierce your shadow on the asphalt
> spilling mouthfuls of pieties (*camándulas*)
> around the fortified walls. (1976, 135)

The irascible voice of *Pandora's Papers* is pious and devotional but stops at nothing. It is as if the wrath of the Gods was here translated into the voice of a fanatic *cum* blasphemer. The voice of the book discusses all, visits every subject from religious worship and pure love, to incest and coprophilia, from cleanliness to defilement, voicing and shattering pieties, conjuring and dispersing taboos, thereby crossing and scattering boundaries created to dominate and tame its impulse. *Cuncta stricte discussurus* (To judge all things strictly).

But the voice in *Pandora's Papers* does not stop at the boundaries of the patriarchal order, as does the voice in *Room for Eros*. It also looks within itself, within its own fortifications. It implacably burrows within itself to find and to reveal, the core of its wrath, the cause of its internal prohibitions, and the source of its self-inflicted wounds: an ancestral force of essential ambiguity and in-differentiation. This source is an impulse that predates the division into object and subject, into native and foreigner, and mother and progeny. It is an energy that loves and hates indiscriminately; a composite force made of desire and repulsion. It is the power of horror at the origin of lack and want that Julia Kristeva calls abjection (1982, 32–55). The subject in Rosario's book emerges as a wrathful voice out of abjection. Indeed, it emerges as a furious sound, an angry rhythm, and an ungrammatical language through abjection. Wrathful and ungrammatical, yes, but it emerges nonetheless as a voicing, as a subject who speaks and lives in speaking.

Nowhere in the book is the complex and paradoxical struggle of the speaking subject with this ancestral impulse clearer than in the story "The String of Pieties" (*"El collar de camándulas"*). Its fluid narrative voice tells a barely recognizable story of intrigue, murder, and vengeance. Despite its opaqueness it is a familiar story. It is the story of a traditional family where the characters perform their familiar roles of implacable *pater familias*, silenced and dutiful wife–servant–daughter, obedient and rebellious sons, and lovers. The story ends with Armantina, the daughter–servant–wife delivering a lethal blow to the stomach of the family; an apocalyptic gesture many times repeated in one form or another throughout Rosario's book.

The word "pieties" doesn't convey the breadth of meanings of the original "*Camándulas*" of the title. My dictionary reads: feminine noun (1) Formal variant of Camáldula (from a town in Italy were the monastic order bearing this name was founded); (2) A rosary of one or three decades; and (3) Figuratively—hypocrisy, artifice, and cunning. Perhaps an ironic reference, a screen, or a mask of Rosario's self (a Rosary of one or three decades), "*Camándula*" is doubleness itself. Is it *Camándula* or *Camáldula*? It is difficult to hear the difference. Whatever the word, its dual meaning signifies doubleness, artifice, and cunning. Indeed, the word is a mirror of doubleness, and can serve as a metaphor for the book: a string of mirrors reflecting and transform-ing, translating (similar to Benjamin's broken vessel in his famous essay on translation) the original language, the mother tongue, into a monstrous sound. Most importantly, however, *Pandora's Papers* translation of this archaic rhythm simultaneously transforms the mother tongue into writing and the ancestral impulse into a speaking subject.

Like the ungrammatical force of the undifferentiated string of words that make up the story's seemingly untranslatable paragraphs, the resistance of the word "*Camándulas*" tests what Benjamin called the hallowed growth of languages: the principle of revelation that ulti-mately sustains the communicative function of language. The creative impulse of the Gospels ("In the beginning was the word") finds its match in the apocalyptic language of "The String of Pieties," which similar to the wrath of God itself, dissolves the very spirit of its age into the glowing ashes of the dead. *Dies irae, dies illa / Solvet saeclum in favilla* (Day of wrath, that day / Will dissolve the earth in ashes).

Language in the story not only does away with the laws of grammar and syntax, it does away with person, gender, and identity itself. Who speaks? It depends. It changes. Sometimes it sounds like Armantina speaking, sometimes it sounds like the repulsive father, sometimes it is the pleading or the swearing voice of the sons, sometimes it is the automated voice of the airport loudspeaker, the impersonal language of the mass media, and sometimes the melancholy collective voice of the family. The circular story ends as it opens with a recipe for a

Venezuelan cake, a recipe for a poisoned *ponqué* that sounds like a timeless and eternal litany.

> [B]eat the yolks one hundred times the whites one hundred times separately until they can be cleanly cut by a knife then a generous amount of sap of Frangipani now I cut the pieces symmetrically even and I distribute them all around everyone pricks them with the end of their forks they take it to their mouths now it is the palate desegmenting the skins of bats the noise made by the utensils exploding as they fall on the plates . . . (1976, 132)

Armantina inherits the lethal recipe, made with the venomous sap from the Frangipani tree (also called in Puerto Rico wedding bouquet, or *ramo de novia*), from her mother, the void and hole at the center of the story. The mother stops speaking after her husband, Armantina's father, kills her lover, when she falls madly in love with him. To be more precise, the mother is haunted and falls under the spell of the eerie sound of his monstrous guitar. Described as a sleeping cockroach, the guitar slowly awakens and moves its "wings." "It devoured all at once all the leaves and all the birds that flew-by quickly overhead as if an endless sound came out of his fingertips screeching over the cold curve of an aluminum cover as if over the arch of another universe" (1976, 123). The mother dies and the family falls apart; but her physical death is incidental. Before she dies, before she becomes silent and mute, before her husband and her family break her, the mother has already left. She has become both a vestal officiant of, and a sacrificial offering to, a force stronger than her husband, her family, and her society combined. "She was wild she left home all the time before they broke her back and when they broke it was already too late she had already jumped the fence and had fearlessly given her skin over as a target" (1976, 128).

The mother absconds to the chords of the cockroach guitar. Seduced and charmed by its sound, the mother internalizes and incarnates the sound of the guitar. She metamorphoses into a monster, dead and alive, speaking a self-censoring language, a mother speaking in tongues. She becomes the mother tongue: a living hole, the mirror image, and the echo of the undifferentiated abject. She is transformed into a sacred witness to the beginning and into the poet and prophet of the end. She incarnates in one impossible figure both David and the Sibylls. *Teste David cum Sibylla* (As David and the Sibyl bear witness). She whispers secret incantations while making her famous *ponqué*.

"Blowing the words through the end of a hole in the throat . . . speaking deliberately slowly mouthing words that nobody hears . . . with her head to one side listening and always giving shape to squalid words that stuck to her lips like shells" (1976, 122).

Armantina memorizes these squalid words and abject sounds to which the mother is drawn and to which the mother becomes subject: a ventriloquist, a medium for the sound of the abject. They are indeed the negatives of Armantina's voice and of all voice or speaking subjectivity. They are negatives that Armantina places over her recollections. By the end of the story she has appropriated her mother's recipe, her litany of sounds, in effect the mother tongue.

Armantina repeats the recipe while making her mother's famous *ponqué*, but she will not identify with her. Indeed, she separates from her to the point of making sure her mother will never return. Unlike her mother, Armantina refuses her role as both witness and prophet and as messenger and ventriloquist of the archaic sounds inside and outside of her. Instead she takes for herself the double role of judge and ax of the executioner. She appropriates her mother's tongue while reversing its direction away from herself and her psyche, out into the world. Like a convex mirror she refracts the mother tongue back to its origins. By so doing, she does not so much prophecy the end as she brings it about.

The end of the story is also the silence at the end of time. It is not so much a glimpse and a taste of Judgment Day as its convulsive performance. *Quantus tremor est futurus. Quando judex est venturus* (What dread there will be / When the Judge shall come). In so doing, Armantina explores one way out of her predicament. She imprints her agency, she exacts her judgment both on and through the voice of the abject, both on and through the mother tongue. In this way, she assures that the ancestral sound will not return the same. Armantina emerges from this struggle with the mother tongue as a subject singing (*Dies Irae*) in a triumphant key. She still faces death, but perhaps now she can avoid suicide: "now I can be sure you'll never come back I can calmly leave singing and walking eroding the road to the other world that disappears far away" (1976, 133).

Lacrimosa

Rosario changes the tone of her voice to a minor key in her book *Fables of the Wounded Heron (Fábulas de la garza desangrada)*, published in 1982. Composed as a negative (a metamorphosis) of the Requiem mass, *Fables of the Wounded Heron* seems rather an Assumption that transforms the opening *Introitus* of the triumphant Requiem into a *Valediction (Envío)* and the final *Communio* into an *Epithalamium (Epitálamio)*. Indeed, as she later describes it, her book is a tempering series of ironic inversions not only of myth but also of her original irascible tone: "Antigone, Desdemona, Ariadne . . . have a very different end from the one they were originally assigned in history. They embody the historical conflicts of women: Antigone defeats Creon, the pater familias; Desdemona poisons Othello; Ariadne aborts the Minotaur" (1992, 109). Perhaps the most striking of these reversals is Ariadne's in a poem entitled "Requiem." In that poem, Theseus is revealed as the maker of the Minotaur. Theseus, convinced that the Minotaur is his destiny, exits the labyrinth and abandons Ariadne inside it, after performing the sexual rites that will conjure the monster. The poem ends with Ariadne, left abandoned in the labyrinth's echo chamber; left to bear in solitude the consequences of Theseus's solipsistic and ritualized desire. Suddenly, she feels the warm wine of blood running down her legs as she begins a painful abortion.

Running blood, flowing tears, falling tissue, and open vessels are the materials running through these poems. The material is an antidote to the fortifications of the male superego, the architecture against which Rosario raised the irascible voice of *Pandora's Papers*. Similar to Theseus, in "Requiem," man conjures the monster again in the poem "Fable of the Wounded Heron." He needs the monster's labyrinths, its echo chambers, and its towers of wrath for support. He needs a threshold, a hole, or an opening to be born. He will build the architecture for his entrance and the dead mother is his lintel: "perfect lintel of the dead mother / her body is marked by movement" (1982, 17). In his imaginary, as well as in the social imaginary, the mother is conceived as a dead certainty, a fixture for movement. The fortifying operation is defensive, and being defensive it is relentless in setting the stage for the equally implacable return of the repressed. Man builds a psychic wall around a void to protect himself from the ambiguity of a shared desire and an equally intense separation and prohibition. Similar to Kristeva's borderline subject, man builds an empty castle. "Constructed on the one hand by the incestuous desire of (for) his mother and on the other by an overly brutal separation from her, the borderline patient, even though he may be a fortified castle, is nevertheless an empty castle . . . haunted by unappealing ghosts— 'powerless' outside, 'impossible' inside" (Kristeva 1982, 49).

The voice of "Fable of the Wounded Heron" struggles against the efforts of this borderline subject to stabilize itself by fixing and silencing the object of its desire. But the voice also confronts the forces that lead the borderline subject to its perverse fortifications in the first place, forces that now return with added strength to build a second layer of stronger impermeable material. Like negativity itself, the voice furiously assaults the double walls around emptiness from inside. But the walls are tripled now, because they are also built as a defense by the "othered" self, the self turned cadaver, object.[2] The walls are built not only by arrogant and vain men or by the returning repressed abject, but they are also built by the voice of the book as a defense against "the fragrance of evil that pursues [her]," against the death that "inhabits and defines her," against the torture of her own breath (1982, 16, 18, 19).

The voice must excavate itself out of this stifling prison working backward, rebuilding itself through abjection. It gives birth to itself in rhythmic waves of sound, expelling out, vomiting, aborting, and liberating what it lost to the void where she is imprisoned. *Lacrimosa dies illa / Qua resurget ex favilla / Judicandus homo reus.* (Mournful that day / When from the dust shall rise / Guilty man to be judged.) Regurgitating matter, flesh, bones, eyes, extremities, and sex she opens the gates, she lets the blood run, the tears flow, and finally voice emerges like a Phoenix from its ashes, and with voice consciousness returns.

> weeping burns and revives her,
> she deliberately breaths in the ethyl smell;
> she fastens it immediately to her underside
> helping herself at the point of birth . . . (1982, 21)

The mournful self-birthing or abortion is aided by a containing placenta-like material, a layer of tissue that envelops the emerging voice. The tissue, made from the flowing tears and gases of abjection, is a returning figure in Rosario's writing. It is the protective skin of the mistress in "From Your Side to Paradise" (*"De tu lado al Paraíso"*). Skin described as a sieve that forces the mistress to remain "on this side of the pores," substantive, with a shape and a form, prevents the mistress from becoming a "useless gush of milk" (1976, 195). It is the envelope of wrath that surrounds, contains, and protects the leaping heart of the ballerina in the poem by that name (1976, 141). It is also the yellow skin, torn into shreds, barely containing and preserving the muscles and vessels of the monstrous but living abortion that is Frankenstein (1980, 38).

> displaying the self in front of men:
> forcing them to touch the skin feeling its weight and shape,
> spying the soul through the secret keyhole of the ear,
> chasing her heart through the bogs of the womb,
> listening to the murmur of desire in relentless flux
> under the sealed eyelid of the navel . . . (1982, 20)

The tissue is the imprint on the abject that keeps the subject alive, which gives life to the subject and preserves it. It is a flexible and porous surface that substitutes the encroaching fortifying walls in an effort to contain while permitting the passage of the abject in and out of the voice. The tissue mediates the recuperation of the being-in-process at the center of the "Fable of the Wounded Heron." It is an acoustic keyhole, a wet spongy surface, through which the fleeting soul and the racing heart are glimpsed, heard, and pursued. The tissue is like the skin of bound Prometheus. It is the merciful savior that keeps him alive in his torment and punishment. *Huic ergo parce, Deus, / Pie Jesu Domine* (Therefore spare him, O God. / Merciful Jesu, Lord). The delicate skin of the eyelid, the tender scar tissue of the navel, are the flexible nets catching the black enigmatic seed of being, and protecting it in its free-fall.

Rosario identifies the regenerating tissue, the imprinted, scarred skin, with language in general and with writing in particular. The poem ends with the Heron, veins open, still bleeding, a version of Alice returned from Wonderland, who raises itself triumphant on the other side of the fortified mirror as she writes. She screams, laughs, and "writes her name with the still-flowing blood at the base of the fragments of the poem / to soothe her delayed vanishing" (1982, 22). The scene captures the essence of *Pandora's Papers*: an abjection (the angry scream, the blood) that turns into writing that imprints the poem and creates the writer.

But the poem also goes beyond Rosario's first book. In this poem, the transformation of the abject (the scream, the blood, the mother tongue) into language (writing) also soothes the Heron. This soothing effect is reproduced in the tone of the poem that sounds more like an elegy than a condemnation. This shift in tone is the result of a second impersonal voice that inhabits the poem and that frames (begins and ends) it. That voice is different from the Heron's. It is visually set apart by quotation marks and by the distribution of the verses on the page. It is also different in tone. Indeed, its mournful tone is the key that allows us to hear the story of the Heron rather than merely repeat it. The framing voice is not the act of a ventriloquist's dummy, a servant to the words of a greater force. Instead, it is the mournful song of a chorus. The chorus keeps a self-defining distance from the monstrous voice of the mother-Heron, from the mother tongue. Like a chorus of supplicants it pleads for the eternal rest of the mother tongue. *Dona Eis Requiem* (Grant them rest).

That soothing voice returns in the poem that closes the book. Titled *Epithalamium*, the poem is an ironic reversal not only of the *Communio* that ends the Requiem Mass in a communion of Lord and Sinner, but it is also a reversal of the traditional meaning of *Epithalamium*: a lyric ode in honor of a bride and bridegroom. Communion and marriage are substituted here by the image of Penelope, the betrothed, unstitching her trousseau in an effort to post-pone the final union. The poem's detached voice describes the betrothed unstitching her feelings from her skin in order to transform them painlessly into a design of silk thread. This design is a second skin that she wraps around her waist, a skin that she rustles with her movement. The poem ends when the betrothed pulls at the strings of this second skin making it, and, perhaps, making herself disappear. The postponement, then, is successful as the betrothed escapes her fate by making and unmaking herself through a second skin. The second skin is the first skin transformed, changed into new beautiful silk, wrapped around the body, rustling but detached, and separated from sensitive skin. This second skin is the poem itself, its reversal and sub-stitution of the lyric ode to marriage and communion. Similar to a sec-ond skin, the poem separates the betrothed from a Classical tradition, which detachment allows her to reverse, manipulate, and appropriate that tradition. While the poem's final verse is a mournful reminder that the reversals are but postponements of an impending disappear-ance that affects us all, it also repeats the willful act of unstitching and unraveling (this time of the thread of the second skin) that makes all the difference.

> unstitched from her own skin
> she allows her feelings to wither.
> she presses them against her thighs, perspiring from wear.
> balancing on the unsteady breeze of her heels
> she makes them rustle like new silk around her waist
> before she pulls on the thread and unravels the design . . . (1982, 74)

Papageno's Tone

We are now ready to answer the first two of the three questions posed at the beginning of this essay. Writing about the loss of the mother is prohibited because the loss of the mother is but a reference to an archaic loss that is necessary for the self and identity to emerge. The speaking self, the poetic voice, Rosario's identity as a writer, all identity, in fact, emerges as a separation, a flight, and as a defense from the material source of words, from the abject origin, from its destabilizing ambiguity. The taboo against writing about the loss of the mother is a defense against the effect of tracing back the loss to a matricide at the origins of the speaking voice. This defense is the thickest wall surrounding and supporting the ego and identity. Its symptoms are the controls and prohibitions Rosario assaults in her writings: the social (external) tendency to contain the threat of the abject by reifying the maternal experience while splitting women into irreconcilable opposites and the psychological (internal) tendency of the writer toward self-violence through self-silencing and self-censorship.

Why is it so important and even necessary to challenge that taboo and write about the loss of the mother? It is necessary to challenge the taboo because to do otherwise is to endlessly struggle with the implacable return of the repressed maternal cadaver. In other words, despite its centrifugal impulse, the speaking subject never fully separates from the rhythms and archaic rumors of the maternal body. The subject's language, its writing, its second skin, is made from the material of the abject, and the speaking subject will communicate its sounds, like it or not. To ignore, deny, or repress those archaic sounds is to build a wall around subjectivity that eventually crushes it with monstrous force. The only way of short-circuiting that return is to listen to the sounds and to the rhythms of the abject as they run through the fibers of language. To do this, however, is impossible by definition. The subject emerges as a speaking subject, and to listen to the sounds of the abject is to listen to the sound of the negative of voice, the sound of the unspeaking, of the unspeakable. Thus, every attempt at writing what cannot be said (as Rosario titles one of her more recent essays) is accompanied by the realization that "one is inclined to censor precisely that which one desperately needs to say" (1992, 106). With each liberating iconoclastic gesture comes the suspicion, if not the realization, that one is keeping something hidden from oneself. And with that realization comes the desire to revisit oneself in order to exceed oneself and overcome self-censorship.

The third question asked at the beginning of this essay is important in this context. What does it mean that Rosario can write about the loss of the mother only by writing in another language? For Rosario, writing in another language is a way of translating the abject mother tongue; it is a way of developing the second skin that is necessary to live. Not surprisingly, writing in another language is also identical with translating herself and coincides with self-exile. She began to write and publish in English in 1986, one year after she moved her residence from San Juan to College Park, Maryland, where she earned a Ph.D. in Literature. At that time, she translated several works from *Pandora's Papers, Room for Eros*, and *Fables of the Wounded Heron*, which appeared in various publications.[3] Since then, she has published several novels in English that she has insisted are English versions of works first written or begun in Spanish. Interestingly, she has translated these Spanish "originals" (often fragments, drafts, or incomplete work) twice: once into English and then from their English versions back into Spanish. Thus, Rosario's work in English is also a circuitous return to Spanish, to her mother tongue.

In fact, her work in English is a version of, or a second look at, her work in Spanish. As has been noted, these translations and re-translations not only contain additions and cosmetic changes but are often ironic reversals of the original.[4] Most ironic is the fact that Rosario's translations into English suggest that the irascible and liberating tone of her work in Spanish also covers-over a self-censoring impulse that keeps something hidden even from herself. After writing the novel *Eccentric Neighborhoods*, for example, Rosario published an editorial in the *New York Times* where she points to this haunting self-censorship, and to the reversals necessary to overcome it. "Our two halves are inseparable; we cannot give up either without feeling maimed. For many years, my concern was to keep my Hispanic self from being stifled. Now I discover it's my American self that's being threatened" (1998a).

Some writers and critics from Puerto Rico have criticized Rosario's decision to write and publish in English and in the United States. They see it as a betrayal. Still attached to the stifling symptoms of the process of national identity and subject formation, they interpret Rosario's reversals and translations as political betrayals of her past ideals. In fact, some believe that these reversals and translations are denials of Rosario's "true" identity.[5] Others believe that Rosario's translations into English are "reductions" and "simplifications" of a complex cultural reality (Aponte Ramos 1997, Irizarry 2001).[6] These critics believe that her so-called reductions and simplifications facilitate her entrance into a growing global book market, and they emphasize that the entrance is gained by submitting to a hegemonic metropolitan (read imperialist) agenda. All of these critics, however, rebuild the melancholy fortifications that Rosario assaults in her work. Participants like Rosario in the vexed colonial history of the island, these writers rush to the ramparts of borderline subjectivity in an ill-fated defense of a national identity and language.

The revelatory power of self-translation has led Rosario in a different direction. It changes the tone of Rosario's writing both in English and in Spanish. After her translations into English, Rosario moves away from the irascible and mournful tone of her earlier writings. Her tone now becomes lighter, ironic to the point of mischief. Indeed, she displaces self-censorship with self-deprecation. Rosario's new tone is not unlike Papageno's self-mocking tone in Mozart's *The Magic Flute*.[7] Like Rosario, Papageno speaks another language. Papageno imitates the sound of birds to catch them. But he also seems to learn from birds. His cheerful, idle chatter, for example, is like a bird song in its obliviousness to the constraining forces that surround him. Papageno is ever merry and his songs are in constant violation of the silence imposed on him by the opera's forces of good and evil (the Queen of Night and Sarastro). *Der Vogelfänger binc ich ja, / stets lustig, heißa hopsasa*! (Yes, I am the bird-catcher, / and ever merry—hopsasa!) Papageno never learns the lesson in self-control that Tamino (the opera's hero) must learn to marry Pamina. And yet, Papageno, like Tamino, finds his beloved (Papagena) and marries her at the end of the opera. Rosario's mischievous translations, and her work in Spanish, similarly resist external and internal (self-imposed) prohibitions on voice.

First published in 1990, *The Bitches' Colloquy (El coloquio de las perras)* is a negative, or an inversion, of *Room for Eros*. It is an often-humorous series of literary essays where Rosario journeys inward, not only to the works of Latin American writers, but also returns to her own early work to comment on it. Indeed, more than half of the collection is a meditation on her own writing and many of the essays are autobiographical. The main theme of the essay that gives the collection its title is a blind spot of many writers from Latin America. Similar to other Latin American women writers, Rosario convincingly argues that male writers from the Latin American "Boom" (ranging from Jorge Luis Borges to Gabriel García Márquez) are blind to the stereotypical characterization of women in their works. Rosario's criticism, however, is not limited to the work of these male writers. She also suggests that the blindness to sexual difference is found not only in the criticism about Latin American writers, but also in the work of women writers from Latin America, including her own. "Before I'm told to consider the beam in my eye ere I behold the moat in my brother's, I admit that most of the masculine characters in a couple of the minor pieces of fiction I have invented are voids, ironic absences around which feminine conflicts develop" (1992, 31–32).

Like Mozart's bird-catcher, Rosario speaks an other language in this essay. The conceit is a reference to Cervantes' own humorous story similarly titled "The Dog's Colloquy" about the conversation between two dogs (Berganza and Cipión) that are in search of an honest writer. In Rosario's version, however, the two dogs are bitches and their names are Fina and Franca. By adopting the language of the animals as her own, Rosario gains the distance necessary to journey irreverently through the works of fellow writers many of whom (usually male and sometimes dead) have been consecrated by academic institutions, by the book market, or by both. The prosopopeia, however, is more than a defensive operation in that essay. Its effect is also a mischievous defacement. Fina and Franca's good-humored conversation goes back and forth from saying what cannot be said to censorship and vice versa. They honestly, wisely, intelligently, detachedly, and coolly say what others are afraid to voice, while simultaneously censoring one another and calling each other names like satiric, braggart, know-it-all, pedantic, aggressive, out-of-control, and obsessive bitch. Thus, the banter between Fina and Franca deflates and challenges any notion of a stable voice of authority, including Rosario's own. Indeed, the voice that frames the essay overcomes external censorship and internal self-censorship by defacing Rosario's voice through prosopopeia, and by metamorphosing the paradoxically self-generating prohibitions into good-humored banter. In other words, Rosario attempts to overcome self-censorship by giving up any claim to identity and to the authority that stems from identity. Instead, she gives herself over to the self-effacing trope and humor of prosopopeia.

In the essay dedicated to translation, Rosario describes the experience of translating her work into English in similar terms. Self-translation, she states, is both a disturbing betrayal and a mischievous second chance, which allows her not only to struggle against the self-censorship she finds in her own earlier work, but also permits her to fix mistakes and to live differently.

[Self-translation] can be diabolic and obsessive: it is one of the few instances when one can be dishonest and feel good about it, rather like having a second chance at redressing one's fatal mistakes in life and living a different way. The writer becomes her own critical conscience; her superego leads her (perhaps treacherously) to believe that she can not only better but also surpass herself, or at least surpass the writer she has been in the past. Popular lore has long equated translation with betrayal: "*Traduttore-traditore*" goes the popular Italian saying. "*La traduction est comme la femme, plus qu'elle est belle, elle n'est pas fidèle; plus qu'elle est fidèle, elle n'est pas belle*" goes the chauvinist French saying. But in translating one's own work it is only by betraying that one can better the original. There is, thus, a feeling of elation, of submerging oneself in sin, without having to pay the consequences. Instinct becomes the sole beacon. "The loyal translator will write what is correct," the devil whispers exultantly in one's ear, "but not necessarily what is right." And yet translation, in spite of its considerable difficulties, is a necessary reality for me as a writer . . . (1991, 162–163)

What first strikes the reader about this description of self-translation is the intense ambivalence Rosario feels toward it. Self-translation is a unique experience that can become obsessive. It is an experience that adds layers to the original self; but those layers can be treacherous. To translate oneself is also to betray the original, to submerge oneself in sin. The distance it provides from the original is prohibited and evil. But self-translation is a necessary evil. And indeed, this passage itself seems to be proof.

The passage above is taken from the English version of the same essay published a year earlier in Spanish. While the overall composition of the passage remains the same in both languages, the mischievous tone of the English version is missing from the Spanish. Instead, the Spanish version reads rather like a censoring self-accusation. While the descriptions of self-translation in English are in part actively and positively inflected, in Spanish the same descriptions are passive and filled with double negatives. In English, for example, the translator says she "feels good" about her/his dishonesty, but in Spanish s/he merely "doesn't feel guilty" about it. In English, the translator submerges in sin and feels elated, while in Spanish the translator "sinks" or "drowns" in sin while experiencing a pathological euphoria (1992, 61). The devil is a mischievous voice in English who whispers that the loyal translator will write what is correct, but not necessarily what is right. In Spanish, however, the devil is much more serious. He whispers a censoring warning, and suggests a prohibition: "The loyal translator will write what is correct . . . but the unfaithful translator will transcribe what suits him best" (1992, 61). It comes as no surprise then that Rosario's conclusion in English is never reached in Spanish. In her mother tongue, Rosario does not claim, and perhaps cannot claim, that translation is a necessary reality for her.

One key to the differences between the two versions of this essay on self-translation is found at the beginning of the essay, which is titled, in English, "On Destiny, Language, and Translation; or, Orphelia [*sic*] Adrift in the C. & O. Canal." The essay begins with a dream where Rosario is ready to leave Washington DC after a productive five-year stay in that city. She is prepared to return to San Juan, Puerto Rico, a place she ambivalently describes both in maternal and military terms. A matrix of cultural meaning, San Juan is on the one hand the source that nurtures Rosario's "hidden springs of consciousness"; and, on the other hand, the city is also a war zone to which Rosario returns as a "war correspondent" (1991, 153, 54). Her dream changes the return trip to San Juan into an allegorical crossing from one shore to another of the C. & O. canal in Washington DC. When Rosario reaches the middle of the canal she hears a voice that warns her that she must take "all the precautions of language" because the water locks will open and the water level will rise (1991, 154). Despite the warnings, or perhaps because of them, the menacing undifferentiated waters of the canal are transformed into "a water of words" that keeps Rosario afloat. Compared to a mirror from childhood that fuses opposites, the water of words both connects and keeps apart the shores of the C. & O. canal.

Rosario interprets the dream to mean that the water of words is an intermediary place where she must learn to live. That place is not only language for Rosario, it is also the place of translation, the place of the in-between: in-between San Juan and Washington DC and in-between the Spanish and the English language.[8] But that intermediary place is not only the place of translation; it is also the unconscious, the place where the dream is found. The unconscious is a place that keeps separate the opposites that threaten to tear Rosario apart even as it connects them. But the unconscious is also the place where Rosario finds a force more menacing and stronger than the irreconcilable opposites of the canal. It is the sound of an impeding storm, its terrible rushing not unlike the rolling thunder and waterfalls of Mozart's Queen of the Night. *Ja, fürchterlich ist dieses Rauschen, / wie fernen Donners Widerhall!* (Yes, fearful is that rushing, / like the distant echo of thunder!) The unconscious is the meeting place with that oncoming and undifferentiated rush of water that threatens to overcome and drown Rosario. Indeed, the unconscious is the meeting point at the center of the unintended slip in the title of the essay. The unconscious is translated into "Orphelia": neither masculine nor feminine, neither the suicidal Ophelia, nor the oneiric Orpheus, but the transformative meeting place of both. In fact, the unconscious is the place where the dream can change Ophelia into Orpheus. It is the place where the dream can change the deadly rush of water, the curse of the vengeful Queen of the Night, into a palpitating life-source.

The operating principle of the dream-work is the opposite of the water's rush. If the rush of water threatens to drown Rosario by condensing all difference into one undifferentiated mass, the dream-work keeps Rosario afloat by displacing water into words and also by displacing Rosario from shore to shore. In other words, the dream keeps Rosario metaphorically alive by turning her into a floating sig-nifier between cultures, languages, and meanings. The dream creates an unstable identity and a malleable self for Rosario. Through Rosario's displacement, the dream makes light of the threatening pre-linguistic rhythms and material without denying or repressing them.

In this third moment of Rosario's writing, she changes yet again the direction of her drive for self-definition. Rather than focus on trans-forming, imprinting, and mourning the ancestral rhythms of the abject, she now mischievously revisits and transforms the sound of her emerging voice as an indirect means of returning to, and transforming, the mother tongue. Rosario's dream-work, her self-interpretation, and self-translation are like Papageno's playful song, like the sound of his silver bells, or like the music of the magic flute. They keep Rosario's voice cheerful and light as she walks through death's gloomy night. *Wir wandeln durch des Tones Macht / froh durch des Todes düstre Nacht* (We walk by power of the music, / cheerful through death's gloomy night).

The Curse of the Queen of Night

Rosario's self-translation (her self-displacement, and self-effacement) allows her to return to the mother tongue to work through (disturb, trouble, and transform) its ancestral rhythmic condensations.[9] The angry sounds and forceful curses made by the Queen of Night against the daughter who betrays her (Pamina sides with Sarastro against the Queen of Night in Mozart's opera) must be disturbed and heard. *Verstoßen sei auf ewig, verlassen sei auf ewig, / zertrümmert sei auf ewig alle Bande der Natur.* (Outcast forever, abandoned forever, / destroyed forever be all ties of nature.) Like the musical notation to

Mozart's music, the mother's curse must be translated into an other language. Transforming the curse of the abject mother tongue into an intelligible sound in turn lightens its heavy burden on the emerging self. By re-suturing its sound to music or voice, by re-membering (i.e., retrieving in memory and reconstituting in body) and working-through the abject, the nature of the subject can also change. No longer outcast, abandoned, and destroyed by the unspeakable curse, the symbolic subject can live again.

Indeed, Rosario's self-translations are to the mother tongue what analysis is to trauma in Freudian psychoanalysis.[10] Like analysis, Rosario's self-translations perform a dangerous but necessary symbolic operation to overcome a destructive tendency contained in the material that constitutes her writing. Like analysis, Rosario's self-translations revisit and provoke the abject material of Rosario's writing. Like analysis, Rosario's self-translations open up an intermediary region between her original writing and its potentially dangerous effect on the psyche. They produce a facsimile, a version, and an interpretation of the abject material contained in Rosario's writing that is the first step necessary to overcome and change the abject's dangerous and destructive effect on the psyche. By disturbing, troubling, and interpreting the original material Rosario gives voice to the abject and to herself.[11] And yet, Rosario's self-translations don't inhabit the exact space of analysis either. Rosario's works in English are not translations but self-translations where she analyzes, interprets, and transforms her own dreams. Unlike the scene of analysis, there is no qualitative difference here between the analyst, who interprets, and the analysand, whose dreams are interpreted. In Rosario's self-translations, the analyst is the facsimile of an analyst. Indeed, Rosario's humorous works in English perform a simulacrum similar to the art of a successful jokester.

According to Freud, "a joke is a double-dealing rascal who serves two masters at once": one master tells the joke and the other listens to it (1905, 155). The apparent circuit traveled by the mischievous joke is but the simulacrum of a circuit because the person who listens to the joke is actually doing the bidding of the person telling the joke. In fact, for Freud the listener is a kind of dummy or servant of the person telling the joke. The joker needs the dummy because its laughter allows the liberation of the repressed material in the ventriloquist. But the "dummy" and the joke's closed circuit are also insufficient. The joker's laughter and pleasure, the release of her repressed material, is only temporary and does not get to the root of the problem. Giddiness and a hysterical noncomprehending laughter could be the recurring symptoms of a melancholy that continues to haunt the joker. Rosario's *Eccentric Neighborhoods* is an example of this persistent haunting. On the one hand, it is an example of her ongoing effort to face and work-through the matricidal impulse at the origin of the process of subject formation, now by translating the mother tongue into voice. On the other hand, it is also an example of the artifice at the center of her efforts to work through the abject; a simulacrum that calls for eccentric readings that interrupt and reinterpret Rosario's work.

Eccentric Neighborhoods is really a constellation of works that includes the 1998 version in English as well as a shorter unfinished Spanish version published in chapters between 1989 and 1992.[12] The first chapter of the Spanish version has recently reappeared in print. It is the first piece in Rosario's latest collection of essays published in 2001 with the title *Under the Shadow of Your Name (A la sombra de tu nombre)*. Originally written in 1989 and titled "Eccentric Neighborhoods," the chapter was transformed into an essay for this collection now titled "Meditations Outside the City Walls" ("*Meditación extramuros*"). That essay describes the original eccentric neighborhoods to which the novel refers in its title: two adjunct and abject places outside the walls of the fortified city of Old San Juan, the cemetery of Santa María dei Pazzi, and the neighborhood of La Perla.

The essay is remarkable because it contains a struggle between Rosario's different voices. On the one hand, we find in it Rosario's mischievous literary voice, which develops the felicitous and ironic coincidence of slum and cemetery outside the city walls. She describes Santa María dei Pazzi as a famous cemetery, where the prominent personalities of Puerto Rico's history lie buried; and she describes La Perla as an infamous slum, where outlaws can hide. She describes both as the unstable positive and negative of the same threatening image: "In the topography of both the two sides of our history will forever be inscribed: the history of our spiritual accomplishments and of our violence" (2001, 19). But the essay also contains Rosario's melancholy voice. The cemetery and the slum are also described as accursed places of sacrifice. While the cemetery holds the remains of the martyrs sacrificed to the colonial history of Puerto Rico, La Perla is "a living cemetery," whose inhabitants are sacrificed to Puerto Rico's vexed economic history. These sacrifices in turn produce living–dead ghosts that curse the island. A metaphor for the return of the repressed, these ghosts exact their vengeance on the city and eat away at its walls. Compared to the pounding surf of the Atlantic Ocean, the ghosts make the fortified walls of the city crumble. "A nationalist sentiment fiercely runs through the tombs giving them the restless and disturbing appearance of cadavers that are not at rest, a restlessness reflected by the rebellious waves stirring around them" (2001, 21).

The melancholy voice echoes a curse embedded in the verses of a Puerto Rican folkloric song (*plena*) that Rosario overhears and transcribes at the end of the essay. "Tanta vanidad / tanta hipocresía, si tu cuerpo/ después de muerto / pertenece a la tumba fría." (So much vanity / so much hypocrisy, when your body / after death / belongs to the icy grave). The verses of the *plena* are sung by an old man from La Perla, and are aimed at the expensive mausoleums and the venerable cadavers that will be his neighbors when he dies and is improbably buried in Santa María dei Pazzi. The old man condemns everything and everyone to a future undifferentiated death. The rhythms of the *plena* and the encompassing movement of his arm echo his all-condensing curse. The curse seems to be the apex of the threats to the city walls. But the curse also suggests a heavier, deeper current, a more unsettling and personal loss at the center of the essay's triumphant melancholy tone. Rosario is personally interpellated by the curse. "I overheard the most moving verses about the Cemetery of Santa María one day when I was visiting" (2001, 23). Like the old man, Rosario has come to the cemetery to pay a visit; but the object of her visit remains a mystery to the reader who may not know that Rosario's mother is also buried in Santa María dei Pazzi.[13]

Rosario's mother, Lorenza Ramirez de Arellano, died in 1969, one year after Lorenza's husband, Luis A. Ferré, became governor of Puerto Rico. Both versions of *Eccentric Neighborhoods* can be read as an account of the decision made by Lorenza to support her husband's political career. Both versions suggest that this decision was a mode of self-sacrifice to a social order, to a philosophy of life, and to an inner impulse. In both versions the mother accepts and curses her fate. But in the Spanish version of the text the curse remains as a violent remnant of the mother's sublimated sacrifice. The curse remains in the untranslated sound of the waves, in the archaic rhythm of the *plena* floating above the words that end the essay. It remains in its melancholy tone overcoming Rosario's mischievous voice. It also remains in the violence that Rosario levels against herself and her own writing in other essays of the collection *Under the Shadow of Your Name*.[14]

Rosario returns to work-through this disturbing remnant in the English translation of *Eccentric Neighborhoods*. The self-translation changes the autobiographical references and instead tells the saga of two families: the Rivas de Santillana and the Vernets. The Rivas de Santillana are a landowning aristocratic family from the South of the island of Puerto Rico. The Vernets are a family of immigrants who become part of the island's cadre of professionals challenging the authority and ultimately supplanting the landowners. The novel is interlaced with references to the colonial history of Puerto Rico: the island undergoes the occupation of two imperial powers (first Spain and then the United States). But the novel also tells the story of three generations of both families. Elvira is the narrator and the great-granddaughter who decides to break with family tradition.

> "No Rivas de Santillana has ever gotten a divorce except for Tía Lakhmé, and everyone knows she's crazy," Mother said. "If you do, your grandparents' ghosts will follow you around and push you down the stairs or in front of a car. Your aunts and uncles will be furious. The whole family will be up in arms. You must be out of your mind, Elvira."
> (1998b, 333)

Curiously, Clarissa's daughter in the novel (Elvira), threatens her mother instead of her husband with a divorce. She refuses to wear the mantle of self-sacrifice proudly worn by her mother, her aunts, and by her grandmother, in dutiful respect of a stoic philosophy of life. The daughter's threat of divorce, or separation, the mother's sacrifice and curse, and the ghost's haunting, are the material that make up this novel. The mother, Clarissa, is a Rivas de Santillana, and she tries to teach her daughter, Elvira, the stoic philosophy of the family. Emajaguas, the fortified family home, is an architectural example of both that philosophy of life and of the borderline subjectivity that has so preoccupied Rosario in all her work. Similar to the borderline subject, the Rivas de Santillanas sublimate and repress the pain, the suffering, and the pleasure of the body into ascetic experiences. Emajaguas, the walled-in, fortified, Paradise where Clarissa and her sisters (Elvira's aunts) grow up, is an architectural example of that philosophy, and it hatches examples of borderline subjectivity. Compared to the Garden of the Finzi Contini, Emajaguas stands as an arrogant claim to a self-sufficient spirituality founded on the denial of the body and sexuality, both of which are displaced on to an evil lurking outside its walls: poverty, revolution, death, and the Caribbean Sea. The "Swans of Emajaguas," Elvira's aunts and her mother, sacrifice their dreams to the guiding principles of the Rivas de Santillana. But Emajagua's fortifications prove insufficient and they all lead miserable, unhappy, and frustrated lives.

Elvira knows better. She knows that her ancestor's stoicism, their fortifications, their denial of bodily pain and pleasure, are insufficient defensive mechanisms against a ghostly energy that must be confronted, translated, appropriated, worked-through rather than wielded as a curse. Indeed, this energy is the same negative spectrum described in Rosario's first book of essays. And Clarissa's death at the end of the novel confirms the spectrum's timeless reach, its effect on the mother even after her death. Clarissa dies a peaceful death only in appearance. "No wounds marked her body, no grimace of pain distorted her beautiful, cameolike profile" (1998b, 338). But when Elvira cleans her mother's body in preparation for burial, she is horrified by a torrent of fresh blood that spills out of her mother's mouth like a curse from the other world. The image is a striking representation of the mother tongue and its silencing effect on Clarissa. Even after death, she chokes on the abject, on the maternal blood that overcomes voice, the blood that substitutes words. Clarissa's horrific "last words" return to haunt Elivra as a recurring nightmare made of untranslatable material that Elvira cannot understand. Eventually, however, the nightmare stops repeating and is replaced instead by the striking dream that ends the novel.

> I dreamed about Mother one last time. We were crossing Río Loco and the family's temperamental Pontiac had stalled on us again. The river was rushing past, but instead of dogs, pigs, and goats being pulled along by the murky rapids I saw Abuela Valeria, Abuela Adela, Tía Lakhmé, Tía Dido, Tía Artemisa, Tía Amparo, all swimming desperately against the current. Clarissa and I sat safely inside the Pontiac, dressed in our Sunday best. She took a dollar out of her purse, rolled down the window just enough so she could wave the bill at the men on the riverbank, who soon came and pulled us out. And as we drove away I could hear through the open window the voices of those I could no longer see, but whose stories I could not have dreamed. (1998b, 340)

Rosario's familiar ghosts tell the story of the English 1998 version of *Eccentric Neighborhoods*, if we believe the dedication "To the ghosts who lent me their voices." These are the ghosts of the maternal ancestors (the mother, the aunts, and the grandmothers) whose haunting curses not only end but also appear to begin the novel. In fact, the novel opens with the original version of the dream that ends it. In that memorable scene of Elvira's childhood, the overflowing and unpredictable dangerous river is explicitly compared to Clarissa's moodiness and to her melancholy tears. "Río Loco always reminded me of my mother, Clarissa. We would be sitting peacefully in the pantry having breakfast . . . when Clarissa would suddenly rise and run to her room. Aurelio would follow hurriedly behind her. As I left for school in the family's Pontiac, I could hear Clarissa's sobs behind closed doors, mingled with the apologetic murmur of my Father's voice" (1998b, 3–4). The dream, which places Elvira in the protective shell of the Pontiac, transforms Clarissa's tearful moods into the rushing waters of the Río Loco (The Crazy River).

If the Río Loco is haunted by the untranslatable sounds of dogs, pigs, and goats, the English version of *Eccentric Neighborhoods* is similarly riddled with remnants of the ancestral curse fortified by social conventions. These remnants take the form of violent, homicidal ghosts like Blanca Rosa, Uncle Basilio, Chaguito's mother, Aztec sacrificial priests, and Aurelio's piano music (1998b, 12, 36, 198, 299, 339 respectively). But like the dream-work, the novel also repeats, revisits, and displaces those sounds into words, into another language, and into English (the language of adventure stories and impish humor in the novel). Through displacement, by writing in another language, Rosario changes the menacing rhythms of the mother tongue into protective shells like the Pontiac. In English, Clarissa's river of blood is transformed back into words. In dreams, she becomes an agent of her own and of Elvira's salvation. Self-translation changes the vengeful old man from La Perla into a guardian angel: Don Félix de Pasamonte.

> They were at the corner of Calle Fraternidad and Calle Salud. The street was busy with horse-drawn carriages and mule carts. Don Félix was carrying his cane, and he swung it in front of him in a semicircle to feel his way. He seemed always to know when some obstacle was in front of him. Chaguito watched in fascination; Don Félix was like a ghost dancer, padding softly down the market's crowded alleys without bumping into anyone. (1998b, 158–159)

Don Félix is light on his feet. He is a mirror image or a negative (a translation if you will) of the old and somber man that ends "Meditations Outside the City Walls," ominously singing the words to the famous *plena*. Don Félix is a stranger, a Haitian immigrant, Adela's father, and Elvira's blind great-grandfather. He might be blind, and he cannot see the obstacles on the road, but Don Félix gingerly dances around them anyway, as he softly pads the market's crowded alleys with his cane. He is a ghost dancer, in the sense that he transforms the people and the things he cannot see, what to a blind man must be ghosts, into his dancing partners. He dances with the unseen living obstacles in front of him without bumping into them. Don Félix, survives in a world of ghosts, by dancing to their rhythms rather than cursing in their wake. A blind man, he nevertheless seems fluent in the language of the seeing. His cane is the mediating support that helps him to survive.

Don Felix's cane, Elvira's dream, and Rosario's self-translations into English, are all repetitions and transformations of the abject. Like her previous work, *Eccentric Neighborhoods* is an attempt to work through the disabling mother tongue. But Rosario's work in English is also unique. *Eccentric Neighborhoods* occupies a singularly peripheral and a hopeful space. It is close to both the material of abjection and to the scene of interpretation and analysis. A simulacrum of both, it is a dance between writing and interpretation.

4

Accidents of Chicana Feminisms: Norma Alarcón, Gloria Anzaldúa, and Cherríe Moraga

The maternal has been at the center of Feminist theoretical and literary debates for the better part of the twentieth century in Europe, Latin America, and the United States. Indeed, the maternal is a point of contact between writers as diverse as Julia Kristeva, Norma Alarcón, Gloria Anzaldúa, and Cherríe Moraga. Not surprisingly, the Chicana and queer authors emerging from the southwestern region of the United States give the maternal a very specific form, particularly after the publication of *This Bridge Called my Back: Writings by Radical Women of Color* in 1981. In this chapter, I discuss how the maternal is represented in the texts of three of the most influential Chicana writers emerging from that book.[1] At stake in this discussion is the place of Chicana writing vis-à-vis both Feminist and postfeminist readings of the maternal.

From their earliest writings in that groundbreaking anthology, Alarcón, Anzaldúa, and Moraga are united by their exploration of a supportive maternal space that challenges the normative separation of language from the body. They question the exclusive categories of language and body from the borders of Feminism, and interrogate imaginaries that hypostasize and essentialize the maternal.[2] Most importantly, however, their works points to the insufficiency of postfeminist readings that conclude that subjectivity is founded on the structural absence of the maternal.[3] The maternal is not always already lost according to these Chicana feminists. Instead, these writers insist that the maternal can be, and perhaps must be, reinscribed, re-membered (i.e., retrieved in memory and reconstituted in body), and implacably pursued.

Alarcón, Anzaldúa, and Moraga pursue the maternal as an enabling accident of life in their works. If the mother literally gives birth unintentionally and painfully, or by accident, the maternal similarly gives life (i.e., meaning and agency) to the Chicanas in these works. The maternal emerges from these works as a changing accident, taking the form of an interstice, an interface, wounded and wounding skin. Writing emerges from their work as a similarly troubled and enabling process. It becomes both the testimony to, and the relentless pursuit of, accident in its changing forms. In short, the maternal and writing surface in these works as complementary events that return meaning and agency to accident and accident to meaning and agency. Maternal writing returns agency to those who suffer the accident of being born Chicana, lesbian, and female in a racialized, heteronormative, and patriarchal society and culture. Conversely, maternal writing returns vulnerability to racialized, heteronormative, and patriarchal society and culture by bearing witness to its accidents.

Alarcón's Interstice

Alarcón returns visibility to the paradoxical position of the Chicana in what she refers to as the socio-symbolic contract, or supremacist and patriarchal discourse, with the metaphor of the interstice. The Chicana subject rises as a radical negation, an erasure, or an exclusion from the confluence of oppositional discourses (African American, White-Feminist, ethno/nationalist, nationalist, juridical, cultural, racist, sexist, etc.) that compete for preeminence in the United States, and struggle most intensely at its southwestern border according to Alarcón. The interstice is a confluence of discursive events that include both figurative and material exclusions of language and body. Alarcón's interstice is the point where all the oppositional forces meet to both repress and silence the voices and the desires of the Chicana subject. Alarcón suggests that psychoanalysis gives this interstice the names of "the phallic mother" and "the unconscious," thereby reducing its complex function to an unintelligible threat. But the interstice is also the site of an enabling and generative aporia for Alarcón. Indeed, Alarcón's interstice is also a place of origin, a place of reunion, where both violent erasures and excessive resistant reinscriptions converge, where straight mother and queer daughter come together to develop a "gynetics," an alternative grammar and lexicon to the patriarchal language. "[I]ndeed, the interstice, discontinuity, or gap is precisely a site of textual production—the historical and ideological moment in which the subject inscribes herself contextually" (2003, 357). In this way, Alarcón's interstice conveys the paradox of a troubled and generative space that Alarcón significantly represents as the margins of patriarchal language in and out of which emerges a textual body with a dissident and supportive attitude. "The speaking subject today has to position herself at the margins of the 'symbolic contract' and refuse to accept definitions of 'woman' and 'man' in order to transform the contract" (1996, 230).

In her numerous critical articles, but perhaps most successfully in her 1996 essays "Making Familia From Scratch" and "Anzaldúa's Frontera: Inscribing Gynetics" (essays written about Moraga and Anzaldúa respectively) Alarcón argues convincingly for a heterogeneous symbolic space. In her work, Alarcón imagines and opens up a hopeful and necessary discursive space between the suicidal and sacrificial phallic mother of Patriarchy (the woman that speaks as Mother), and the fiction of the "self-aware" female speaking subject, the "choice maker," the "history producer" (1989, 83). Alarcón acknowledges her debt to Kristeva as an important guide for tracing this third space while admitting to limitations in her theory (1996, 230; 2003, 365). Wielding concepts from Kristeva's *Revolution in Poetic Language* and from their controversial application to the horizon of Feminisms in Kristeva's 1977 essay "Women's Time," Alarcón similarly searches for a way out of the double bind where women are left by the Patriarchal Law and its linguistic domain. Following Kristeva, Alarcón argues that the symbolic order produces and genders the subject–object split. Procreation, the maternal, but also the phallic mother figures of Guadalupe and Malinche in Mexican and Mexican American culture are examples of this ideologically inflected symbolic order and of its silencing effects on Chicanas. "The female-speaking subject that would want to speak from a different position than that of a mother, or a future wife/mother, is thrown into a crisis of meaning that begins with her own gendered personal identity and its relational position with others" (1996, 221).

Also following Kristeva, Alarcón suggests that the female speaking subject must go through the symbolic in order to get beyond that stifling contract and its roles, including the maternal role. It must be critical, but only after-the-fact, always through the symbolic, through language. It must revise, appropriate, expropriate, reinscribe the symbolic contract, but it must not abandon, reject, and expel its figures. "[S]exuality, especially as ascribed to the maternal, and language" must be kept in sight (1989, 76). In fact, this is one of the most intriguing aspects of Alarcón's thought. She argues that Chicana feminists must evoke something that precedes the symbolic entrance into language, something that precedes the splits of the symbolic, but it must do so from the symbolic, from language, indeed from the very interstice of a split. "[A] female speaking subject today has to walk with one foot inside and another outside the *interstice* that would stake the boundary of what a 'woman' may speak" ([My emphasis] 1996, 230).

Alarcón describes this interstice in various ways. She calls it the margins or the periphery of the socio-symbolic contract (1996, 230). She calls it a delay in the process of subject formation (1996, 231). A translation that is also a revision and appropriation (1989, 63); a negativity (1996, 230). She calls it an interrogating and critical attitude (1989, 87). She calls it a position after-the-fact: a look back, a will to begin from scratch (1996, 226). Perhaps her most sustained attempt to date to describe the interstice is found in her essay "Anzaldúa's Frontera: Inscribing Gynetics." In that essay, published originally in 1996 and reprinted in revised form in 2003, Alarcón describes the interstice as a confluence of material and linguistic practices. This confluence is paradoxical, in that it both produces the erasure, the exclusion, of the subjectivities of women of color, and it also gives rise to a "gynetics," an alternative discourse that remembers and recovers them.

Perhaps the most intriguing aspect of Alarcón's interstice is its heterogeneous nature. The interstice cannot be reduced to either material or linguistic events. Throughout her work, Alarcón is at pains to sustain its unsteady combination of body and language. On the one hand, Alarcón locates the interstice in language in general and in the Patriarchal Law in particular. It is an aporia both within and between discourses that Alarcón identifies with arguments and narratives, with their tropes, figures, and myths. Indeed, the interstice is the effect of oppositional discourses that together, and sometimes unwittingly, configure the unstable center of the supremacist and symbolic order, an order that consistently displaces women of color to its borders. Alarcón comes closest to a linguistic definition of the interstice when she uses the Lyotardian concept of the *differend* to describe it: "a case of conflict, between (at least) two parties, that cannot be equitably resolved for lack of a rule of judgment applicable to both arguments" (1999, 70; 2003, 357). She also uses the metaphor of a gap in patriarchal language to evoke this interstice and to suggest the precariousness, and the fragility, of the symbolic order, always open to accident. In this way, Alarcón opens up the possibility of an alternative signifying system by finding and describing accidents, or the interstice, in a Patriarchal Law that is described and experienced as impermeable and categorical more often than not.

On the other hand, Alarcón's image of a gap also evokes a material aspect to this interstice, which is not only the place of linguistic aporias, but also the site of military conflicts (or otherwise), and the place of a geopolitical struggle for the development and control of nation states. Most importantly, the interstice as gap is also the forgotten place of an archaic struggle for subjectivity and selfhood.[4] Alarcón writes that the interstice is that from which the split self of woman is split, it is a different bond, an "old dream," a recollection of closeness, of a transfusion (1996, 222, 226, 225, 229). It is an embodied and maternal site that engenders a dissident *attitude* in a body that walks strangely in and out of the interstice, the discontinuities, or gaps of patriarchal language (1996, 231 n.1). Not surprisingly, the maternal interstice provokes both excessive hungers and urges, as well as a "*push* toward the production of another signifying system" in the subjects that emerge from its porous and accidental site ([My emphasis] 2003, 366). These hungry subjects are desirous to re-member, recover, and rediscover not only their multiple names and languages or voices, but also languages inflected with the body: its instincts, libidos, and lesboerotic desire for Alarcón. She insists for example that "*Borderlands/La Frontera* is an '*instinctive urge* to communicate, to speak, to write' " ([My emphasis] 2003, 367).

Alarcón's maternal interstice, then, is a vexed site where the reader finds a struggle for predominance between two forces that sometimes appear to belong to different material and linguistic orders. "Gynetics," for example, is Alarcón's central metaphor for a generative, reproductive process that transforms and even undermines the violent and competing discourses at the borderland of nation states, even as it repeats them. "The polyvalent name insertions in *Borderlands* are a rewriting of the feminine, a feminist re-inscription of gynetics" (2003, 361). Gynetics is an interstitial process that produces both a testimonial chronicle of self and an overdetermined series of signs: a speaking subject that is also already spoken for. But while gynetics is clearly meant to suggest an embodied form of text, Alarcón's analysis, as well as her own critical practice, emphasizes the linguistic nature of its process: a form of border poetics that nevertheless leaves Alarcón dissatisfied.

On the one hand, Alarcón defends, develops, and even practices this form of border poetics, a nonrational aporetic thinking accompanied by an excessive troping with standard grammatical devices such as the hyphen, the parenthesis, and the slash.[5] Alarcón argues that only such an ambiguous practice of signification can lead women of color in general, and Chicanas in particular, out of the nonsymbolizable space where the patriarchal supremacist discourse has placed them. Only through this practice can women of color reinscribe a body that has suffered a symbolic fragmentation, dismemberment, and an erasure from the body politic. Alarcón insists that Chicanas turn their violent experience (their silencing and dislocating experience through a multiplicity and confluence of discourses, material and narrative) into text: "Chicanas want to textualize those effects" (2003, 367). And she rightfully suggests the need for a poetics of linguistic excess as a *pharmakon*, a cure that is as intense as the experienced loss of meaning.

On the other hand, Alarcón is also wary and suspicious of what seems to her to be the overly symbolic nature of her own solution. In all of her critical pieces, Alarcón interrogates her own place in the Academy, and troubles the limits of postmodern postfeminist theorizations not unlike her own. She never forgets the materiality of the effects of the symbolic order on women in general and on women of color in particular. Indeed, she walks with the attitude of the body that Alarcón herself describes as stepping in and out of academic discourses. She displays a mastery of abstract language. And she insists on the relevance of both normative and alternative symbolic practices to particular and distinct bodies. To her credit, Alarcón consistently leaves us with an open question: "The contemporaneous question, then, is . . . what [the interstice] might imply . . . especially for women of Mexican descent and others for whom work means migrations to the electronic, high-tech assembly work on both sides of the U.S.-Mexican border" (2003, 367). Alarcón's questions keep open the intermediary space between theory and practice, but also between discourse and person, between body and language.

Anzaldúa's Interface

"I grew up in the interface" (1999, 60). Instead of representing the maternal with the aporias of language, Anzaldúa represents it with the symbol of a wound, and calls this wound an interface. "It was only there at the interface that we could see each other" (1999, 170). The interface is Anzaldúa's metaphor for an embodied inflection, an organic writing and an intuitive reasoning, that comes from a polyvalent wound that is also (but not only) a maternal womb. "Between the two eyes in her head, the tongueless magical eye and the loquacious rational eye, was *la rajadura*, the abyss that no bridge could span" (1999, 67). She associates the interface and it's embodied inflections with the vicissitudes of the maternal body: its joys, its rhythms, its generative potential, but also its history as a site of violence. "The U.S.-Mexican border es una *herida abierta* where the Third World grates against the first and bleeds" (1999, 25). Anzaldúa's interface resists patriarchal mystifications: the reduction of the maternal to a purely biological and destructive event. But sometimes Anzaldúa herself reduces the maternal interface to a purely organic event, even if its effect is creative as well as pleasurable. "A cool tendril pressing between my legs / entering" (1999, 172). Like Alarcón's interstice, Anzaldúa's interface goes a long way in the pursuit of the accidental and supportive function of the maternal. But if Alarcón's interstice sometimes seems to turn the body into a transcendental word, the embrace of pure body limits Anzaldúa's interface from the opposite direction.

Anzaldúa's *Borderlands/La Frontera: The New Mestiza* (first published in 1987), offers more insights into the intriguing intermediary zone between body and language explored by Alarcón in her essays. "Petrified, [the woman of color] can't respond, her face caught between *los intersticios*, the spaces between the different worlds she inhabits" (1999, 42). Anzaldúa's emphasis, however, is on the maternal body and not so much on Patriarchal Language. Indeed, she aims at changing the role of the maternal figure in subject formation from its traditional inscription both in Mexico and in the southwestern United States as a treacherous woman who betrays the Mexican nation, race, and identity.[6] Rather than circumscribing her to a biological body that must be abandoned in order to attain sociality, language, and subject-status, Anzaldúa instead argues for the need to redefine the maternal role and the body in the process of subject formation. "White America has only attended to the body of the earth in order to exploit it, never to succor it or to be nurtured in it" (1999, 90). The maternal function for Anzaldúa is analogous to the Kristevan semiotic chora, or to the *structuring* disposition of the semiotic.[7] Anzaldúa associates this function with an embodied mode of writing. "And for images, words, stories to have this transformative power, they must arise from the human body—flesh and bone—and from the Earth's body—stone, sky, liquid, soil" (1999, 97). In *Borderlands/La Frontera*, this writing is performed through the symbolic bodies of multiple mythical mother figures including Coatlicue's "cavernous womb" (1999, 68).[8]

The matricidal, if not suicidal, effect, of fortified subjectivity as it is generated within Patriarchy motivates Anzaldúa's rejection of the mythical figure of Malinche. It also explains her development of an alternative way to figure the maternal, and her elaboration of a constellation of concepts related to the maternal experience that is analogous to the main structuring operations of the unconscious: displacement and condensation. At the figurative level, Anzaldúa substitutes la Malinche by Coatlicue, the ancient Aztec goddess of both creation and destruction. But Coatlicue (and its many other forms such as "The Shadow Beast," "The Serpent," or "Leyla") is nothing for Anzaldúa if it is not a figure for the unsettling forces that nevertheless must be allowed to give *structure* to our psyche. "Coatlicue is one of the powerful images, or 'archetypes,' that inhabits, or passes through, my psyche" (1999, 68).[9]

In other words, Anzaldúa's maternal is not reduced to what Alarcón calls "the inarticulable site of the Freudian/Lacanian unconscious" (1996, 231 n. 1). Instead the maternal interface resonates with Kristeva's semiotic chora in its singular deployment by Anzaldúa.[10] It is a border state between opposing spiritualities (1999, 60) or between the physical and the noumenal world (1999, 170). Coatlicue (or "The Serpent," or "Leyla") is the embodiment of this interface. The Coatlicue State is the structuring unconscious force that inflects our bodies with instinctive reasoning and "organic writing" (1981, 172).[11] Similar to the semiotic chora, both organic writing and instinctive reasoning bear the uncanny traces of the unconscious operations that nevertheless give structure to the psyche. "Organic writing" works similarly to alchemy and *condenses* body and language into something different that surprises even the subject who performs it. "It's not on paper that you create it but in your innards, in the gut and out of living tissue— *organic writing* I call it" (1981, 172). "*La facultad*," on the other hand, is a vestige of a "proximity sense" that is sensitive to that which is *displaced* from view but is still strangely present in front of us. "*La facultad* is the capacity to see in surface phenomena . . . the deep structure below the surface" (1999, 60). "Organic writing" and "*La facultad*" are Anzaldúa's terms for the enabling forces of the unconscious drive, the accidents, the slips, the dreams, the jokes, the *susto*, or "sudden shock or fall that frightens the soul out of the body" that both trouble and produce life (1999, 60).

Anzaldúa criticizes the tendency of Western and European positivistic and spiritual thought to erase these accidents that she associates with the maternal body, with its productive rhythms and creative pleasures. "We are taught that the body is an ignorant animal; intelligence dwells only in the head" (1999, 59). This defensive erasure distorts the ambiguous force of accident (and of the maternal) in the process of subject formation. "We're supposed to ignore, forget, kill those fleeting images of the soul's presence and of the spirit's presence" (1999, 58). She suggests that the subject that emerges from these erasures and distortions is a matricidal subject that defensively inverts the value of the very operations of the unconscious, turning them against the maternal body. The treacherous maternal figure of La Malinche is one example of the effect of the erasures at the center of matricidal subjectivity. The myth of La Malinche changes the structuring effect of intuitive reason and organic writing, turning them instead into operations that erase, forget, or de-structure the maternal. La Malinche emerges from this myth as a rattling chest of bones threatening the Mexican subject with perdition.[12] On the one hand, the myth creates and promotes specific or normative versions of identity and authority based on the process of *condensation*. La Malinche *condenses* and circumscribes abjected, racialized, and sexualized subjects, within organic, natural, and biological envelopes or receptacles. Normative subjectivity is then formed in opposition to, or through separation from, these condensed and biologically determined (if phantasmatic) structures that then render silent the Chicana subject. In other words, normative subjectivity depends on *displacing* the maternal abject onto women who are then made into an object or an other.

But these self-deluded matricidal operations are also spiral in form and stifling in effect. The best example of this matricidal operation driven to its logical conclusion is perhaps Octavio Paz's description of the "mythical wound" in his *Labyrinth of Solitude*. Anzaldúa writes against this and similar definitions of what she calls "*la rajadura*": "This Indian flesh that we, Mexicans, despise, just as we despise and condemn Malinali, our mother. We condemn ourselves. This defeated race, enemy body" ([my translation] 1999, 44). The mythical wound *condenses* the maternal object into the Indian skin that covers the body of the Mexican, a skin that the Mexican subject must then abject in order to develop a stable, rational, spiritually, racially, and sexually normative subjectivity. Anzaldúa and Alarcón instead remind us that the mythical definition of the wound *displaces* the literal wounding and violent penetration of women in Conquest, and the historical figure of Malintzin to the invisible margins. Most importantly, however, the mythical wound hides from view the enabling accidents, the organic writing, and the intuitive reasoning, also associated with

the maternal body, *condensing and displacing* its ambiguous operations away from both the sight and the site of normative subjectivity.

The tragedy of these matricidal operations is that they unwittingly
do what they seek to prevent. Instead of resulting in stable and fortified subjects, they multiply figures for wounded subjectivities. For
Anzaldúa, grasping the social origins of the now reversed structuring
operations is of paramount importance to understand the disabling
effect of the mythical wound. But it is also important to understand
that the reversed operations of the Malinche myth are inseparable
from simultaneous and similarly reversed operations bearing on the
individual psyche for Anzaldúa. In fact, social and familiar distortions
and erasures find their analogy in an internal self-violence for her.
These internal operations mirror the external ones, and similarly
rearrange and distort the operations of subjectivity in such a way so as
to allow the normative subject to emerge. They create prejudices
against an abject, or an ambiguous process that is found within the
subject and even constitutes it. "When I was older I would look into
the mirror, afraid of *mi secreto terrible*, the secret sin I tried to conceal—
la seña, the mark of the Beast" (1999, 64). This self-violence combines with social violence to produce the haunting internal and external, homeless and displaced form of the mythical wound that
Anzaldúa' tries to re-member in her text. Indeed, this mythical wound
appears in every form and in every subject as a psychological, linguistic, individual and collective, and private and public reminder of
matricide.[13] "And I think *la Jila is Cihuacoatl*, Snake Woman; she is *la
Llorona*, Daughter of Night, traveling the dark terrains of the
unknown searching for the lost parts of herself" (1999, 60). The mythical wound is both abstract and omnipresent, but its effect (Anzaldúa
reminds us) is particular to, as well as materially violent for, those who
are identified with its abject forms of sexuality and race.

Through the body in general, and lesboerotic desire in particular,
Anzaldúa returns a vital structuring effect to the operations of the
unconscious and to the symbol of the wound. "A cool tendril pressing
between my legs / entering. / Her finger, I thought / but it went on and
on" (1999, 172). Through the accidents of the interface (organic writing and intuitive reasoning), Anzaldúa brings the supportive and
enabling aspect of the maternal back into view. By practicing intuitive
reasoning (or *La facultad*) and organic writing, by claiming them as
part of her cultural heritage, by allowing them to shape her self in
writing, Anzaldúa implicitly returns structure and meaning-making to
the maternal. In doing so, Anzaldúa takes a number of risks. To write

organically and to think intuitively as Anzaldúa claims to do in *Borderlands* is to risk derision, ridicule, and even violence in a matricidal culture. It is as risky a practice as it is to claim a lesbian identity in a patently homophobic culture.

But Anzaldúa doesn't only risk being pathologized, as Alarcón has rightly remarked. She also risks experiencing the unsettling effects of these processes. "Writing is dangerous because we are afraid of what the writing reveals: the fears, the angers, the strengths of a woman under a triple or quadruple oppression" (Anzaldúa 1981, 171). To allow the body and its drives, instincts, and desires to inflect one's voice, writing, and language, is to both reveal and disavow the erasures of the maternal in our culture. "I sometimes get sick when I *do* write. I can't stomach it, become nauseous, or burn with fever, worsen" (1999, 92). In this sense, *Borderlands* is a hopefully perverse, creatively fetishistic book that denies the radical loss of the maternal in the face of widespread symbolic matricide. In so doing, *Borderlands* preserves what Teresa de Lauretis has called the uncertainty, the radical motility, and the sustained mutation of desire (1994, 203–253 in passim). *Borderlands* returns meaning making and desire to a context and to a body where both are made impossible. "But, in reconstructing the traumas behind the images, I make 'sense' of them, and once they have 'meaning' they are changed, transformed" (1999, 92). By living in the uncomfortable interface that she calls the Coatlicue State, Anzaldúa removes the self-delusions that distinguish matricidal, suicidal, and normative subjectivity. Instead, she embraces its disavowals, and opens up the possibility of a different kind of subject that she calls the new *mestiza*, a border subject. "Living in a state of psychic unrest, in a Borderland, is what makes poets write and artists create" (1999, 95).

Borderlands suggests that life requires more than a joyful, triumphant, and uncritical abandonment to, and identification with, the archaic and primitive forces that constitute the maternal body in a matricidal context. Anzaldúa suggests that life requires the reinscription of the bodily drives (organic and instinctive) as structuring accidents that contain death. In this way, by calling attention to an inheritance of instinctive knowledge and organic reason, by insisting on re-membering the Mexican mythical wound as a lesboerotic fetish, Anzaldúa underscores the necessary means to sustain life at the uncanny borderlands of the United States. By insistently inflecting her writing with the ambiguous rhythms of a racialized and sexualized maternal body, Anzaldúa goes a long way in the effort to preserve its life. By re-membering wounds of the maternal body and by celebrating and singing its vicissitudes, she returns our faith in its meaning-making potential.

In *Borderlands*, Anzaldúa advises that we "let the wound caused by the serpent be cured by the serpent" (1999, 68). But in the effort to *cure* the wound by acknowledging the simultaneously haunting and enabling operations at the center of subjectivity, Anzaldúa also seems to forget her own warnings. In her 1981 essay, she writes "We can't transcend the dangers, can't rise above them. We must go through them and *hope we won't have to repeat the performance*" ([My emphasis] 1981, 165). In *Borderlands*, however, she comes close to reifying the maternal body, sometimes triumphantly, and perhaps romantically, describing it as a divine and undifferentiated state of pleasure. "I collapse into myself—a delicious caving into myself—imploding, the walls like matchsticks softly folding inward in slow motion" (1999, 73). This description of an imploding body threatens to erase the productive tension Anzaldúa herself struggles to preserve. She argues that a tension must exist between the structures and accidents (the vicissitudes) of the maternal. By going too far in an idealizing direction, Anzaldúa comes dangerously close to hypostatizing a death driven unconscious. "It is this learning to live with la Coatlicue that transforms living in the Borderlands from a nightmare into a numinous experience" (1999, 95). Sometimes the reader feels that Anzaldúa's homage to the maternal is romanticized to the point of freeing the body from its unsettling nature and effect. "All the lost pieces of my self come flying from the deserts and the mountains and the valleys, magnetized toward that center. *Completa*" (1999, 73). Conversely, the reader also perceives an intermittent reduction of the border subject to a similarly passive figure, now a wounded victim of external oppressive forces, or of self-destructive internal forces. "*La mojada, la mujer indocumentada*, is doubly threatened in this country. Not only does she have to contend with sexual violence, but like all women, she is prey to a sense of physical helplessness" (1999, 35). Resisting these romantic temptations, Cherríe Moraga instead insists on the promise of the wounded maternal skin, and of the self-wounding agency of the Chicana.

Wounded Skin

Moraga takes advantage of Alarcón and Anzaldúa's complementary insights into the maternal, represented by their respective elaboration of the interface and the interstice. Their search for the maternal as both an accident and an enabling event is her point of departure. And

Moraga also refers to the maternal as an intermediary space between body and language. But Moraga also turns their search into an urgent and uncanny pursuit. She refers to the maternal both as wounded skin and as a self-wounding process that pierces skin. Indeed, Moraga suggests that we are all responsible for the precariousness and the perviousness of a skin that is both ours and not ours, which hinges language and the body, which makes us vulnerable and yet protects us. Her self-wounding writing has an ambiguous effect on the symbolic subjects that emerge from her works, and a similarly troubling effect on the forces oppressing them. Writing is both painful and pleasurable, oppressive and liberating. It is not only an aesthetic but also a revolutionary practice that aims to return troubling agency and voice to the silenced Chicana subject.

Waiting in the Wings (1997) is Moraga's latest effort in a series of attempts to contain the sources of the pain and radicalism of oppressed people. "I think, what is hardest for any oppressed people to understand is that the sources of oppression form not only our radicalism, but also our pain" (1983, 134). Throughout her work, Moraga describes the source of radicalism and pain as a hole in the body, a premature "cutting out" from the maternal body, an interruption and a loss of maternal plenitude. Characters like Dolores in *Heroes and Saints* (originally published in 1986), for example, describe giving birth as a violent act of appropriation or theft. "You are a chain to that baby. It doesn' matter how old they get or how far away they go, son tus hijos and they always take a piece of you with them. So you walk around full of holes from all the places they take from you" (1995, 130). Corky, the character of Moraga's play *Giving Up the Ghost* (originally published in 1989) cries out "He made me a hole!" associating rape with a similarly painful hole (1995, 29). In *The Last Generation* (1993), Moraga recasts this hole as "a primordial state of female hunger" and associates it with lesbian desire (107). "My first Chicana lover . . . was . . . 'without holes in her body.' Still, like those Mexican pots, she had a wide-open mouth, ready to devour everything surrounding her. This was lesbian, I discovered" (119).

In these early works, Moraga describes lesbian desire as a haunting return of an archaic void, of a primordial loss, hunger, and desire, repressed (tamed and domesticated) by a tradition of ancient rituals and contemporary narratives that graft a symbolic hole onto the body of the Mexican mother. The Aztecs, Moraga will remind her readers, were responsible for the patriarchal myth of the Hungry Woman: an archaic mother figure with a body covered by a skin of insatiable mouths (Bierhorst 1984, 23–25). Moraga will set out to rewrite this myth in her later works. But lesbian desire emerges from her early works as a liberating form of this truncated, archaic, hunger for, and by, the mother. Lesbian desire returns joy to the skin of the body in these early texts by Moraga; and joy returns in the form of a memory of uninterrupted if lost maternal *jouissance*: "as if our bodies still beat / inside the same skin" (1983, 14). As de Lauretis has compellingly argued, Moraga displays an enabling perverse desire that fetishizes an always already lost mother in works such as *Giving Up the Ghost*.

But it is her later companion works "*The Hungry Woman: A Mexican Medea*" (2001) and *Waiting in the Wings* that interest me here. The maternal is not always already lost, but is recovered instead as a powerful if troubling force in these later works. Moraga pursues this archaic loss to the point of literally becoming a lesbian mother, meeting the maternal in its uncanny, troubled, but also powerful site. Similar to *Waiting in the Wings*, the play tells the story of a lesbian mother, and stays close to the painful and disturbing edge of her losses and desires. The play also describes a mysterious power that comes from that edge. Moraga describes this power in a later interview. "If you feel that as a woman, as a Chicana, that you have been born hungry, that fuerza, the power of what you could be, comes to you . . . that memory of being something bigger than this racist world" (Kevane 2000, 107). Medea, the main character in the play, uses this troubling and yet powerful memory. She kills her own progeny as a desperate last measure against the violence of a future Chicano patriarchy. Indeed, the gesture of the Mexican Medea is homicidal. But it is also enabling in so far as it returns humanity, meaning, and willful agency to impulses that are made unthinkable and irrational by matricidal narratives such as the Aztec myth and Euripides' *Medea*.[14]

Moraga rewrites this troubled and powerful edge between loss and recovery in *Waiting in the Wings*. In this memoir, Moraga describes her lesbian motherhood as an ambiguous and ambivalent experience. The maternal emerges from her memoir as a fragmented, perforated, and troubled state that gives birth to a similarly fragmented, perforated, and troubled life: Rafael Angel, a premature baby artificially conceived in a racist and homophobic society. Moraga writes that the birth of Rafael Angel makes both loving and writing more difficult, troubling, nigh impossible for her. "It is hard to write when there is no fixed me to be" (1997, 166). Tired and haunted by the fear of the message of death paradoxically delivered with (and by) Rafael Angel, Moraga's life changes. She separates from her lesbian companion, and wonders at her transformed self and writing: "The writing isn't any less challenging, but now a hole has been created through which my child passed. (Don Juan speaks of this.) Now the work—the art—passes through me differently. I can't say how, exactly" (1997, 95). The memoir bears witness to these painful vicissitudes, but it also represents Moraga's deliberate, willful, and implacable pursuit of accident, her development of a thick protective skin that is nevertheless "all wound" (1997, 65).

The metaphor of life-preserving skin screens (both covers and reveals) the holes disseminated throughout Moraga's texts. Skin is both thick and porous in *Waiting in the Wings*. Moraga describes it as the body's protective layer, as a "thick-membraned blood-smell," as a "thick, rich, yellow liquid" (1997, 67, 99). Skin is both the physical envelope covering the body, and a fluid metaphor, a membraned smell, a thick liquid, and even a network of queer relations (*comadres*, doctors, nurses, family, caregivers, spirits, colored queerboys). Skin is a "smooth glove of dried parchment" that nevertheless contains a secret, a hunger, the archaic holes that inspire *susto*, an endless fear, but also holds a promise of relief and joy (1997, 116). Indeed, thick and porous skin is a metaphor for a form of writing that joins the body and language in Moraga; a transformative form of writing both human and animal, ancient and new. It is a figurative space similar to Anzaldúa's interface and to Alarcón's interstice in its evocation of the ambiguous edge of the maternal experience. Like the interface and the interstice, Moraga's skin challenges and demystifies the rhetoric that distinguishes between language and body, a rhetoric that parses them into different gendered categories.

If porous, fluid, ambiguous skin is a metaphor for writing in Moraga, writing is, in turn, a mnemonic excavation of, an unearthing from, and a passage through, skin. Writing is a place similarly marked by both absence and presence, "where the work possesses us and our pitiful egos take flight" (1993, 176). Writing is also ambiguous, both a source of strength and of torture (1983, 132). It is a place in conflict with itself, inhabited by hybrid words and rhythms (1983, 55). Writing is even a practice beyond symbolic language for Moraga (1993, 185). It is a pursuit of the body's accidents, its heterogeneous language: the symptoms of illness as well as the fluttering of health; pregnancy, but also the body's reaction against it; conscious memories but also dreams. Autobiography is a transcription of her body's signs, a symbolic transformation of its drives, to "get to the heart of [her] feeling" for Moraga (1997, 26, 38). Self-writing approximates

Moraga to what she calls a "prememory," an experience before the insufficient displacements and condensations of a cultural memory that Alarcón calls "the incompletely Angloamericanized Southwest" of the United States (Alarcón 2003, 358; Kevane 2000, 107).

Writing and skin combine in Moraga's image of tattooing, and together they work as poetic anamnesis, enabling survival at the border by provoking pain, but also by transforming pain into prayer. "I pray as you cut. I pray deep and hard and if it pusses, I pray harder for the pain. In the center of the pain, there is always a prayer" (2001, 21). Moraga locates both the uncanny source of pain and the relief for that pain, not only in our permeable and thick skin, but also in a perforation, a writing, that bears witness, pays homage, or remembers a collective wound. Wounded skin is the place where a supportive community returns to Moraga. "A prayer where you get up to leave and a whole army of people is there to carry you away. You aren't alone anymore" (2001, 21). In short, the tattooed skin of Chac-Mool in "*The Hungry Woman,*" and the traumatized skin of Rafael Angel in *Waiting in the Wings*, are figures for a testimonial form of writing. Their tattooed and lacerated skins bear witness to the accident of being born. But they also testify to the specific accident of being born in the contested ground between national borders. Writing on skin is a testimony to the deeply ingrained violence of persistent homophobic rituals and racist master narratives. Wounded skin is both a reminder of, and a paradoxical cure for, a complex form of violence perpetrated on the body at the border.

Wounding Skin

Chac-Mool and Rafael Angel suffer the pain and endure the testimony of their wounded skin. But Moraga offers an even more powerful and compelling representation of a border subject in her autobiographical *Waiting in the Wings*. A young female student is described there, both defensively writing in her notebook and violently sticking needles into her skin. She goes further than Chac-Mool and Rafael Angel in her intensely paradoxical form of agency. Rosie goes so far as to wound her own skin in an effort to contain and transform the material and linguistic forces that disable her.

> Rosie hunches over the pages of her notebook, blocking her tight-fisted scrawl with the draping sleeve of her flannel shirt. She is my student. At fifteen, Rosie has more piercings etched into her flesh than her number

of years on the planet. She puts down her pen and looks up at me with wide eyes. "Am I doomed," she asks with those eyes. I know her family history—the brutal fact of abuse, the white rapist father, the silent latina mother. So she cuts at her body and drives ink and all matters of rings into her skin. She sticks liquid needles into her veins and wonders if she'll survive the season. The season of being young and queer and on the street because home is a more dangerous place to be. She is my daughter. (1997, 18)

The image is a figure for a wounded and self-wounding writer, simultaneously pursued by, and pursuing pain. "I dig at it, *esta herida vieja* / remind it to bleed" (1993, 67). Moraga often repeats this self-wounding practice in her own writing, emphasizing its accidental nature: both its risks and its promises. "Possibly the greatest risks yet to be taken are *entre nosotros*, where we write, paint, dance, and draw the wound for one another in order to build a stronger *pueblo*" (1993, 71). And Moraga's poetic pursuit of accident is relentless. It is clearly manifested in her unflinching drive to ask herself hard, even self-wounding questions in her writing. For example, she undertakes an examination of the intimate "places we feel we must protect unexamined at all costs" in *Loving in War Years* (1983, 134); she interrogates her "unyielding need to re-live the rape, understand the rape, the loss . . . the truth" in *The Last Generation* (1993, 114); she questions her conviction that lesbians on the more masculine side of the spectrum aren't really women, and later she asks "how is it I can be pregnant and write the story of killing a child?" in *Waiting in the Wings* (1997, 20, 33). Indeed, Moraga's autobiographical writing is similar to Kristeva's poetic anamnesis in its deliberate pursuit of the constitutive instability and heterogeneity of the subject. In other words, Moraga's writing makes its troubled home in the space left open by Alarcón's unanswered questions.

Perhaps Felman best described the practice of these self-wounding writers calling it a surprising and momentous poetic testimony. "What makes the newness and the radicality of the poetic . . . performance of a testimony which is both 'surprising' and momentous is . . . not just the inescapability of the vocation of the witness in so far as the accident pursues him, *but the witness's readiness . . . to pursue the accident*" ([My emphasis] 1992, 24). In *Testimony; Crises of Witnessing in Literature, Psychoanalysis, and History*, Felman describes the pursuit of accident as the deliberate repetition of a process of invocation and apostrophe, as the insistent return to a quality of addressability. She argues in that book, that limit-events such as the French Revolution, the entrance into Modernity, the World Wars, and the Holocaust, have annihilated (more successfully and categorically with each successive event) this process of invocation and quality of addressability. For Felman, life depends on the return of this process and quality. This return depends on the continued attempt by poets like Paul Celán to pursue accident, to invoke, apostrophe, or address incomprehension, a missed encounter, an implicit violence, a trauma, or a wound.[15]

Most importantly, this return depends on a self-wounding pursuit. According to Felman, Celán means to approximate language to an accident that annihilates its addressability by inflecting the pursuit with the accidental quality itself, with the violence inherent in accident. By doing so, the pursuit of accident, or poetic testimony works a fundamental reciprocal transformation. The self-violent pursuit transforms the implacable nature of the pursuing accident, and it changes the dehumanized fate of the witness who is pursued (or "elected") by accident. Felman writes that to pursue accident in this self-wounding way, "is to give reality one's own vulnerability as a condition of exceptional availability and . . . attention to the relation between language and events" (Felman 1992, 29). Poetic testimony (understood as the self-violent pursuit of accident) reopens a passage between accident and testimony, between events that are beyond thinking and language. This passage allows accident to once again become intelligible, meaningful, and therefore vulnerable. It returns the witness to the exceptional position connecting language and events. Indeed, this passage is the condition of possibility for continuing life after the accidents of history, accidents that also include the oppressive experience of Chicana lesbians in the United States at the turn of the twenty-first century.

Moraga suggests that a self-wounding writing can be a similar poetic testimony, and that its painful sources, its accidents, can also be paradoxically protective, enabling, and even empowering. Wounding skin is the radical poetic practice of the student in the passage by Moraga quoted above. Rosie's "writing" (cutting at her body and driving ink and rings into her skin) is surprising because it is both painful and poetic. But her writing is truly momentous because the student actively pursues its painful source. By painfully pursuing the source of writing in the same way that oppression pursues her, the poet affirms her agency in the face of those very oppressive sources threatening to erase and silence her. By wounding herself, she reveals the vulnerability of those sources and the limits of their oppression. By wounding herself, she performs a poetic testimony that returns meaning to the accident of being young and queer and on the street; she bears witness to the only mode of agency made available to her, even as she appropriates and transforms it. By wounding herself, she poetically testifies to the silencing discourses that surround her. Hers is a paradoxical testimony that reopens the necessary passage connecting writing and oppression even as it wounds her. Rosie finds, opens, and speaks to, and through, the wound that her context is so eager to displace and graft onto her.

But Moraga's passage also goes beyond Felman's account of this necessary poetic testimony. Felman also closes the passage she opens through her insightful analysis of Celán's poetry. If Felman implies a necessary connection between the body and language through a discussion of the wound, she also brackets out the figure of the maternal body from the enabling passage, from the open wounded writing that connects language and accident. Felman again imprisons the maternal body in the place of darkness, of incomprehensibility, of trauma beyond language.[16] Instead, Moraga locates the maternal on the edge of the ambiguous (oppressive and protective) source of writing. On the one hand, the source of the student's pain and writing is "the white rapist father, the silent latina mother." But on the other hand, the source of the student's painful writing is also Moraga herself ("She is my daughter"). More importantly, Moraga represents writing or poetry as a painful passage through a maternal membrane that is both thick and perforated. In the quotation by Moraga cited above, she answers her student's question whether she is doomed by recognizing Rosie's self-violence as an enabling if painful form of writing. Moraga seems to say to Rosie and to her readers that writing is the thick but necessarily porous, pervious skin that both protects us and makes us vulnerable. And indeed, Moraga suggests in her work that writing is the membrane that mediates between organic drives that are always already invested with structure and a language that is always already pierced by accidents. Writing is the "receiving membrane," the buffer zone, the zone of contact that links and separates the building blocks of language and speaking subjectivity for Moraga (cf. Kristeva 1984, 240 n.13).

Moraga's writing membrane is also a politically inflected. In *Revolution and Poetic Language*, Kristeva praises high modernist writers like Joyce and Mallarmé for a form of writing that represents "a total exploration of the signifying process," but she also concedes that their *experimental* writing dispenses with "political and social signifieds" (1984, 88). Moraga's autobiographical writing instead describes in detail the harassment and the interrogations suffered at the hands of the sometimes homophobic, sometimes racist hospital staff (orderlies and doctors), and the institutional effect of the absence of legal status for the lesbian co-mother in her book (1997, 75–76). Indeed, Moraga engages in a paradoxical politics of remembering what cannot be remembered in what I would call instead an *experiential* mode of writing. "I am trying to write about the impossible" Moraga writes (1997, 117). By reaching "that memory of being something bigger than this racist world," Moraga's poetic performance, her deliberate pursuit of accidents, her writing of a wounded maternal membrane, changes the brutal facts that abuse her and her student. The racist world becomes smaller, its homophobic families become more precarious and vulnerable. "It's like making familia from scratch each time all over again" (1997, 14). Moraga makes family possible again by scratching at, or repeatedly cutting into, our most familiar and, for that reason, our most oppressive sites.

I end by focusing on Moraga's *Waiting in the Wings*, not because I find that it balances the different forces that constitute the maternal, but because the memoir transforms the recovery of the maternal into an implacable pursuit of accident. I am struck by the fact that the memoir insists so remarkably on the painful agency of meaning-making. Writing is a self-wounding chase of accident for Moraga, and her figure of the writer–mother, her maternal body language, and her testimony to lesbian motherhood are different forms of this urgent chase. As a pursuit of accident, her memoir is a form of compelling poetic practice that I associate with testimony. Indeed, together with Alarcón's interstice and Anzaldúa's interface, Moraga's relentless pursuit of accident and her wounded and wounding skin, constitutes a testimonial poetic practice. The combined maternal testimony of these writers returns vulnerability and intelligibility to the accident of being. More specifically, however, their works return a painful but hopeful meaning-making agency to Chicanas and *lesbianas* that suffer the particular accident of being born in a place and at a time when defensive economic, social, and cultural imperatives and judgments turn their lives into impenetrable, silent, and irrelevant objects beyond comprehension.

5

Memoirs for the Abject: Irene Vilar's *Memoria*

At the end of *The Ladies' Gallery* (1996), Irene Vilar writes "Mother has died, therefore I am" (323). She repeats this provocative and striking association between her life and the death of her mother, Gladys Mirna, in a recent televised interview.[1] Identifying with Anne Frank (whose diary she read when she was nine years old), Vilar suggests that the loss of her mother undermines and transforms her. Her mother's suicide turns her into a "traveling child." She describes the experience as waking up in somebody else's house, as having to relate to "weird people with . . . weird antics," and most poignantly as having to "ask permission to exist every morning." But Vilar also states that this loss not only delegitimizes her, but it transforms her into something more fluid, giving her a new identity as a writer. She says that the loss of her mother is the origin of the writer's "fluid" point of view, of her ability to imagine other people's thoughts, a point of view and an ability that Vilar also calls, more mysteriously now, an "internal dialogue" and "a translation."

In her memoir, Vilar also mourns a loss of national origin and national identity resulting from the effects of colonialization on Puerto Rico—her now "portable" homeland. Vilar is granddaughter to Lolita Lebrón, "martyr" of Puerto Rican independence, and nationalist icon of Motherhood.[2] The violent colonial situation turns Lolita Lebrón into a prisoner for life and into an epic figure with a haunting and ghostly voice. Vilar mourns the loss of national identity together with the loss of her grandmother in her memoir. More specifically, she describes and underscores the catastrophic effects of the loss of national identity on her and on her family. The losses of the colonial process turn Lebrón and Vilar into melancholy writers bent on regaining what is lost by identifying with it and by silencing their own voices.

Similar to Gladys Mirna, Lebrón and Irene Vilar become suicidal figures.

And yet, Vilar's memoir also translates Lolita Lebrón's ghostly voice, transforming it in the process and allowing a human voice to surface alongside the epic voice of martyrdom that proclaims "A Message from God in the Atomic Age" (the title of Lebrón's book of poems written from prison). Similarly, the memoir also allows a space for another voice to accompany Vilar's melancholy and suicidal voice. Indeed, the memoir is an internal dialogue between Vilar's two voices, set side by side, and transcribed in two types. As a result, the memoir transforms the petrified and even mythical personas of Lolita Lebrón, her daughter, and her granddaughter into something more fluid. *The Ladies' Gallery* is then a testimony to the catastrophic nature of the limit-event at the center of melancholy writing. It mourns the loss of nation and origin, but it also transforms the symptomatic identification with this loss into something unstable but human: a *memoria*. "Mother has died, therefore I am. Not a nation, it is true, but a presence that remains. A book" (323).

The Ladies' Gallery does more than describe Vilar's transformation into a writer. Indeed, it describes the vexed process of subject formation itself. In her memoir, Vilar struggles to understand the absence of the necessary components of the process of subject formation in a late capitalist era that globalizes, accelerates, and intensifies loss. "Nation, ethnicity, belonging, even the word history, all of these things are changing. It's not any more some sort of French translated theory book that we were reading ten years ago and we said 'oh, you know, we are all citizens of the world'. Now it's very concrete."[3] Such comprehensive loss produces a nostalgic identification, an obsessive need to stabilize our origins by affirming and recovering our lost identity. But identity so configured, Vilar insists, emerges troubled and vexed by its damaged (if not entirely absent) components, by its "wounds." Vilar's autobiographical memoir confronts the reader with the catastrophic effect of this self-constitutive cycle of loss and recovery. But the memoir also suggests the need to transform the reactive process of subject formation that drives this suicidal cycle. *The Ladies' Gallery* remembers unstable lost material; it reclaims the beauty of the wounds of identity; it listens to the sacrificed voices of Lolita Lebrón and Gladys Mirna, the irretrievable maternal losses. By remembering, reclaiming, and listening to the abject, *The Ladies' Gallery* transforms loss into living and speaking subjectivity. She calls it a presence that remains. She writes a book.

Memoria: Between Narrative and Memory

Memoria in Spanish is comparable to *mémoire* in French. Unlike the English "memory," *memoria* means slightly (if significantly) different things. On the one hand, it means remembrance, or the psychological process of remembering. As such, it is a process opposed to forgetting, to the loss of memory. On the other, it means narrative or report, and as such, it is a process based on forgetting. Plato famously opposed memory to writing in the *Phaedrus*, where the god Ammon mourns the end of memory and laments the invention of writing: "The fact is that this invention will produce forgetfulness in the souls of those who have learned it. They will not need to exercise their memory, being able to rely on what is written, calling things to mind no longer from within themselves by their own unaided powers, but under the stimulus of external marks that are alien to themselves. So it's not a recipe for memory, but for reminding, that you have discovered" (Plato 1956, *Phaedrus* 68.275). In his essay "Mnemosyne," Jacques Derrida maintains and transforms this opposition of memory and writing by mourning the end of narrative and lamenting his love of memory. "But what happens when the lover of Mnemosyne has not received the gift of narration? When he doesn't know how to tell a story? When it is precisely because he keeps the memory that he loses the narrative?" (Derrida 1989, 3). While Plato asked his readers to practice the "living and breathing word" (of which the written word is only the image) for the sake of memory, Derrida challenges his readers to inhabit instead the unstable common ground of memory and narrative, of remembering and forgetting.

Derrida locates this uncanny site in *mémoire*. According to Derrida, the memory of a loss before narrative, and the narrative of the remembering self inhabit *mémoire*. For him, "memory" and "narrative" refer to different versions of the same mourning for an irretrievable loss. Together, these processes constitute *mémoire*: the impossible affirmation of otherness, and the possibility of its narration through technics, in a report, in a recording, or in writing. In other words, for Derrida *mémoire* is both possible and impossible mourning, and its specular process has the paradoxical effect of constituting a similarly precarious self and other. *Mémoire* constitutes a threatened remembering self that resists dissolution, and a threatened remembered other that resists the closure of our memory.

Mémoire, understood as possible and impossible mourning, is the condition of possibility for deconstruction. For Derrida, deconstruction is the study of the resistance that *mémoire* generates. He describes *mémoire* as "the procession of a mobile army of metaphors, metonymies, and anthropomorphisms" (30). This procession demystifies essence, truth, nature, self, identity, and so on, by getting us to consider that these concepts not only have their opposites inscribed within them, but more importantly they contain the trace of what Derrida calls "the other on the very eve of meaning." This uncanny and unnerving revelation encounters resistance, and deconstruction is its study and the study of its symptoms. According to Derrida, deconstruction is the very opposite of this resistance. It endures the precariousness of *mémoire*. Indeed, deconstruction is "born" from *mémoire* as mourning. It endures the experience of possible and impossible mourning and remains "in sufferance there" (30).[4]

What is this precarious state or site that includes presence and absence, self and other, remembering and forgetting, and memory and narration? How does the state or site of *mémoire* arise? Why must we inhabit it? Derrida describes *mémoire* as the ambiguous gift of Mnemosyne. This gift, the reader learns, is also the gift of loss. Derrida finds this gift in the remnants of an archaic language. He finds it in everyday expressions, such as the persistent but strange dative of the idiom "*to* the memory of." In Latin, the dative case would be a part of a word; it would not stand apart from it. It would emphasize the action of giving (the word "dative" comes from the Greek *dotike* transformed into the Latin *datus*, the past participle of *dare*, to give). The dative is a generous action embedded in the word. It also marks the recipient of the action from within the word. In the case of the expression "*to* the memory of," however, the action, the recipient, and the grammatical intimacy between them (once preserved by the dative case) are now absent. This loss of intimacy should make giving more difficult if not impossible in language. And yet the expression means the very opposite. "*To* the memory of" means that it is precisely these losses that compel the act of giving in language, that oblige us to give, and that make the dative necessary once again even in its awkward prepositional form. We give in mourning of the lost recipient. We give to mourn a loss of intimacy with the other, an intimacy lost along with the archaic mother tongue (Latin, in the case studied by Derrida).

Significantly, Derrida also finds a similar law of loss in the body of Mnemosyne. If deconstruction is born from *mémoire*, *mémoire* is born from Mnemosyne's maternal body: "*tes tôn Mousôn metros*, the mother of all muses, as Socrates recalls in the *Theaetetus*" (1989, 3). While memory and narrative are not reconciled in Derrida (the self-proclaimed "lover of Mnemosyne") memory and narrative are Mnemosyne. And they are Mnemosyne quite literally, materially, and corporeally for Derrida. Indeed, memory and narrative are the lessons learned from two rhythmic movements of the maternal body, movements inflected with violence and cruelty according to Derrida. Not surprisingly the maternal body is deeply interred within Derrida's essay, for it is a dangerous maternal body that devours and aborts an unborn child (35). As such, Mnemosyne embodies a voracious law of consumption and an implacable law of abandonment.

The self emerges from Mnemosyne both wounded and articulate. It learns to act similarly. Devouring the other in us becomes the minimal condition for self-constitution according to Derrida (34). Aborting and leaving the other alone shows the necessary respect for the other, and allows the self to survive (35). For Derrida, devouring and aborting the other are as impossible as they are necessary acts. Doing both simultaneously is the aporetic law the self learns from the maternal body of Mnemosyne. This law is the command, the trace left by her body before it both abandons and consumes the self. It is the law that obliges the self to live what Derrida calls "the aporia of mourning" (35): the simultaneous memory and narrative of the lost other.

So it is that the gift and the law of loss are combined in Derrida's analysis of *mémoire*, and they are united by the figure of the mother. On the one hand, according to Derrida we must inhabit the unsettling site of *mémoire* because of an ethical responsibility. *Mémoire* is a reciprocal gift to the intimacy of the mother tongue we have lost or perhaps have abandoned. On the other hand, we must inhabit the suffering site of *mémoire* because we are indelibly marked by the corporeal lessons of the maternal body in the throes of the maternal experience as described by Derrida: its simultaneous need to abort and devour. We are shaped by its movements and we will repeat them whether we like it or not, in familiar and unfamiliar (i.e., uncanny) ways.

The Ladies' Gallery inhabits an unsettling and uncanny site similar to Derrida's *mémoire*. It is a *mémoire* or *memoria* understood as the aporia of mourning, as both possible and impossible mourning. On the one hand, it is "a memoir of family secrets," the narrative of a remembering self, a possible narrative that paradoxically erases the maternal body. But it is also an impossible memory that affirms the maternal experience, the memory of a loss before narrative: "A missing mother—and one of whom not even her photographs remain—is a problem. Memory works on its own, it invents, draws circles that never end" (Vilar 1996, 29).

Possible Narrative: Vilar's Odyssey

Similar to Homer's *Odyssey*, Irene Vilar's *memoria* is a song of survival that screens something that is nevertheless left unspoken. Her memoir weaves two alternating narrative threads, registers, or voices. One voice tells the story of the circumstances that lead Vilar to her first suicidal attempt. This voice sometimes takes on a historical register and discusses the colonial situation of Puerto Rico, presumably as part of the explanation for Vilar's suicide attempts. Paradoxically, this voice ends on a personal even hermetic note. The end of this narrative thread of the memoir finds Vilar unsuccessfully trying to explain to a psychiatrist the feelings of guilt keeping her from following through with her suicide. The psychiatrist listens to her and decides to commit Vilar to Hutchings Psychiatric Hospital.

The second voice of the memoir (a part of the text written in Italics) tells the story of Vilar's experiences first in Hutchings and then in Syracuse University Hospital, where she is eventually admitted. It is a sometimes hermetic, sometimes ventriloquist, and sometimes split voice. This unstable and troubled voice tells the story of Vilar's second suicide attempt. Paradoxically, it also tells the story of, and even sets the conditions of possibility for, Vilar's recovery. The end of this other thread of the memoir describes Vilar's release from University Hospital: "I left like Odysseus, the way one always leaves a labyrinth, traps, encirclements: by means of a subterfuge" (Vilar 1996, 317). Indeed, similar to wily Odysseus, Vilar leaves her own labyrinth (the clinic) by telling a lie, by saying what her doctor wants to hear.[5] Vilar is pregnant and wants to abort, but she tells Dr. O. that she will give birth instead. Vilar compares her "subterfuge" to Odysseus's cunning with the Sirens. "When the doctors questioned me, or when Dr. O. wanted to know what I was going to do about my pregnancy and showed me the picture of a little girl with an enchanting look, they were also saying Hurry up, you can only be one of us. They were the Sirens too. Except that their songs were not as seductive" (320).

The Sirens were mythical creatures: half-human and half-bird. Their song was lethal to sailors in a particular way. In Homer's account, the song made them sever all familiar affiliations, their ties to home, wife, and children. "Woe to the innocent who hears that sound!/ He will not see his lady nor his children/ in joy, crowding about him, home from sea;/ the Sirens will sing his mind away . . ." (*Odyssey* 1963, 210). The myth told of sailors forgetting everything and dying of hunger. In the *Odyssey*, however, Odysseus heard the song of the Sirens but he escaped the lethal amnesia by having himself tied to the mast of his ship and by plugging the ears of his sailors with beeswax. Some post-Homeric narratives make the opposition between Odysseus and the song of the Sirens even more explicit. In them, Odysseus silences and even kills the Sirens merely by surviving them. According to Kafka's further elaboration of the myth of the Sirens, they become silent or even die suicides because they fail to seduce their prey.[6] Further silencing the Sirens, both Odysseus and Homer leave the song of the Sirens outside of narrative, despite the fact that the song is the very pretext of the narrative. In fact, it has been argued that for existence men depend on displacing, if not silencing, the song of the Sirens and the unspeakable knowledge for which it stands.[7]

The Ladies' Gallery is a memoir that similarly silences and displaces the song of Sirens. This song stands for a knowledge that threatens Irene Vilar with the loss of reason. The song is both the pretext for, and the surplus of her life-sustaining narrative. It is a constantly repeated and forever displaced knowledge that threatens her with madness and suicide. It is embodied in the doctor's question about Vilar's pregnancy. In this question, Vilar hears her mother's "overpowering" voice invading her, getting inside her, asking her to "hurry up," to take her place in the island of Sirens. *The Ladies' Gallery* is the narrative of survival that Vilar writes both in spite of, and because of, her mother's plea and command to "hurry up." More specifically, Vilar writes her memoir both in spite of, and because of, the maternal urgency that inflects that idiom. "I had been shuttling between the library and my room armed with index cards that were becoming increasingly oppressive, but Mama's overpowering voice went on; hundreds of voices sprang from hers, talked among themselves, spoke to me, about me, on my behalf, voices from my index cards—the illusion of a busy life—notes for a diary I would one day turn into a critical book about Three Sirens, or cycles: the Child, the Nymph, the Old Lady, three generations of women in my family" (Vilar 1996, 13).

If, according to the myth, Odysseus silences the Sirens through his subterfuge, there is sense in Vilar erasing her mother's voice by writing *The Ladies' Gallery* and by becoming a writer. Similar to the Freudian dream-work, *The Ladies' Gallery* screens the processes (the condensations and displacements) responsible for the mournful and melancholy nature of identity. The two-toned memoir hides and reveals the transformations and erasures, the losses both personal and national, responsible for making identity such as it is, vexed as it is.

These transformations and erasures trouble the memoir. Its current title, for example, displaces a former title: *A Message from God in the Atomic Age*. Significantly, the text reveals the latter to be the title of Lolita Lebrón's book of poems, which were written during her imprisonment. Vilar troubles the identity of her memoir, *The Ladies' Gallery*, by both covering over and revealing Lolita Lebrón's haunting apocalyptic voice, the spell of the sacrificed Mother of the nation, the message that lies underneath. And it does so quite literally by printing the former title in smaller caps at the bottom of the cover page.

Something similar occurs with the name of the author–narrator, Irene Vilar. The name is also the result of processes that screen (hide and reveal) the loss of the mother, the erasure of the maternal name, Gladys Mirna. At the beginning of the memoir we find Vilar in the waiting room of Hutchings Psychiatric Hospital. She has voluntarily walked into the hospital at dawn. While she waits for the doctors to decide what to do with her, she looks at herself in the two-way mirror. She experiences a "larval feeling" that she describes as the growing death inside her. We know that she is in Hutchings with the hope of being cured of this feeling. But instead of a cure, a painful scene ensues that only intensifies the feeling of death. She is taken to a room where a woman dressed in white sits at a desk with Vilar's belongings strewn all over it. The narrator describes them, one by one: a bottle of perfume, earrings, pens, jacks, eyeliner pencil, seashells, checkbook, and letters written but never mailed. Vilar ends the list of these disconnected fragments of her identity scattered over the table with a significant reference to the empty black purse that once contained them: "My black purse was there on the floor with a tag with my name: 'Myrna Irene Vilar' " (12).

The scene repeats the most unforgiving and unforgettable scene of Vilar's memoir: the scene of her mother's suicide. The scattered fragments of Vilar's identity are transformed duplicates of her mother's similarly scattered pieces: her "turban floating in the ditch, the broken hand mirror, the gold purse, the high-heeled sandal . . . a strip of artificial eyelash" (158). Significantly, the returning purse is on the floor again. Purse is *cartera* in Spanish, from *charta* the Latin word for letter. Literally, *cartera* is a bag for letters. Similar to the letters Vilar writes but never sends, the purse never really leaves her original owner, and, when it does, it returns to sender. A haunting corpse, the purse is tagged with a name that screens the maternal name by condensing it. The composite "Myrna" tagged to this corpse-turned-purse reminds the reader of Gladys Mirna. It also reveals the erasure that precedes the name of the author of the memoir, Irene Vilar, an erasure that simultaneously makes the author of the memoir possible even as it troubles her.

Rituals of Defilement

The Ladies' Gallery also troubles the similarly partial and ultimately unsuccessful erasures of a maternal body and experience by social master narratives. Of these, perhaps the most striking and provocative are the patriotic discourse of Puerto Rican Nationalism during the 1950s, and the commercial and advertising discourse of Puerto Rican television during the 1970s and 1980s. Vilar represents the former with the speeches of Pedro Albizu Campos (the founder of the Nationalist Movement who fought for political, economic, and cultural sovereignty of Puerto Rico) and the latter with a popular game show (Climb Kid Climb, hosted by Puerto Rican television personality Luis Vigoreaux) and with ubiquitous advertisements by the tourism industry.

While appearing to compete against one another, these temporally successive master narratives also overdetermine the instability of the Puerto Rican subject and its precarious national identity by defensively constituting it through rituals of defilement. On the one hand, these narratives separate the Puerto Rican subject from a symbolic Mother, both sacred and defiled, fortifying them against it. On the other hand, these rituals unwittingly return the same subject to a palpitating raw, unstable, and resisting archaic material guaranteeing its instability. If nothing else, these rituals establish the need to work through this material in a different way.

The Ladies' Gallery tells the story of the struggle for Puerto Rican independence that tragically results in the loss of Vilar's mother. It tells the story of Lolita Lebrón's political commitment to the cause of Puerto Rican Nationalism. Wrapped in the Puerto Rican flag and shouting "Freedom for Puerto Rico" from the Ladies' Gallery of the Congress of the United States, Lolita Lebrón sprayed the chamber of the House of Representatives with bullets in 1954. The attack was ironically carried out from a small balcony overlooking the legislators's semicircle presumably reserved for women visitors during the nineteenth century, and an architectural reminder of a sexually segregated government. The decidedly unladylike attack led to Lolita Lebrón's incarceration for 25 years, her ascension to Virginal and martyr status, in Puerto Rico and not surprisingly to her separation from her young children.[8] Replying to a reporter who asked her about her children,

Lolita Lebrón answered "They need a mother . . . that's true. But later on they will need to be free even more" (Vilar 1996, 95). Sadly, both of her children died while her mother was in prison, and the narrative suggests that they were caught in a cycle of suicidal repetitions that possessed Lolita and that now haunts Vilar. "To a question from Prosecutor J. Edward Lumbard, Lolita replied: 'I didn't come here to kill but to die' " (Vilar 1996, 96).

The memoir is careful to place the losses within the larger frame of the violent struggles of a colonial situation. Lolita Lebrón's suicidal attack and the "accidental" death of her young son and daughter are all casualties within a vexed and long-standing colonial narrative. The memoir insists on the ceremonial nature of these suicides, and particularly on their purifying and sacralizing roles. Describing the scene of Lolita Lebrón's ascension, as she goes up the steps of the Capitol building, the narrator describes Lolita as a participant in a purifying ritual. "From up above, a guard noticed them coming, dressed as if for a baptism. They did indeed look ceremonial in the photographs taken a few moments later. Are they coming to kill? No, sir. They're coming to die . . . That's called sacrifice" (92). Contemporary Nationalist speeches quoted in the narrative repeat the underlying description of the occupation of the colony by a metropolitan invader as a sin, and most importantly as a sin of which the colonized body needs to purify itself. "The brazenness of the Yankee invaders has reached the extreme of trying to profane Puerto Rican motherhood; of trying to invade the very insides of nationality" (47). Nationalist sentiment not only emphasizes that the colonizing outsider profanes the Nation, but it also insists that the Nation is both a sacred Mother and a defiled maternal body. Significantly, when he heard of Lolita Lebrón's attack on Congress, Pedro Albizu Campos declared: "A Puerto Rican heroine of sublime beauty has pointed out once more for the history of nations that the Nation is a woman and that she cannot think of her mother as a slave" (95).

For Albizu Campos, it is better to be dead and sublime than alive and impregnated by evil. And he warns Puerto Rican women against participating in the unwitting defilement of their bodies. "When our women lose the transcendental and divine concept that they are not only mothers of their children but mothers of all future generations of Puerto Rico, if they come to lose that feeling, Puerto Rico will disappear within a generation" (Vilar 1996, 47–48). Albizu Campos states that the Puerto Rican Woman must not lose the concept of motherhood. He warns that she must not give in to her body's suffering and hunger: "neither pain nor hunger nor death is cured by murdering nationality in its very insides" (48). Pleasure and materialism are the snares of the new empire, and Woman must resist them, he warns. Indeed, her body is the site of a struggle between carnal pleasure and divine reproduction for Albizu Campos. Not only does the "yankee invader desire her" but she is threatened by desires that she must learn to curb, sacrificing them to the divine responsibility of motherhood. "The Puerto Rican mother has to know that above all she is a mother, and that motherhood is the greatest privilege God has given the human species" (48).

The future of the Nation depends on the outcome of this struggle between the pure and the defiled within the same maternal body. According to the Nationalist discourse, the Puerto Rican subject will emerge only if the maternal body is sacrificed for this "sublime beauty." Thus, the founder of the Puerto Rican Nationalist Movement interprets Lolita Lebrón's suicidal attack as self-sacrifice. Lebrón sacrifices her life as a slave to the body in order to produce a sublime beauty. This sacrifice or ritual of defilement sacralizes her. It turns Lolita Lebrón into an icon of Motherhood for Nationalists. But by turning Lebrón into a paradisiacal origin from which the Puerto Rican subject has been expelled, Nationalist discourse also produces a desperate urge to return to a lost place: a nostalgia bred from a forceful and radical separation. This return is only possible through self-sacrifice, and so the subject emerges from the ritual of defilement in a melancholy mood. Identifying itself with the mother's self-purifying act, with her sacralizing self-erasure, the subject promotes the repetition of future rituals of defilement and insures in this way similar representations of the maternal body.

Nationalist rituals of defilement in Puerto Rico then produce antithetical and complementary figures. On the one hand they produce the cult of Lolita Lebrón, a Virgin and an icon of immaculate Motherhood. But it also produces a maternal body betrayed and defiled by its own desires, a body that must sacrifice itself rather than give in to its impure longings. *The Ladies' Gallery* suggests that subsequent rituals of defilement produce similar representations of the maternal body betrayed by its own desires and in similar need of self-sacrifice. To make this point, Vilar tells the story of Luis Vigoreaux. A television personality from the 1960s and 1970s in Puerto Rico, Vigoreaux was the master of ceremonies of several widely popular game shows including "Climb, Kid, Climb" (*Sube nene sube*) and "Go up, Daddy, go up" (*P'arriba papi p'arriba*). The centerpiece of both shows was a greased pole. Members of the audience were selected to climb up the pole for prizes. The memoir emphasizes the simultane-ously grotesque, familiar, and ceremonial aspects of the show: "It was a family program. Luis Vigoreaux, with that melodious voice that needed no microphone, directs the ceremony; beside him are his wife, wearing a wig of blond curls, and his two daughters dressed as clowns" (55). The story ends tragically. Luis Vigoreaux was found burned to a crisp in the trunk of his car. Accused of planning the murder, his wife and mother of two ended up in jail.

The story stands out as an irreverent mirror image of the Catholic rituals performed by the Puerto Rican Nationalists. Instead of an ascending Virgin, the deadly Siren floats to the surface of this story. The ceremony and its main characters, however, remain virtually the same. Here, the role of the evil agent is still played by the "yankee invaders" now visually transfigured into a totemic phallus, both sacred and defiled. The melodious, pleading and commanding voice of Luis Vigoreaux is at the service of this evil (conspicuous consumption) ensnaring the Puerto Rican audience with false hopes of a better future: "Get going, there is hope, it's just a matter of using your knees right and hugging the pole tightly. Get going, come on, make an effort" (Vilar 1996, 55). If all explicit allusions to a pure, natural, and inno-cent mother have disappeared, the sacred mother survives through her defiled negative. The mother wears a wig and is the mother to two clowns. She is both defiled and sacralized by her proximity to the greased pole. As the participant tries to climb the pole, the mother and her daughters surround it, touch it, and shriek, "Climb, kid, climb!" (55).

Curiously, though, the outcome of this televised ritual is similar to the purifying self-sacrifice promoted by the Nationalists. Like Lolita Lebrón, Lydia Echevarría (Luis Vigoreaux's wife) ends up in prison after a brutal and violent attack on the insidious voice of evil. She silences the melodious voice of materialism and conspicuous con-sumption and transforms it into charred remains: "a black blob, fried bones, teeth, the Rolex . . ." watch (Vilar 1996, 56). Indeed, to hear Vilar tell it, Vigoreaux's death is a local and syncretic purifying ritual that combines pagan and Christian symbols. "I, listening attentively, imagined Vigoreaux all toasted, his skin crisp and shiny like a suckling pig at Christmas time, like one of those piglets with the indifferent look that inspired so much respect in me as a child . . . They seemed calm, as if they'd transcended the fire consuming them" (56).

The surprising end of Vigoreaux's story reveals the superior and unrelenting power of the sacred embodied in the defiled maternal body. If in the television show the greased pole seems to contaminate the mother when she touches it, the outcome of the story reverses the relationship. Indeed, the powerful and contaminating agent is now revealed to be the mother, Lydia Echevarría, who touches the totem. As in Freudian psychoanalysis, the defiled maternal body is at the base of the totemic phallus and produces the fetish. Similarly, the melodious voice of Luis Vigoreaux is but a refined echo of the maternal "Climb, Kid, Climb!" and these "shrieks" are in turn but a transformed version of the Siren song that haunts Vilar throughout the narrative: "As I stepped down from the chair, the other voices faded away, but Mama's went on. It started to invade me, to get inside me. It said, 'Hurry up, Irene! You can only be one of us' " (13–14).

Coupled with the Nationalist discourses of Albizu Campos, the story of Luis Vigoreaux illustrates the effect of repeating these rituals of defilement without working through the matricide performed at their center. Not only will the subject emerge prone to suicide, it will also emerge haunted by the return of the abject. The possible narratives of the *memoria* are accompanied by impossible memories. The excluded material that sets the conditions of possibility for narratives such as the cult of the Virgin does not simply disappear. Its subterranean repository or crypt, if you will, is not impermeable, and the material finds its way out through memory and through antinarratives such as the haunting voices of Luis Vigoreaux and Albizu Campos. Not surprisingly, the power with which the subject invests the cult of the Virgin (the power to bring about the future of the Nation) finds its antithesis in the equally powerful Siren and in its ability to bring about the downfall of the Nation. The subject of nationalist discourse then emerges melancholy, suicidal, and pining for a lost origin or maternal Paradise. He also emerges torn apart by the conflicting powers with which he invests a divine maternal experience and a defiled maternal body, the power to create and to destroy him.

Feminine *Jouissance*

The Ladies' Gallery describes successive and interrelated rituals of defilement as well as their corresponding unstable subjects (Lolita Lebrón and Gladys Mirna) and sacred or mythical symbols (the Virgin and the Siren).[9] The *memoria* emphasizes that the relationship between social rituals and psychic economies and between the resulting symbols and subjects, is a relationship of correspondence, not one of cause and effect.[10] Social rituals do not merely produce subjective economies. Unstable subjects do not simply produce sacred or mythical symbols. Rather, subjectivities and socialities, subjects and symbols emerge simultaneously and in interaction with one another in this *memoria*.

Subjects and social rituals arise in a relationship of correspondence, and they also emerge from a fluid common ground. This unstable ground is the borderland of an event screened by the sacred maternal experience and by the defiled maternal body. This event is "feminine" *jouissance* screened by the aporetic abject.[11] According to Kristeva, "feminine" *jouissance* is an in-between state perhaps best, but not solely, represented by the mother-child dyad.[12] "Feminine" *jouissance* is a painful state, and Kristeva argues that rituals of defilement produce both taboos as well as linguistic functions like naming to defend and protect against this pain. But she also argues that "feminine" *jouissance* is a pleasurable state, and these defenses are also ways of coding a journey to this pleasure. Through defensive and protective coding, societies accompany the speaking subject on this journey as far as possible.

Kristeva also insists that "feminine" *jouissance* is not merely the passive object of the manipulation of rituals of defilement. In fact, she argues that rituals of defilement code the archaic relationship of the mother–child dyad as passive object, as abject object, in a defensive attempt to screen the agency of "feminine" *jouissance*. Kristeva states instead that rituals of defilement emerge in relation with "feminine" *jouissance*. That is, rituals of defilement emerge in active and ambivalent interaction with that incestuous state in-between subject and object.

The implications of Kristeva's analysis are far reaching. One of its most important corollaries is that defilement, the threat to the symbolic order, issues from the weakness of the symbolic order, from the risk to which it is permanently exposed. In other words, the danger of defilement is structurally built into the symbolic order. "The danger of filth represents for the subject the risk to which the very symbolic order is permanently exposed, to the extent that it is a device of discriminations, of differences. But from where and from what does the threat issue? From nothing else but an equally objective reason, even if individuals can contribute to it, and which would be, in a way, the frailty of the symbolic order itself" (1982, 69). From this perspective, social orders and symbolic systems are either the synchronic or structural effect of this weakness, or the diachronic or historical effect of the struggle with "feminine" *jouissance*.

Kristeva suggests that without an authority or a law strong enough to balance or settle supremacy, two powers must exist. For Kristeva, these two powers are the symbolic and the semiotic, rituals of defilement and "feminine" *jouissance*. While the symbolic order represses "feminine" *jouissance*, its authority returns with the breakdown of the symbolic order. "Feminine" *jouissance* also returns when the subject that emerges from that order tries to think through its advent in an effort to be a more effective speaking subject. *The Ladies' Gallery* is an example of just such an effort. Its narrative displays the struggle between these two powers, and it allows an ambivalent journey back to the "feminine" *jouissance* that also separates the subject from its painful pleasure. The myth of the Siren and the cult of the Virgin that emerge from this *memoria* are the defensive screens, the symbolic rituals, that allow Vilar to approximate the lost archaic dyad through the sacralized maternal experience and the defiled maternal bodies of Gladys Mirna and Lolita Lebrón.

But "feminine" *jouissance* is not only the uncanny foundation of socialities and subjectivities. It is also at the origins of the *memoria*, the source of its possible narrative and its impossible memory, of its remembering subject and of its memory of a loss before narrative. Not surprisingly, for Kristeva "feminine" *jouissance* is central to the production of both defilement rituals and writing practices. On the one hand, the uncertain event of "feminine" *jouissance* is at the foundation of the rituals that constitute the sacred maternal experience and defiled maternal body. On the other hand, "feminine" *jouissance* is also the pretext of practices that allow a more inclusive relationship with its life giving painful pleasure.

Naming language, the linguistic derivative of the rituals of defilement, is only one extreme in a continuum of "language" that extends back and forth from symbolic rituals to semiotic "feminine" *jouissance*. Under this definition, language contains both signs and something that exceeds names or signs. Language also contains matter, flesh, rhythm, and light. For Kristeva, language is more than a meaning driven device, a technique, and a narrative. Language is also something closer to a biological organ that produces a "non-meaning meaning," if you will, an uncanny music and poetry.[13] "Feminine" *jouissance*, or the semiotic, is a language in this sense, which Kristeva calls the mother tongue in *Strangers to Ourselves* (first published in 1988). It is also the language of bodies interacting in the mother–child dyad. But in being a language, "feminine" *jouissance* (or the semiotic) is also indelibly associated with, it is inextricably linked to, and it inhabits the rituals of defilement of the symbolic order. In fact, the rituals of defilement of the symbolic order are attempts to translate "feminine" *jouissance*, the music of the semiotic, the mother tongue, into a meaning-making language. Speaking subjectivity is the successful translation, transformation, transcription, coding, or symbolization, of the mother tongue while preserving, and even insisting on, its organic aspect, its rhythms, matter, and flesh. Speaking subjectivity is not and must not be a rupture with or separation from the mother tongue. Similar to Vilar's *memoria*, speaking subjectivity instead must inhabit the tense and unstable link between the music of "feminine" *jouissance* and the rituals of defilement.

Kristeva suggests that the structural weakness of the symbolic order and its rituals of defilement allow for different ways of accompanying the subject in its journey to "feminine" *jouissance*. While names and taboos, as well as myths and cults, allow a narrative journey that simultaneously separates the subject from "feminine" *jouissance*, poetry is unique in its attempt to reconcile the subject with the mother tongue. For Kristeva, the poet and the musician inhabit the privileged, fluid, and intermediary ground of language as defined above, the closest symbolic approximation to "feminine" *jouissance*. "At the intersection of sign and rhythm, of representation and light, of the symbolic and the semiotic, the artist speaks from a place where she is not, where she knows not. He delineates what, in her is a body rejoicing [*jouissant*]" (1980, 242).[14]

So, "feminine" *jouissance* is both the unstable ground below corresponding socialities and subjectivities, between symbols and subjects, and it is the uncanny language at the origin of *memoria*: the fluid combination of narrative and memory that is also the Derridean *mémoire*. Indeed, the abstract correspondence between sociality and subjectivity, symbols and subjects, finds its analogue in the correspondence between narrative and memory in Vilar's *memoria*. *The Ladies's Gallery* narrates or describes the rituals of defilement particular to Puerto Rican society. It establishes the links between these rituals and the material these rituals are meant to control in the effort to produce pure and proper Puerto Rican subjects. But the *memoria* also gives a visual trace and performs the sound of the resistant raw material destabilizing those very subjects. Perhaps the two most prominent examples of this visual and acoustic rendition of the material is the unrelenting repetition of the mother's haunting call "Hurry up," and the italics that mark and inflect the narrative voice that speaks from inside the psychiatric hospital.

The *memoria* does not neatly parse these abject sounds from the ensuing rituals of defilement. The mother's call transforms into Luis Vigoreaux's melodious voice. Lolita Lebrón's book of poetry contains the apocalyptic tone heard in the speeches by Albizu Campos. The flow between the sounds of the abject and the rituals of defilement triggers a defensive maternal sacrifice that is exposed in Vilar's *memoria*. It leads to a defense that often takes the form of a maternal body that is either defiled or sacred according to Vilar. But the same flow leads Vilar to the realization that the sound of the abject and the rituals of defilement are not irreducible experiences. Indeed, the flow suggests that sounds and rituals are susceptible to change and transformation. *The Ladies' Gallery* is also written from this realization, and it offers a different response to "feminine" *jouissance*. Rather than matricide, Vilar shapes a troubled narrative from the unsteady flow between the sounds of the abject and the rituals of defilement.

Impossible Memory: The Siren Song

The Ladies' Gallery opens with an epigraph from Franz Kafka's "The Sirens." "The Sirens, too, sang that way. It would be doing them an injustice to think that they wanted to seduce; they knew they had claws and sterile wombs, and they lamented this aloud" (vii). Like Euripides before him, Kafka suggested that the song of the Sirens was in fact a mournful lament at the loss of their humanity.[15] They mourn the loss of their hands and feet, and they mourn the loss of their reproductive ability. More importantly, they mourn the knowledge of this loss. The Sirens lament the memory of their humanity. They are hybrids in more than one sense. Physically, they are half-human and half-bird. Psychologically they are inhuman monsters that remember their humanity. Humanity returns to them, and this memory of a lost humanity is the beauty of the song of the Sirens according to Kafka. This memory is the quality that turns the mournful lament of the Sirens into a seductive song. Humans cannot turn away from their mournful song because it is a paean to humanity. The Sirens remember humanity even after their absolute and radical loss, and this makes them human again for Kafka. Having lost their humanity, however, they cannot hear the lament of the humans as they fall prey to the beauty of their song. It is the inability of the Sirens to hear humanity, even in their own song, that kills the sailors according to Kafka.[16] The Sirens did not intend to kill their victims, he insists. Their song was not intentionally deadly; they "could not help it if their laments sounded so beautiful" (Kafka 1971, 93).[17]

Echoing Kafka, Vilar's *memoria* suggests that the song of the Sirens is not the opposite of narrative. It is the memory of a loss before narrative. The haunting voices of Gladys Mirna and Lolita Lebrón contain a resistant humanity that will not be forgotten despite the rituals of defilement that transform them and turn them into monsters. But Vilar also leaves out Kafka's last sentence from the epigraph to her book. She preserves the violent agency of the Sirens. Vilar suggests that their voices resist, and even strike back against those that abandon these women to their monstrous fate. Their call is similar to the plaintive song of the Sirens, but also to the mournful complaints of the Freudian melancholic whose song expresses both a great loss, and performs an oblique violence against another. "Their complaints are really 'plaints' in the legal sense of the word; it is because everything derogatory that they say of themselves at bottom relates to someone else that they are not ashamed and do not hide their heads" (Freud 1953–1973, vol. 14, 169). Their suicidal calls are both a wail that bears witness to their loss of humanity, and a violent reaction aimed outward: a vengeful protest against the agents responsible for their loss.

In the *Odyssey*, the sailors turn away from the Sirens. They skirt their island and remain deaf to their complaints. They reject the humanizing memory of their fertile womb. They move away from the memory of birthing that troubles the Sirens and makes them sing. Vilar, instead, listens to the fluid language and uncanny music of her Sirens. She suggests that the song of the Sirens is the voice of a threatened self that actively resists dissolution. She also suggests that their song contains a remnant of the loss in memory. Unlike the *Odyssey*, Vilar's *memoria* condenses Odysseus narrative and the memory of the Sirens into one vexed text. It endures the experience of possible and impossible mourning and remains, like Derrida's Mnemosyne, "in sufferance there."

The Support Beyond *Memoria*

And yet, Vilar's *memoria* also suggests that to remain in sufferance at the threshold of memory and narrative is not a sufficient condition for life. From its solitary and unstable condensation of narrative and memory, *The Ladies' Gallery* also hints at the need for a support outside *memoria*, outside itself. If the *memoria* remembers the music of "feminine" *jouissance*, it also transforms naming language, it returns to what Kristeva calls the symbolic order. The *memoria* calls for, and imagines, the help of a supportive third: a fluid language between "feminine *jouissance*" and rituals of defilement, self and other, subjectivity and sociality, memory and narrative, as well as remembering and forgetting. There are two moments in the *memoria* that illustrate the difference between the absence and the presence of this loving third. One scene is full of anguish while the other is hopeful.

At the end of the book, Vilar recounts a shocking experience she had while on a trip to Haiti on her last year of high school. She sees a black woman giving birth or aborting (it is not clear) on the street while a white man in a white cassock goes over "to her with a pail of water and a bottle of ivory dish-washing liquid" (253). The scene is inflected by a monstrous tone, both repulsive and playful. The narrator both performs and censures a modern ritual of defilement that brings together a white cassock and a bottle of "ivory dish-washing liquid." The ritual is further complicated by the simultaneous erasure of racial difference. The body at the center of the ritual is enveloped in a monstrous aura that results from a double abjection. It is abject because it is delivering a daughter, and it is abject because it is black. The ritual abjects the maternal body and sacralizes the maternal experience turning it into part of an allegorical, transhuman, and even mythical world of poverty. "What I saw was nothing like what I was accustomed to seeing in Puerto Rico" (253).

Vilar, horrified at the scene and partaking of its unexamined rituals, feels "the gastric touch of vomit coming up her throat" (253). She transcribes but significantly does not translate the solitary song, the mournful sounds of the mother. "She was making an effort, consoling herself with mumbled phrases while a gelatinous mass blossomed from between her legs," and later, " '*Ma fille, ma fille, ma fille . . . ,*' the woman was sobbing" (253–254). Horrified by the abject, the adolescent Vilar confesses that she "didn't know what to do." She runs up to the cathedral, but finds it closed, and when she finally decides to go over to the woman to help, she notices the disapproving look on the face of the priest. Both judged and intimidated by his judgment, Vilar holds back: "I was about to go over but I noticed that the man in the cassock didn't look too kindly on my presence. After all, I was just another tourist, one among so many amateurs in the contemplation of other people's misery" (253–254).

The scene is the mirror image of another, this time clearly the scene of a birth. Earlier in the book, Vilar describes her experiences in Boynton School in Orford, New Hamphsire. Vilar describes her entrance to the school both as a separation from history and from "the family crypt," and as the entrance into a religious and contractual world, a world of "fellowship" that promises no harm "to each other or to nature" (185). The central and even constitutive experience of this mythical world is the birth of a lamb. The symbolic scene is a ritual of defilement and includes an abject maternal body, a witness to the scene, and an officiant. If Vilar was drawn before by the smell of the abject body, now she is awakened by the "bleating," "monotonous weeping" of a ewe, "a weeping as persistent as the rain that had been running down my window for some days" (196). In what amounts to an allegorical scene of an archaic maternal experience, the sheep gives birth to a lamb and the bodies at the center of the experience are abject. As before we witness "a gelatinous pink bundle . . . peeking out from between her hind legs" (197).

But unlike the sobs of the Haitian woman in the scene described above, the animal sound of the trembling sheep is translated or humanized. She describes it as "an almost mournful moan" (196). The ritual also includes an officiating "priest" that is similarly humanized. Rather than the antiseptic judgmental priest in the forbidding white cassock, here we find a loving lay man. Mr. Boynton's love is represented both by his voice and his touch during and after the birthing process. Vilar describes Mr. Boynton kneeling down in front of the ewe and talking to it. He murmurs, winks, and caresses the sheep and is unafraid to stick "his hands between the legs where the bundle had become stuck" (197). After the lamb is born, Mr. Boynton speaks to the mother who is quiet and seems to have fallen asleep in a pleading and commanding tone of voice. "Come on, wake up, you've got a son to feed" (197). Initially described as a "drowsy lump" the mother is transformed by Mr. Boynton's voice and by the literal support of his hands. "Finally he made her stand on four feet, almost carrying her in his arms" (197). The sheep begins to lick the lamb and finally allows it to nurse.

Mr. Boynton is not afraid to touch the abject sheep. His hands are not the cleaning hands of the officiant in Haiti. They do not compensate for the threat of loss by defiling the maternal body with a matricidal and erasing gesture. Instead, they help to bring out the lamb and hold up the mother. Mr. Boynton is not afraid to touch and even caress a body that is still covered by abject material. Indeed, before he intervenes, Mr. Boynton covers his hands and arms with a yellow liquid, transforming the abject into a protective coating and film for his own body. Mr. Boynton's commanding plea also resists the effect produced by the rituals of defilement that repress "feminine" *jouissance*. Unlike Luis Vigoreaux's message of self-empowerment, "Get going, there is hope, it's just a matter of using your knees right and hugging the pole tightly," Mr. Boynton's "Come on, wake up, you've got a son to feed" emphasizes the responsibility to an other. Neither do his words pledge allegiance to a totemic phallic order that mournfully separates the "Kid" from a defiled maternal body. Instead, Mr. Boynton emphasizes the importance of the mother's life to the son's survival. The scene approximates "feminine" *jouissance*.

Several things set this scene apart from the rest of the *memoria*, from its flow between rituals of defilement and "feminine" *jouissance*. The scene's triangular structure is different from the binary structure of *The Ladies' Gallery*. Mr. Boynton is part of a triangle that includes him, the animal, and Vilar, the witness. He occupies a position that is neither self nor other. Moreover, unlike the empathic, suffering, but paralyzed witness to the scene, Mr. Boynton makes a stand. He opts for life, pleads, commands, and shows similar impatience with the fluid state of slumber, and with passive contemplation. Finally, Mr. Boynton's actions invert the direction of the journey that informs much of the *memoria*. Rather than repeat the often-catastrophic return of "feminine" *jouissance* after unsuccessful rituals of defilement, Mr. Boynton appears to transform a ritual of defilement, soiling himself, to approximate the abject. "When my will flags, when nothing is going right, it's nice to think of hands like those. My talks with Dr. O. should have begun there, with things like that" (198).

The Ladies' Gallery: A Memoir of Family Secrets memorializes the loss of "feminine" *jouissance*: a loss that is both personal and national in scope, and that is both creative and catastrophic in its effects. In her *memoria*, Vilar describes "feminine" *jouissance* as an ambiguous event sacralized into the maternal experience and defiled into the maternal body. It is a vexed condition (both supportive and destructive), and a contradictory state (in-between life and death). But "feminine" *jouissance* is not only troubled and contradictory, it also threatens the very process of subject formation, the process responsible for identity, nation, family, and culture. Incapable of bearing the ambiguity of "feminine" *jouissance*, we deploy and perform rituals of defilement aimed at cleansing it, and at differentiating the emerging subject from the messy abject. We constitute our subjectivity by repressing and/or reifying "feminine" *jouissance*.

The Ladies' Gallery bears witness to the catastrophic effects of these processes when left unexamined and unchanged. It attests to the destruction that is left in their wake, and to the reaction of the resistant material. The rituals of defilement at the center of the process of subject formation produce a reaction in the resistant abject. And this reaction becomes the hallucinations and the dreams that haunt the emerging subject. *The Ladies Gallery* describes these hallucinations. The book represents the avenging return of the abject, of the defiled maternal body, repressed or idealized into an other. It also represents the trap where the subject is left when it fails to interrogate these rituals. The subject that emerges from this memoir to the memory of the abject is often caught in between contradictory psychic economies. Between mourning and melancholia, the subject that emerges from *The Ladies' Gallery* is torn and split. It is both repulsed and seduced by a sacralized maternal experience and by a defiled maternal body. The subject that emerges from this *memoria* also emerges haunted by the song of the Sirens.

To escape from the influence of the Sirens, the *memoria* works through, and rewrites the repressed and reified material of its otherworldly song. Such writing is different from rituals of defilement in that it allows the emerging subject to experience again the painful pleasure of "feminine" *jouissance*. By remembering the abject, by suturing the abject material back together through writing, the emerging subject also bears witness to its life-sustaining work.

Writing also allows the emerging subject of the *memoria* to understand and transform the complex nature of the process of subject formation. Writing recasts the language of the symbolic order. It helps Vilar to witness her own investment in a matricide. Repetitions reveal the erasures that precede Vilar, repetitions that trouble her authority, her identity as the author of a memoir of family secrets. These repetitions memorialize or bear witness to her own participation in the matricide at the center of the process of subject formation. They are ethical epitaphs that stand in solitary memory of "feminine" *jouissance*.

Finally, writing also provides a loving space from which to take a firm stance against this matricide. If Vilar grasps the importance of the rituals through which matricide was (and continues to be) performed, she also comes to understand the need for a loving third, a transformed and transforming version of the symbolic order. Through writing, the process of subject formation promises to regain its human, contradictory, and paradoxical dimensions. By remembering the abject and interrogating our rituals of defilement *The Ladies' Gallery* transforms both the process of subject formation and the abject, opening the possibility to a less violent world.

6

From Revenge to Redemption:
Julia Alvarez's Open Secrets

"Keep it to yourself!"
my mother said, which more than anything
anyone in my childhood advised
turned me to this paper solitude

      —*Julia Alvarez*, By Accident

Julia Alvarez's latest book of poems *The Woman I Kept to Myself* (2004) is her best effort yet at a melancholy form of writing that she practices throughout her work. Alvarez's writing is a form of melancholy regression to an archaic negation that is both depressive and constitutive of subjectivity. Similar to Freudian melancholia, Alvarez's poetic writing is determined by the loss of a loved object, which sometimes takes the form of an abstract ideal (like the nation or the motherland), and at other times remains invisible to the subject, taking instead the form of an indeterminate all-encompassing grief. Her writing is an example of what Kristeva calls an intimate revolt, an experimental and poetic mode of Freudian melancholia and negation.[1]

Alvarez's poetic writing revolts against the defensive fantasies of an epitaphial tradition, in literature and other cultural practices, responsible for the loss and for the symbolic interment of the lost object.[2] Indeed, Alvarez in her writing both echoes and disturbs a cultural and literary tradition that erects itself on the foundation of a lost origin, of a blank page, first produced and then displaced on to the feminine and maternal body as the original lost object.[3] Kristeva best describes the revolt against this tradition as that which brings to the fore "the permanence of contradiction, the temporariness of reconciliation . . . the drive, the unnamable feminine, destructivity, psychosis," in short everything that puts to the test the very possibility of unitary meaning (Kristeva 2002, 10). Similar to Kristeva, Alvarez helps us to see that our culture and literary tradition displaces (and then circumscribes) the so-called destructive components of the body to the maternal (i.e., negation, negativism, abjection, psychosis, and the death drive). But most importantly, her poetry suggests that this apparently negative material also permeates and helps to constitute the language necessary to survive.

Similar to the other works examined in this book, Alvarez's melancholy writing is a life-affirming testimony to the continuous line that must run between the maternal body and language. The maternal body and language are registers of a continuous event that we experience as divided into opposite orders only to our own peril. Her melancholy writing aims to recover the necessary aporia of the maternal experience. She both remembers and re-members a limit-event that is impossible to circumscribe or contain within the separate spheres of the self and the other, an event that has a similar bearing on the individual and on the social. Together with Lispector, Garro, Ferré, Vilar, Anzaldúa, and Moraga, Alvarez associates this limit-event with the maternal body, and with its effect on the development of language and on the process of subject formation. Indeed, the maternal aporia is a type of "intimate revolt": the key, not only to personal transformation but also to social, political, and economic change according to all of these women writers.[4] To revisit the aporia at what Alvarez calls the "dead center of the human heart" is also to resist the matricidal defense against its unstable ground. In opting for a melancholy mode of writing modeled after the uncanny maternal origin, Alvarez struggles against the nationalistic, authoritarian, identitarian, and fortifying fantasies that have given way to our catastrophic and suicidal modes of being.

During an interview conducted after the publication of Alvarez's latest novel *In the Name of Salomé* (2000), Bridget Kevane asks the author about the influences on her writing. Alvarez replies by referring to the maternal command to be silent that opens Maxine Hong Kingston's *Woman Warrior* (1975): " 'You must not tell anyone,' my mother said, 'what I am about to tell you' " (1975, 3). Alvarez continues "Hey, I thought, my Mamí told me that too! Not just my Mamí, but the whole culture she represented" (Kevane 2000, 24).[5] And indeed, Alvarez's latest novel abounds with similarly questionable advice for its female protagonists from its overbearing male characters: " 'That tone of voice is not becoming, Salomé,' [Pancho] said, one hand tucked inside his vest in the manner of a statesman making a pronouncement;" " 'Yes I do have some advice,' Pedro says [to Camila], 'I think the poet should keep writing for her own pleasure' " (Alvarez 2000, 177, 124).

Four years after that interview, the Cuban American playwright and journalist Dolores Prida asks Alvarez a similar question, this time about the origin of the title of her latest book of poems, *The Woman I Kept to Myself*. Alvarez again replies by referring to a maternal injunction to silence, this time in her poem "By Accident." "I actually took Mami's advice," she says, "I became a writer who 'both keeps things secret and broadcasts my heart for all the world to hear' " (Prida 2004, 128). What does it mean to model writing after the maternal command to keep it to yourself? What does it mean to write in a mode that by Alvarez's own account "keeps things *entre familia*," that never betrays the so-called Catholic, female, Old World culture, even if it simultaneously broadcasts the heart "for all the world to know?" (Kevane 2000, 24; Prida 2004, 128). What does it mean to write by taking to heart this negation of voice, by taking the advice "do not speak what I am about to tell you" as a model for writing?

In the case of Alvarez, it means to write in a negative but necessary way. On the one hand, it is a difficult mode of writing because it involves a metaphorical un-becoming. It is a mode of writing that does not abandon, but rather reverses the direction, or writes against the grain of an epitaphial cultural tradition deeply embedded in literature, and more so in autobiographical writing.[6] It is a provocative mode of writing that unwrites by reversing itself: "like a film put in reverse" (Alvarez 2004, 103). On the other hand, it is also a necessary mode of writing because it reverses the matricide at the center of that cultural tradition. Alvarez's melancholy writing, modeled after the maternal command to keep it to yourself, both obeys and revolts against that command. It clearly listens to the maternal voice that tells the writer to keep silent. But it also listens for the revolt contained in and by the maternal voice. By listening for the maternal revolt, and taking its advice, Alvarez ironically succeeds in challenging the matricidal ventriloquist behind the maternal command to keep it to herself. Alvarez's writing redeems what amounts to the productive negativity, or revenge, that lies at the source or the origin of her poetry: "Yes, it was revenge that set me on the path of becoming a writer. At some point, though, revenge turned into redemption" (Alvarez 1999, 140–141).[7]

Through A Glass Darkly

Various poems of *The Woman I Kept to Myself* develop a negative mode of writing, and "Winter Storm" is one of its more violent, and perhaps dramatic, examples. The poem suggests an image for poetry that condenses the event of a deadly snowstorm, a "deepening depression that descends / and deadens everything," with the violence of Abraham's unstoppable and unhinged knife-wielding hand "plunging doubt's knives into what I love" (Alvarez 2004, 79–80). The poem represents a mode of writing as a violent undoing, a negation of writing, a form of the maternal command to keep it to oneself, by suggesting that the snowstorm and Abraham's hand are metaphors for the poet's depression and for the violent writing that results from it. But the poem also practices what it describes as it implacably leads the reader to the white emptiness of the page that follows its final verse: "until nothing's left / except the emptiness of the blank page" (Alvarez 2004, 79–80).

"Disappearing" similarly condenses a beginning image of unbirthing ("shunning the lavish spray of eager sperm," Alvarez 2004, 83) with an anorexic mode of writing, a writing that is modeled after the uncompromising refusals of a deliberately slenderizing, rebellious, and self-impoverishing melancholy subject.[8] "Better not compromise the seed of self / to whatever power wields the watering can" (Alvarez 2004, 83). Death is the host that lords over the "feast of summer" in this poem. It is the master of ceremony that commands the company to eat single-mindedly, like gluttons, "like the bully who wants it all" (Alvarez 2004, 83). Faced with its injunction to indulge in the binge of life, the poetic subject instead prefers to barely eat: "A nibble, a sip, a swallow—and I'm done" (Alvarez 2004, 84).

Indeed, the poem is an example of Alvarez at her minimalist best ("I am the pope / of the particular, imam of mites, / a god in the minus numbers," Alvarez 2004, 131). It infuses the histrionic melancholy gestures that characterize "Winter Storm" with a redeeming reduction in poetic tone and breadth. It does not aim for public drama but for a private serenity that nevertheless maintains the negativity of writing.[9] If writing is compared to an erasing violence done to the page in "Winter Storm," here it is compared to the gradual shriveling of leaves in autumn. The goal of writing is still to vanish, to disappear.[10] Alvarez follows the silencing command like a "good girl," but she also leaves almost nothing for death to take. "What will be left for death if I succeed?" she asks (Alvarez 2004, 84). Nothing, she answers, but the remainder in language of an internalized negation, a minimal, intimate, but also a foundational revolt: "a trail of print on a page as clean / as the dinner plate of a goody-goody child" (Alvarez 2004, 84).

The foundational character of this intimate revolt is perhaps best expressed in "Anger and Art," a poem possessed by a similarly intense melancholy that is nevertheless transformed into a different perspective and a new mode of writing. "Anger and Art" suggests again that a melancholy self-directed rage is at the origin of Alvarez's art. It re-members a child reacting to her own mortality by holding her breath, a fruitless protest against the dying world. "I held my breath, / hoping to make it stop" (Alvarez 2004, 22). The child's melancholy and spiteful revolt, however, is also a necessary rite of passage. After passing out, the child wakes up to a different reality. The dark light of the star that was lost eons ago now shines on her face, an image for the transition to a different, a darker life: the life of a sleepless insomniac who both lives in the shadow of this star, and transforms its "old sunlight" into poetic language.[11]

The melancholy writer of Alvarez's work is often figured as a sleepless insomniac who is both heartened and scared by the *sereno*, or the night-watchman, in her novels, essays, and poetry.[12] Indeed, "El Sereno" is a poem dedicated to the symbolic translation (and transformation) of an intrusive darkness in Spanish into poetic language in English: "Sereno was the name I knew him by / Serene and dew of night, his homonyms" (Alvarez 2004, 143). The sleepless poet both draws strength and recoils from this memory of an "old *sereno*," a figure that accompanies the poet in the dark nights of her childhood, but also shoos her off by day, who untangles her kite strings but also baits her lines. The *sereno* reminds the poet of the haunting yearnings at her core in the beginning of the poem (" 'What do you want?' He'd shoo me off to play," Alvarez 2004, 143), while simultaneously representing the graceful and stoic translation of that yearning by the end of the poem into "Serenity, to bear the heavy load" (Alvarez 2004, 145). As such, the *sereno* becomes a model for a transformative mode of writing that nevertheless remains disturbing. Writing for Alvarez becomes the repetition and translation in language of the darkness witnessed by the *sereno*, "of all he'd seen during his dark patrols" (Alvarez 2004, 143). The darkness is embedded in the *sereno*'s open question to the poet that she repeats by the end of the poem: " 'What do I want?' the ancient question lurks" (Alvarez 2004, 144). The impossibility of answering this question suggests an archaic desire that is impossible to satisfy. Poetry then becomes a struggle to serenely repeat and translate that dark desire, a practice that must not alarm but should nevertheless disturb a tradition of sleepers, a graceful warning to "those dreamers who will soon be waking up" to a similar light (Alvarez 2004, 144).

The poem "Spring at Last!" gives yet another account of the archaic negativity that determines Alvarez's poetic writing. After listing a series of devastating losses (including an oblique reference to the wars that followed the violent attacks that destroyed the World Trade Center in New York City) the poet describes the arrival of an "incredible" spring. Her husband admonishes her to "Calm down. It's annual. It's only spring" (Alvarez 2004, 103). But spring after such an accumulation of losses is temporally uncanny for the poet. It appears to reverse time: "and back into the intact Towers flew / stick figures, like a film put in reverse" (Alvarez 2004, 103). This eerie spring back in time suggests to the poet that life itself "works in sad reverse" . . . "like the star's light, beamed eons ago" (Alvarez 2004, 103–104). Clearly, her spring is different from her husband's. It is a much darker season—its black light seasoning the poet with loss. The negative light of this spring colors the poet's writing as much as her perspective. It allows her to write in a similarly reverse and negative mode that contains loss in both of its senses. It contains loss in that it gives loss a shape, a limit, and a form in poetic language. But it also contains loss in the sense that it evokes again all that the poet "wasted, overlooked, [and] bypassed" (Alvarez 2004, 104).

The Novel as Anamnesic Narrative

Many of Alvarez's novels turn on an overtly anamnesic structure[13] that reveals the importance of temporal reversal in her writing. Indeed, regression, or time in reverse, could be said to be at the heart of her first and latest novels (*How the García Girls Lost Their Accent* (first published in 1991) and *In the Name of Salomé*). Narratively and structurally speaking, both of these works tamper with the temporal line.[14] They tell the story of two exiles, Yolanda and Camila, but they tell it backward, leading the reader back in time to a traumatic memory. In both novels, this memory is a dark place where time itself is jumbled. In both novels, the collapsed time of this memory is identified with a maternal body and voice. It is worthwhile to briefly examine this memory, which has changed slightly (but nevertheless significantly) as Alvarez has continued to write. While it is unquestionably traumatic in the first novel, it becomes far more ambiguous in the second.

Yolanda is the protagonist of *How the García Girls Lost Their Accent*. She is one of four sisters in a family that is harassed and threatened by the Volkswagen-riding officers of General Rafael Leonidas Trujillo's (1891–1961) secret police, the infamous SIM, a lynchpin of the General's 30-year dictatorship over the island. The novel tells the story of the family's rushed exit from their home in the Dominican Republic and into exile in the United States in 1960, one year prior to the assassination of Trujillo. The novel begins with Yolanda as an adult, and ends with the same character as a child paradoxically describing the scene that explains how she grew up to be a woman "prone to bad dreams and bad insomnia" (Alvarez 1992, 290). The novel locates this original trauma well beyond the scene of escape from the island, to a guilty moment when little Yolanda removes a fragile kitten from her litter. The ending shuttles back and forth in time as it describes Yolanda haunted through adulthood by the ghostly sound of the mother cat loudly mourning her loss. The last sentence of the novel is unhinged from the temporal line. It inhabits a ghostly present when the voice of little Yolanda paradoxically evokes the older Yolanda. The voice describes the returning, insistent, uncanny sound from a "black furred thing": "her magenta mouth opening, wailing over some violation that lies at the center of my art" (Alvarez 1992, 290).

Camila is the protagonist of Alvarez's latest novel, similar to Yolanda she is driven into exile in the United States. Camila is the youngest daughter of Salomé Ureña and Francisco Henríquez, a couple famous in the Dominican Republic for their resistance (in both political and verse form) to General Ulises Hereaux (1839–1899). The novel figures Lilís (short for Ulises) as Trujillo's nineteenth-century predecessor, and describes his rule over the Dominican Republic as a dictatorship over a ten-year period. Like Trujillo, Lilís was assassinated at the end of his violent rule. Similar to Yolanda, Camila turns back into a child by the end of this novel. Before the last pages of the book, she hides from her father in the bowels of a steamship. Camila sinks back into a memory that both threatens and comforts her. It is the memory of a time when time itself collapses. She describes this memory as a "plunge" into "the dark center of herself where her mother waits to take her by the hand and lead her to heaven where they will start a new life together" (Alvarez 2000, 331).

The second novel ends in a temporal no-man's-land similar to the last line of Alvarez's first novel. After the scene in the steamship, an epilogue introduces for the first time in the novel the first person voice of Camila who tells the story of her visit to her own grave from the present of the narration. Camila-turned narrator is now blind and worried about the right spelling of her name on her tombstone. She describes a little boy tracing and retracing the lines of writing that eerily materialize on the last page of the novel as Camila's epitaph: a mark for the book's ending, and a trace that returns the maternal name that gives the novel its title: Salomé.

Both novels then end on a melancholy note. They configure a final and irreducible memory trace, an allegorical black-hole (an indentation in stone in the last book) where an unhinged present shuttles between the future and the past, where the self struggles against, and gradually blends with, the mother who is also a radical other: a memory trace evoked by the narrator into which she gradually slips and disappears. In both novels, the trace is either an embodied abject sound, or a maternal and deadly invitation at the end of a narrative journey. It is also an archaic temporal event before the displacement of a post-dictatorial and migrant self, and beyond the time of dictatorship and exile.[15]

The Anacahuita Turn

The effect of this temporal journey back to a moment when linear time itself disappears is not unambiguously traumatic in Alvarez's novels. The traumatic effect of the memory is associated with art in the first novel, and with an uncanny serenity at the end of *In the Name of Salomé*. But perhaps we find the most ambitious representation of the ambiguous and even contradictory effect of this regression in time in Alvarez's second novel, *In the Time of the Butterflies*.

This novel tells the story of the lives of the four Mirabal sisters, famous in the Dominican Republic for bravely resisting Trujillo's regime. Alvarez allegorically represents a journey back in time in the scene that begins the novel: a turn in the road at the place of an Anacahuita tree that the traveling narrator must make in order to meet Dedé, the surviving Mirabal sister. The turn also marks the entrance into a time of a different order from chronological time in the novel. The turn confronts the narrator with the time of Dedé's memory, a "Dominican time" that is different from the clock time of the narrator. " 'It's just the road by the anacahuita tree. We don't name them,' Dedé says . . . 'About what time?' the voice wants to know. O yes. The gringos need a time. But there isn't a clock time for this kind of just-right moment. 'Any time after three or three-thirty, four-ish,' 'Dominican

time, eh?' The woman laughs. '¡*Exactamente*!' " (Alvarez 1995, 4).
Most importantly, however, the turn leads to a paradoxical moment
without time, a "moment zero" when time itself stops: "And I see
them all there in my memory, as still as statues, Mamá and Papá, and
Minerva and Mate and Patria . . ." (Alvarez 1995, 321).

The journey back in time allegorized by the turn at the Anacahuita
tree has a strengthening and therapeutic effect on all four sisters at
critical times of their lives when they require a strategy to survive
incarceration, madness, or impending death. The turn is a form of the
memory games Minerva plays to survive solitary incarceration
(Alvarez, 1995, 198). It is also a mode of the survival strategies used
by a Holocaust victim that Dedé finds described in an article she reads
in a beauty salon (Alvarez 1995, 7). It leads back to a family scene that
helps the remembering subject by instilling within her a serenity analogous to the therapeutic effect of the Anacahuita tree whose fruit and
leaves are used to treat several diseases.[16] It also leads back to the
maternal storytelling voice, whose effect is similarly soothing. "They
are sitting in the cool darkness under the anacahuita tree in the front
yard, in the rockers, telling stories, drinking guanábana juice. Good
for the nerves, Mamá always says" (Alvarez 1995, 8). Contrary to the
moment zero of Dominican time, the Anacahuita turn is actually a
reversal in time, and it works as an antidote for the time deprivation
experienced in imprisonment.

It is worth noting that the reversal signified by the Anacahuita tree
reappears in Alvarez's last novel, *In the Name of Salomé*. Camila, now
blind, visits her grave and hears something drop with a bang. When
she asks about the sound, her brother Ignacio explains "The
anacahuita tree . . . There's a great big one next to the grave" (Alvarez
2000, 351). Camila as narrator then goes on to explain the meaning of
the explosion. "The pods of the anacahuita are known for exploding
when they hit the ground. Oh dear, I think, there goes my peaceful
eternity!" (Alvarez 2000, 351). Once again, the Anacahuita appears as
a temporal event, but now it appears in time. Camila imagines the
sound of the exploding Anacahuita pods interrupting eternity, disturbing her eternal sleep. More importantly, the pods stop the melancholy tone of Camila's image of herself in death. The pods, described
as dropping "with a bang like a firecracker," suggest the image of a
mischievous child playing a prank. For a second, the exploding pods
allow humor to enter the scene, to disturb the hold of the timeless and
morbid thing that appears to possess Camila's imagination and the
imagination of so many of Alvarez's characters.

Similar to the black hole or the epitaphial trace at the end of Alvarez's novels, the Anacahuita is also a disturbing mode of reversal. It leads the protagonist of *In the Time of the Butterflies* to the obverse of the soothing familiar scene. "And when it doesn't work, she thinks, I get stuck playing the same bad moment. But why speak of that" (Alvarez 1995, 7). Dedé describes the terrifying effect of this turn as a familiar nightfall, right before the death of the sisters. "A dark night was falling, one of a different order from the soft, large, kind ones of childhood under the anacahuita tree, Papá parceling out futures and Mamá fussing at his drinking. This one was something else, the center of hell maybe . . ." (Alvarez 1995, 199). Finally, the very last line of the novel suggests the negative and melancholy effect of the Anacahuita turn on Dedé. She is left stuck in between time and the timeless in a temporally uncanny scene. She is present in time but also paradoxically present as an absence. Eerily, Dedé is an absence from a timelessness that she herself misses, as if she were both alive and also already dead. "And I see them all there in my memory, as still as statues, Mamá and Papá, and Minerva and Mate and Patria, and I'm thinking something is missing now. And I count them all twice before I realize—it's me, Dedé, it's me, the one who survived to tell the story" (Alvarez 1995, 321).

The endings of Alvarez's novels leave the reader asking questions about a scene of return to what appears to be a particular mode of the uncanny of Freudian psychoanalysis.[17] The endings return to a familiar place that is also radically other, but most importantly they go back to a time that is also the opposite of time.[18] This place is figured in Alvarez's writing as the Anacahuita turn, which leads the reader to two related questions. What is the meaning of this temporal uncanny reversal? and What is the nature of the relationship between the temporal reversal and Alvarez's writing?

The Paradox of Familial Time

Alvarez goes some distance in answering the first two of these questions in her essay "Imagining Motherhood," an important key to understanding the relationship between time and writing in her work. The essay is part of a collection titled *Something to Declare*. It begins with an announcement by her baby sister that she is now a mother, that she has adopted a baby from the Dominican Republic. This announcement then produces both a desire to become a mother and a visit from an "old monster" of childhood, an archaic jealousy in

Alvarez. These responses in turn become the springboard for the description of a complex experience that Alvarez calls "familial time," a temporality at the center of the temporally uncanny event that ends all three novels.

The essay begins with a temporal opposition between motherhood and writing. Alvarez tells herself and her readers that time was the reason for her choice not to become a mother. Writing takes time and she doesn't have the time for motherhood. Time is limited, she tells herself, and writing and motherhood are temporally exclusive. There is no time for both writing and motherhood because both consume time, eat up time, they leave no time for the other. In other words, both motherhood and writing are experienced in chronological time, watch or clock time. The publishing or professional world of writing is ruled by deadlines and these in turn impose a timeline that is difficult if not impossible to break. The world of good-motherhood is ruled by a different set of temporal coordinates that nevertheless are just as difficult to break: Suzuki recorder lessons, birthday celebrations and so on. The chronological times of writing and motherhood are times of apparently endless movement and change, filled with, and driven by, specific, unique, but also relentless and endless demands, tasks, deadlines, and goals. Their similarity lies in their apparently endless exclusivity extending forever in different directions, to different futures, but always in time.

Her sister's adoption coincides with Alvarez turning 40 years old, and both of these events confront her with a different order of time. They remind her again that time is limited; but this temporal limit is not a reference to the fact that there are only so many hours in a day, the driving reminder of chronological time. This limit doesn't refer to a choice, a plan, an agenda that implies an exclusion of other parallel but similarly endless time-lines. Instead, this reminder refers to the so-called biological clock, the limited time of the body. The body ticks away at its own peculiar time, and at 40 it reaches a halfway point in its gradual but implacable progression to the end of time. The impending end of time, the fact that the balance of time in the body now leans toward the end rather than the beginning of time, produces a particular sensation in Alvarez. She feels a sense of urgency and a radical anxiety that works in an altogether different way from the pressures of motherhood and writing in chronological time.

Alvarez calls this temporality familial time; and it is of a fundamentally different order from chronological time. She illustrates familial time by telling "the old story of women living together in a house; their menstrual periods will eventually synchronize" (Alvarez 1999, 96). The "old" story tells of the disappearance of the time that makes the women separate individuals. Different women become one simultaneous menstruating body when brought together in this story. Their bodies are synchronized, and they lose their individual chronological time-lines when they enter the temporal home of the familial. Alvarez even suggests in her essay that her decision not to have children is an effect of this familial time. Alvarez's decision is part of a temporal balance between four sisters, two of whom decide not to stay in long-term marriages and not to bear children.

But when the youngest sister decides to adopt, she unwittingly upsets the balance. The harmony, of familial time is made evident and is expressed in the shared childlessness with Alvarez. Her sister's decision to adopt creates a rift in familial time that seems to put into question the ability of the subject to remain within this time, to continue to inhabit familial time. The youngest sister (perhaps all too easily) breaks the familial bond with Alvarez, and follows this with an overwhelming expression of joy which generates an intense feeling of loneliness, an "old," "jealous" need in Alvarez. The youngest sister's statement that "nothing in the world compares to this, nothing," is followed by Alvarez's emotional bursting into tears, and by her pleading request to "please stop saying so, please" (Alvarez 1999, 97). On the one hand, Alvarez experiences a jealousy, a need for possession of something that is radically lost to her, of something that was never really and truly hers to begin with: a familial time that was never hers to own. On the other hand, Alvarez lives this jealousy again describing it as an "old" feeling, a feeling that has never left her: a trace of the haunting, archaic, surviving familial time that still possesses her.

Both statements are signs of what is really at stake in this chapter. Their affective load suggests that familial time is an untenable paradox. On the one hand, familial time, like motherhood, appears to be well beyond Alvarez's reach. The effect on Alvarez of the younger sister's decision underscores its fundamental otherness. Indeed, familial time appears to approximate the timelessness of a maternal experience defined as the very negation of the chronological time of the solitary subject. Familial time is symmetrical while chronological time is chronometrical. Familial time is inclusive of modes of being that are different only on the surface. It produces a unity of being while chronological time produces a radically exclusive set of life choices. Familial time is balanced and harmonious. It is based on the notion of a steady and even static equilibrium, while chronological time is uneven and extreme in its endless movement from past to future. Familial time is the fundamental expression of a link or a bond, inflected by a common past, present, and future, while the arbitrary or deliberate appointments of chronological time are of an altogether different order. And yet, despite the fact that familial time is radically lost to Alvarez, it is also too close for comfort.[19] Her sister' s choice to adopt combined with her fortieth birthday provoke an insistent need in Alvarez that suggests that familial time is closer than ever to the chronological time of the temporal subject.

The paradox of familial time is at the center of Alvarez's essay: an event that cannot truly ever be the property of a temporal subject, even as it leaves its profound, indelible, and timeless mark on her. And the deeply and fundamentally paradoxical nature of the temporal disturbance of familial time is also at the origin of the contradictory responses the sisters have to it. Familial time keeps Alvarez in a lingering depression evidenced by her uncontrollable bouts of crying. Its disturbing paradox is also at the origin of her young sister's catastrophic euphoria who insists on the negativity of the experience even as she joyfully celebrates it: "*Nothing* in the world compares to this, *nothing*" ([My emphasis] Alvarez 1999, 97). But such a disturbing repetition of a triumphalist negation also provokes an ironic interpretation of the statement. It suggests to Alvarez the simultaneous identity of the absolute plenitude of motherhood with an existential nothingness (nothing is compared to motherhood). From this perspective, familial time also produces a request to stop repeating the statement, a negative request that is both defensive and self-affirming. If familial time is paradoxical, its paradox is that of a maternal experience that both threatens and seduces the self with an absolute nothingness, a paradox that provokes a similarly ambivalent reaction in Alvarez (and therefore in chronological time). She both cries and says "I'm so . . . happy . . . so, so happy"; she tells her sister to stop acting the proud mother, but catches herself acting as if she were the proud mother of the new baby (Alvarez 1999, 97).

The inherently paradoxical nature of familial time is not the only force driving Alvarez's ambivalent reaction. She suggests that a social narrative that unequivocally affirms motherhood also helps to create the conditions of possibility for the submission by women to the sometimes catastrophic demands of familial time. Bowing to the unforgiving disdain of so-called Latin culture for maidenhood, Alvarez's aunt decides to have "her one child" and echoes the tone of Alvarez's youngest sister when she exclaims "I won't deny . . . that [mother-hood] has been *the most* significant event of my life" ([My emphasis] Alvarez 1999, 99). Conversely, the social tendency to identify women with the experience of motherhood reduces their choice not to have children to a form of suicide. Indeed, Alvarez suggests in her essay that our current social narratives leave women between two forms of self-erasure. Women in Western and so-called Latin cultures find themselves between a rock and a hard place. They face the impossible choice between motherhood as triumphalist self-sacrifice, or childlessness as a form of "genetic suicide" (Alvarez 1999, 99). Either way, women are repeatedly forced to prematurely face the end of time.

When faced with the paradox of familial time and its multiple pressures, Alvarez calls for help. She asks her husband Bill to consider the possibility of adoption. Bill, however, appears to be immune to the pressures that assault Alvarez. Not only has he already had a family, but more importantly his relationship to that family is from chronological, not familial time. At 50, Bill seems to feel neither the urgency of the biological clock, the passion of the impending end of time, nor the jealousy of a haunting timelessness. Instead, he remembers and understands his own experience of fatherhood in chronological terms, as an event with a beginning and an end. Bill claims that the basis for his refusal is the unattractive prospect for him of starting that process again. Perhaps the absence of social pressures to be a father allows Bill the luxury of inhabiting an exclusively chronological mode of time. Perhaps his excuses contain an implicit disavowal of the pressures of familial time. Whatever the case may be, he responds to Alvarez's request with a dangerous sacrifice of his will that also relieves him of all responsibility, placing all the weight of agency on the shoulders of his wife. "If it's something you really think you have to have, I'll do it for you" (Alvarez 1999, 98). Alvarez suspects the catastrophic implications both for Bill and for her of accepting Bill's offer in the terms given. She is left not knowing what to do. "With the choice presented in terms of what only I wanted, the same indecisiveness struck again" (Alvarez 1999, 98).

At the end of the essay, Alvarez refuses motherhood, but her refusal is fundamentally different from Bill's. Rather than disavow familial time, or entrench herself in the barricades of chronological time, Alvarez instead enters familial time and transforms it by stubbornly keeping chronological time inside of it. Alvarez first acknowledges, accepts, and interiorizes the double assault of familial time and the lack of social support for her decision to remain childless. She then transforms this assault into the very material that supports her decision to remain childless, ironically reversing the effect of familial time on her.

A Turn of Phrase

Alvarez responds to the temporal and social pressure to have a child (and to the impossible position where this pressure leaves her) with a turn of the screw in this essay: by remembering an interiorized maternal reconvention that is both frustrated and frustrating. Alvarez ambivalently tries to close the impossible possibilities of familial time in our social context (i.e., self-sacrifice or suicide) by repeating a "rude" fact, something her mother might have told her as a response to her "old" jealousy: "You can't have everything" (Alvarez 1999, 100). She shouldn't feel cheated, Alvarez tells herself, if she can learn her mother's lesson. She must accept childlessness as a necessary choice given the constraints of a radically single life. Most importantly, she must accept the consequences of a radical separation: the maternal "rude" reminder (and implicit warning) that one lives outside familial time only at one's own peril. She must face the "rude fact" that one will die in the end outside of familial time. So, implicit in the mother's lesson to accept childlessness as a chosen loss, the reader and Alvarez find the oblique reconvention that one must accept the choice to be separate from one's mother, to be outside the timeless familial time. The maternal lesson boils down to accepting the consequences of an existential condition that is unreasonably framed as a choice. The maternal injunction paradoxically warns Alvarez that to choose to be alive, to choose to be outside of familial time, is to take responsibility for choosing to have an identity, for choosing to be a writer, for choosing to be one, and for choosing to be mortal.

But the ending of Alvarez's essay also suggests that the maternal injunction might be too radical perhaps in its absolute displacement of responsibility and agency away from the mother figure at the center of familial time. It suggests that the maternal lesson might be instead but a mirage, a false belief in the independence of the self-aware, self-contained, single, and also fatally wounded writer of chronological time. Indeed, Alvarez suggests that her attempt to close the possibilities opened by familial time (by "accepting [her] chosen loss," by choosing writing as her end, by choosing and taking full responsibility for her identity as a writer) might be insufficient by the end of the essay. In a reverse twist, she suggests instead that writing is not merely an identity assumed against motherhood, but that writing is perhaps the very source of the desire for motherhood.

Despite, or perhaps because of, her realizations, Alvarez subordinates writing to the experience of motherhood up to the end of the essay. "Yet I still felt the pressure to at least say I wanted to be a mother" (Alvarez 1999, 99). But things stand differently at the end of the essay when Alvarez performs a temporal inversion that subordinates motherhood to writing. Rather than having a child for the sake of motherhood, Alvarez begins to suspect that the reverse might be true. Perhaps she wants to have a child for the sake of writing, or in order to be a better writer, she tells both herself and her reader. In fact, she even goes so far as to state that her desire for a child might be a form of mourning for a loss *to* writing, suggesting that her desire to be a mother mourns or compensates a loss of creativity. By making the desire for motherhood into a mournful process that compensates for this loss, by having the desire for motherhood be a way of overcoming a loss of writing, Alvarez returns responsibility for being a good writer to the maternal in an ironic way. The desire for motherhood is responsible for an improvement in the writer. Moreover, if such desire is responsible for the improvement of a being that exists in time (such as a writer), then chronological time might also be a part of the maternal. Not surprisingly, Alvarez's ironic inversion turns writing into a playful act that saves both mother and child from an untimely and monstrous mother who stands outside of time. To imagine motherhood, to write about motherhood, might "[s]pare the poor kid a grandmother-mother who wears dentures," Alvarez writes (Alvarez 1999, 101).

Alvarez's reversal associates a certain kind of writing with the timeless imagination even as it also reverses familial time and its catastrophic effects on the temporal subject. Alvarez infuses familial time with the peculiar temporality of an ironic mode of writing at the end of the essay. When she travels to her "native Dominican Republic," her aunts ask her whether she feels "inspired" to have a child (Alvarez 1999, 101). The aunts mean to put the pressure of familial time on Alvarez. But instead of pleading for her aunts to stop asking the familiarly disturbing question, Alvarez repeats their words while simultaneously transforming and even inverting their meaning. Winking at her husband for a necessary and complicit form of external support (a mode of social support, if you will), she answers ironically "Yes, I feel inspired" (Alvarez 1999, 101).

The phrase is ironic at a number of levels. What Alvarez means by this inspiration is not what her aunts mean by it. She does not mean that her sister's adoption has inspired her to have a child. Instead she means that she is now inspired to imagine motherhood in writing. "Inspired, that is, to come home and write about it" (Alvarez 1999, 101). Indeed, the phrase means that she is inspired to write about the experience of motherhood rather than experiencing motherhood itself. The turn of phrase is also ironic because inspiration is an experience traditionally associated with writing. In other words, Alvarez returns the phrase "to be inspired" to a more familiar lexicon than the vocabulary surrounding motherhood, a lexicon where the word is more at home, if you will. But most importantly, the turn of phrase underscores the uncanny mode of homecoming that is triggered by the aunts' question. In other words, the aunts' familiar question about inspiration perhaps unwittingly, but certainly ironically, both evokes writing for and provokes writing in Alvarez. The aunts' question begins a paradoxical movement of return in Alvarez, an ironic return to a home that is also not a home. "To come home and write" suggests a return to Vermont, a place of dwelling for Alvarez very different from her "native Dominican Republic." But "to come home and write" also suggests an important redefinition of home as the temporally uncanny act of writing itself. In particular, it suggests coming home to an ironic mode of writing that is also a form of temporal return. This mode of writing not only returns time to the maternal through ironic inversions in content, but it also returns time to the timeless through similar inversions in the negative tone and asynchronic rhythm of poetic language as we shall see below.

"Imagining motherhood" then goes some distance in answering the first question posed by the temporal uncanny and repeated in Alvarez's novels. The uncanny temporality of the Anacahuita turn is the result of a struggle to bring chronological time back into familial time, to find chronological time already within familial time. At stake in this effort is the survival of a symbolic feminine subject interred by social pressures in familial time and twice denied existence. Damned to self-sacrifice if they give in to familial time and damned to suicide if they resist it the protagonists of Alvarez's fiction dare to take the temporally uncanny Anacahuita turn, a turn that returns the timeless past into the present. A turn that is keenly different from nostalgia in its drive to survive a disturbing present and to project an unfamiliar future, as Dedé, the protagonist of *In the Time of the Butterflies*, reminds us. "I'm not stuck in the past, I've brought it with me into the present. And the problem is not enough of us have done that" (313).[20]

The essay also answers the second question posed by this repeating scene, namely what is the relationship between the temporal uncanny and writing for Alvarez? Writing as an ironic repetition, an inversion, or a turn of phrase, seems to be a mode of the temporal uncanny for her. To write in this mode is also to allow a way out of familial time for the female subject. But with the temporal uncanny also comes the disturbing effect of the paradox of familial time. The way out is not easy or free from disturbance and Alvarez's ironic mode of writing requires a sympathetic interpretation of this difficulty and disturbance. It requires that we acknowledge the productive irony of the turn. Only such a reading will reverse the wounding effect of familial time and counter the absence of social support that further compounds it. Alvarez's redemption of the untimely, the negative, the comic, and the revolting, in short, of the abject in poetic language, goes a long way in this direction.

Asynchronic Rhythm and Negative Tone

Both Kevane and Juanita Heredia insightfully point out in their book of interviews that Alvarez, a successful novelist, is really "a poet at heart" (Kevane 2000, 20). When asked why she decided to tell the story of the Mirabal sisters in narrative form for example, Alvarez remembers that she began writing the critically acclaimed *In the Time of the Butterflies* as poems. The poems were in the voice of the characters and were meant to head each chapter. They eventually fell away but survived in folders. Significantly, Alvarez points out that the poems were necessary to the narrative. They contained an essential rhythm that allowed her to hear in a certain way. "I guess I needed them in order to hear essentially, rhythmically, each voice" (Kevane 2000, 27). Later in the interview she describes this rhythm as a pulse: "the heart of language" (Kevane 2000, 30).

It is interesting to consider Alvarez's revelation that the chapters of *In the Time of the Butterflies* were originally headed by poems that gave a rhythmic form to its characters, when one considers the intricate and temporally uncanny rhythmic structure of her latest novel, *In the Name of Salomé*. In that novel, Alvarez preserves the poetic origins of the chapters and heads each one of them with the title of a poem by Salomé Ureña (1850–1897), the mother of the novel's protagonist, Camila. The novel is divided into two parts. Each part is divided into four chapters, and each chapter is divided into two sections. Each section carries a title from one of eight different poems by Salomé, and each title alternates between Spanish and English. Halfway through the book, however, the relationship between the language and the titles of the poems is reversed producing a confusion of a temporal order. If the first part of the novel begins with an original Spanish title, "El ave y el nido," and ends with the English translation "Shadows," the second half begins with a reversal to the Spanish original "Sombras," and ends with a return to the first title now translated into the English "Bird and Nest."

The structure of the novel, then, is a dizzying combination of two rhythmic patterns. One is based on repetition, while the other is based on succession or change. One is best represented by the symmetrical movement back and forth of the pendulum of a clock, alternating between one title in English and another title in Spanish, while the other is evoked by the successive movements of the hands of the clock. The latter is a movement that begins with one poem and returns to the same poem at the end of the novel. The strange mixture of repetition and change has a temporally uncanny effect on the titles as well. Spanish originals appear to change into Spanish "translations," and English translations reappear as English "originals," when the same title is repeated but in the inverse order and in a different language from the beginning of the book. Significantly, the narrative is the counterpoint of this rhythmic tension. The novel tells the story of two women narratively trapped in asymmetrical temporalities: the story of Camila told in reverse time, and the story of her mother Salomé told in progressive time.

Repetition and change, quotation and translation, progression and regression together constitute the temporally uncanny pulse of Alvarez's writing figured as a root, a living language in her novel. " 'I shall recite a little-known poet,' [Camila] says, taking a deep breath. Among her poems, one particularly has received a positive response . . . 'La raíz,' it is called, a root probing in the dark earth for water, dreaming of flowers" (Alvarez 2000, 116). This pulsating root has a life-affirming function in the novel. Not only does it join the symbolic and the organic, but it also establishes a necessary connection between the self and the other. "This must be the beginning of death, [Salomé] thought, the tendrils of language unable to reach beyond the self and catch the attention of others" (Alvarez 2000, 312).

Not surprisingly, Alvarez represents writing in this novel as the metaphorical umbilical cord that connects the temporally asymmetrical lives of Camila and Salomé. At the end of the novel, Camila describes her survival strategy with the image of such a cord that is also an image for the novel itself. "I learned her story. I put it side by side with my own. I wove our two lives together as strong as rope and with it I pulled out of the pit of depression and self-doubt. But no matter what I tried, she was still gone. Until, at last I found her the only place we ever find the dead: among the living" (Alvarez 2000, 335). At the end of her rope, Camila finds a way to recover her lost mother not by finding her in any one place, but by finding her a place among the living. The space of writing is this disturbing place among the living, an organic and symbolic connection, a pulsating cord (inspired by Salomé's poetry) that contains the temporally uncanny rhythm and the negative tone of the lost maternal body.

The temporally uncanny rhythm at the center of the pulsating cord of Alvarez's latest novel, takes poetic form in the verses that return to her during moments of loss or impending loss in her latest book of poems. She remembers verses that span three centuries of writing in English in "Life Lines." But they offer her ambiguous comfort. "And yet I mourned the deeper for that line" (Alvarez 2004, 101). They spring back to Alvarez's memory, on their own, from a canonical list that includes William Shakespeare (1564–1606), George Herbert (1593–1633), Oliver Goldsmith (1728–1774), and W.B. Yeats (1865–1939), when her parents return to their motherland, and when her mother dies. Here, Alvarez selects verses from poems or plays that explore the connection between loss and language; and she chooses lines that are marked by a negative tone aimed at similar losses in the external world. The verses convey a heterogeneous series of negative emotions that range from Yeats' jaded rejection of youth in "Sailing to Byzantium," to Herbert's weary surprise at feeling the will to live again in "The Flower"; from Goldsmith's spiteful rebuff of a foolish woman in *The Vicar of Wakefield* to Shakespeare's angry impatience with time in *Macbeth*.

But it is the tone of these verses that best conveys Alvarez's negative mode of saying in poetry "what can't be said in words": a break with meaning or sense, a departure from the sensuous, material world, and a melancholy death wish. The jarring tone of these verses suggests the ambiguous function of poetry as disavowal: both the negation of loss, but also the confirmation of loss. An unseemly loud clapping and song both negate and affirm, hide and reveal, the wounds in Yeats' lasting image for the mortal body. "Soul clap its hands and sing, and louder sing / For every tatter in its mortal dress" (Yeats 1928, 2). The discordant tone sends the poet on a journey to Byzantium, a metaphor for poetry as the disembodied country of artifice. The same negative tone, however, is the *goal* of Alvarez's poem. "Life Lines" ends with a modified version of Yeats' famous line, suggesting Alvarez's simultaneous repetition and reversal of a literary tradition. Contrary to Yeats, Alvarez seeks to articulate the wounded and lost body that gives language its disturbing meaning, its uncanny sense. Rather than inter the dying body in a tomb of language, escaping, obscuring, or silencing its mortality by opposing it to eternal art and poetry, Alvarez instead returns the tattered, wounded, mortal body to language through a negative tone.

In "Life Lines," Alvarez revolts strangely against an epitaphial poetic tradition that identifies the body in general, and the feminine body in particular, with the blank page, the stone, or the loss on which the mournful writing of these poets is engraved as a memory. Goldsmith warns a "foolish" woman in his poem that "The only art . . . / To give repentance to her lover, / And wring his bosom is—to die" (Goldsmith 1939, 145). Alvarez writes that she almost quotes his poem to her headstrong cousin, but thinks better of it. Instead, she writes in her poem of biting her tongue in time. "I almost said—but bit my tongue in time— *When lovely woman stoops to folly*" (Alvarez 2004, 101). Ironically, Alvarez quotes Goldsmith and the others in her poem even as she bites her tongue. She allows the wounding tradition to spring back at the very moment she describes the act of repressing it. To do so, she suggests, is also to listen for the negative tone of this tradition, to trace its violence back to its source, as she does in "Life Lines," which takes back the verses to the haunting "prayers mothers whisper over cribs" (Alvarez 2004, 102). In this way, the poet turns the act of biting one's tongue in time into a metaphor for poetry as a reverse journey back to an uncanny and wounded first tongue. "Life Lines" puts back the painful and melancholy act of self-censorship in time. Alvarez keeps her anger to herself but does so in poetry. She turns her melancholy self-violence into a poetic rhythm, a spring back, a temporal regression in language that remembers the lost maternal voice at the source of a violent poetic tradition. Rather than obscure the jarring sound of the maternal, instead of abandoning its unseemly gestures, "Life Lines" listens for the pulse of the body in language. "The winds of time would carry me away / but for the words which when my life breaks down / rise up and clap their hands and louder sing!" (Alvarez 2004, 102).

A Comic and Revolting First Tongue

Alvarez eloquently describes the regression in language back to a place pulsating with an asynchronic rhythm in the poem "Passing On": a journey back to "some place dead center in the human heart" (Alvarez 2004, 139). The poem, like many others in this collection, performs a reversal of writing in writing. It takes us from the intimate indirect voice of Emily Dickinson (1830–1886) and the loud, in-your-face voice of Walt Whitman (1819–1892) in the first stanza back to the familiar Spanish sounds of women gossiping, malaproping clichés, singing sad *boleros* (ballads in Spanish) and salsa songs, and to the litany of rosary beads in the second stanza. The journey appears to come to an end at the beginning of the third stanza, when the poetic subject comes close to the maternal rhythm that she also calls the "first tongue." "When all I knew was heartbeat and the hum / of Mami's murmuring blood becoming mine" (Alvarez 2004, 140). But instead, the first tongue marks a strange beginning.

Echoing, but also reversing the direction of Yeats' "Sailing to Byzantium," the end of "Passing On" evokes the image of the poem as a ship sailing out to the end of time. But Yates compares poetry to an artificial vessel that reaches eternity because it rejects the body. "Once out of nature I shall never take / My bodily form from any natural thing" (Yeats 1928, 3). Instead, Alvarez recalls the biblical image of Noah's ark as a metaphor for the mixture of the animal and the human in her poetry. Indeed, Alvarez's poem struggles to contain the heartbeat and hum of a first tongue, a rhythm beyond a nation, beyond a species, and beyond time but not beyond the body where Yeats pretends to go. Indeed, the organic remains of the body reappear to constitute that first tongue in Alvarez's poem. Yeats evokes the image of the poet as an artificial bird whose privileged vantage point (he sits on a golden bough) allows him to sing "Of what is past, or passing, or to come" (Yeats 1928, 3). Instead, Alvarez conjures the biblical image of the Tower of Babel as a metaphor not so much for the punishment of poetic hubris, but as a symbol for the promise of human limitations. Alvarez's ship of poetry contains the babble of Babel: and it is this uncanny voice (a voice both possessed and possessing the poet, a voice that is also the negative of voice) that takes her to the limit of language, to the border of self-possession, and to the edge of time. "I now pass on, my own, and not my own" (Alvarez 2004, 140).

In "First Muse," Alvarez again revolts against the stunning effect of a similar cultural and poetic injunction against the body that forces her to identify with Spanish, her lost mother tongue. She quotes a famous poet who proclaims that "One can only write poems in the tongue / in which one first said *Mother*, I was stunned" (Alvarez

2004, 39). And again, her answer is to write, but to write negatively, in a stunned tongue if you will. She follows the famous poet's "advice" to keep poetry to herself, but does so strangely. "And you know how it happens that advice / comes from unlikely quarters?" (Alvarez 2004, 39). Alvarez not only transforms her subsequent writer's block into a poetic subject, but she turns her descent into depression into a symbolic pre-text for her writing. She turns from writing to watching TV, and finds a model for her dramatically unlyrical mode of writing in the televised voice and dance of a caricature. The poetically abject sounds of commercial advertising, the exaggerated rhythm of Chiquita Banana's comic body dancing to the jingle's beat, the exotic lilt of her foreign accent, become not only the source of Alvarez's writing, but even turn into the uncanny sources of her identity as a writer. "I touched the screen and sang / my own heart out with my new muse, *I am / Chiquita Banana and I'm here to say*" (Alvarez 2004, 39).

The irony of tracing back her writer's identity to a caricature is not lost on Alvarez. Indeed, the comic is a form of ironic reversal in Alvarez's writing. Comedy is a mode of the negative in her writing, which is also modeled after maternal malapropisms. Perhaps the poem "Spic" best represents this comic mode of poetic negativity that is also present in her poems to the animals and to their ambivalent revenge against humanity (See, for example, the poems "Naming the animals" and "The Animals Review Pictures of a Vanished Race" in *The Woman I Kept to Myself*). "Spic" describes the comic reversal of a defensive taunt that does violence both to a different body and to an irregular language that threaten the so-called normalcy of sameness: "lifting my sister's skirt, yanking her slip," "Irregular verbs crumpled under tires" (Alvarez 2004, 27). "Spic" moves from the traumatic site of the insult to the comic moment of the mother's joke in the second stanza. The mother figure reverses the force of the silencing slur "spic" into its speaking opposite by deliberately inverting the order of the verses of the national anthem, and tracing back the racial slur to the implicit xenophobia of patriotic discourse. "The anthem here invites its citizens / to speak up. *Oh see, can you say*, she sang" (Alvarez 2004, 27).

The migrant mother's funny malapropism has the added effect not only of reversing the silencing command, but also of pointing out the negative, or the opposite meaning already embedded in xenophobic language. "Our classmates had been asking us to speak" (Alvarez 2004, 27). The poet listens for this disturbance of unitary meaning in language, and takes her mother at her negative word. Following her mother's advice, the poet does the opposite of what her classmates order her to do. She speaks up in class; and her negative speaking has a disturbing effect on her classmates. They modify their slurs with revealing qualifiers. Spic becomes "Spic ball!" and "Spic trash," and both changes suggest the organic and unstable nature of the threat that the slur turns into untouchable, expectorated, rotting, and abject material. The poem similarly approximates language to the abject, but does so in reverse. Alvarez promises that she will "learn their language well" and indeed she does. She follows the xenophobe's advice and *spics* just like her mother. She humorously puts into language the silencing violence she has seen in America. She allows the unstable material made morbid by the slur to surface as the comic excess of a joke.

It is important to emphasize, however, that Alvarez's poetic language neither takes on a ludic performativity of ethnicity, nor does it celebrate multiculturalism. Instead, she seems painfully aware, rather than blissfully ignorant, of the consequences of assuming a vexed identity, of articulating what she calls "a hyphenated voice" (Alvarez 2004, 139).[21] That is, Alvarez's identity and her poetic voice are deliberately revolting. She takes on the revolt implicit in the caricature and the slur as the key ingredient of an unstable identity.[22] In other words, she takes to heart their unstable source and shaky ground. Indeed, Alvarez traces back her negative form of writing to the disturbing material excess that the racial slur and the caricature screen in an autobiographical essay with the same title as the poem "First Muse."

Maternal Desire and *Jouissance*

In the essay "First Muse," Alvarez traces back the unpoetic figure of Chiquita Banana to her memory of a traumatic scene from childhood. " 'No speak eengleesh,' [children] taunted my accent. 'I'm Chiquita Banana and I'm here to say . . .' They glared at me as if I were some repulsive creature with six fingers on my hands" (Alvarez 1999, 140). Indeed, the children's taunt is an apt symbol for Alvarez's hyphenated voice in her latest collection of poetry. The children mock Alvarez, but also unwittingly perform a paradoxical negation of English in English for her. Their taunt is an ungrammatical, syntactic, and phonetic distortion of English that later becomes the sign of Alvarez's distinctly negative mode of hyphenated poetry (which is not to say that her poetry is ungrammatical or distorted). But the essay also suggests that the jeer is a defensive reaction by a Dominican tradition to the threat of a monstrously excessive body associated with the maternal outlaw. Earlier in the essay, Alvarez tells the story of a similar monstrosity (in this case the body with the sixth finger is male) where the corporeal excess is a mark of divine punishment against a mother who breaks the law. "You know, Chucho, the man born with a sixth finger on each hand because when his mother was pregnant, she stole a piece of *pudín de pan* from a neighbor, and so God punished her by putting an extra, shoplifting finger on her son's hand" (Alvarez 1999, 138). The story is a Dominican cautionary tale where the outlaw maternal body is punished by adding a monstrous appendage to its offspring, and by characterizing its excess as an unseemly hunger: an unlawful desire for the *pudín de pan*.

The Dominican pairing of the abject maternal body and its excessive evil desire is part of a familiar, longstanding matricidal cultural and literary tradition that takes many forms including the biblical figure of Salomé. The unruly desires of this mythical maternal outlaw also place her outside the law, and she is vilified for her transgressions centuries later in Western opera, short stories, and plays.[23] Indeed, the figure of the criminal mother is a red flag that screens (that unwittingly reveals even as it hides) the unstable and revolting sources of language (English and Spanish) and of the Divine Law. In fact, the figure suggests the productive interdependence of the constraints of language and the sensations that are the object of its defenses, what Kristeva calls *jouissance:* "the pleasure of sensory meaning or of the sensory in meaning . . . and pain" (Kristeva 2002a, 48). The Dominican and the Biblical matricidal traditions perceive and represent this interdependence as an evil. In doing so, these traditions guarantee the outcome that they seek to prevent. They disavow and petrify the revolt, the questioning, so necessary to representation and to all modes of signification (Kristeva 2002a, 10).

Alvarez is clearly interested in reversing this tradition and its symbols. She revolts against them by containing, rather than disavowing, the excess of maternal desire, by writing in an ambivalent mode that redeems its negativity that allows *jouissance* to return to the surface of language. In a central passage of that novel, the biblical and maternal namesake of the poet Salomé Ureña appears to her as an abject figure, alarmingly naked, reeking of urine and sweat, and only able to scream when she opens her "rotted mouth" (Alvarez 2000, 97). The encounter happens when the character is a child, and she is held and then repelled by this abject body. The novel emphasizes that the "probing desire" of the figure "to know who I was" fixes Salomé in place until "she opened her rotted mouth to scream" (Alvarez 2000, 97). As an adult, however, Salomé allows the figure's probing desire and uncanny voice to influence her poetry, which develops into an excessive and similarly vexed mode of passionate writing she knows to be outside the law. "But even as I wrote, I knew such frank passions in a woman were not permissible . . ." (Alvarez 2000, 143).

Indeed, Salomé's poetry is excessive in its sentimentality. It contains a disturbing intimacy to the point of offending the gatekeepers of the Dominican literary tradition. Salomé's husband and her sons circumscribe their mother to the disembodied role of muse of the motherland, and go on to edit the offending poems out of their posthumous anthologies. It is an unfortunate, defensive, but predictable response to a mode of writing that tries to reverse an ancient, biblical punishment, and that tries to take back the divine Law into flesh. "I wanted . . . that hushed and holy moment that all poems aspire to when the word becomes flesh" (Alvarez 2000, 88). Their reaction suggests the threat provoked in Dominican tradition by the excess, the disturbance, the desire, or *jouissance* contained in Salomé's intimate poetry. They excise it, deaden it, petrify it, and write over it. Camila's response to Salomé's poetry is somewhat different, however. Her mother's poetry provokes a similar fear in Camila that leads her to silence. But it also provokes a pleasure that she allows herself to feel and calls a "funny sensation," though she knows it is forbidden. "But there is a secret Camila cannot admit even to her best friend: the funny sensations she has when they have sat together in bed, propped up on pillows, reading her mother's poems" (Alvarez 2004, 288). If maternal desire leads Salomé to an intimate mode of poetry that aspires to transform the word into flesh, maternal pleasure leads Camila to a mode of teaching that returns the body back to writing. "Together we trace the grooves in the stone, he repeating the name of each letter after me. 'Very good,' I tell him when we have done this several times. 'Now you do it by yourself' " (Alvarez 2000, 353).

Alvarez models her own negative poetic voice on an ambivalence that is similar to the simultaneous sacrifice and revolt of Salomé's writing and Camila's teaching. Perhaps the poem "By Accident" best represents her attempt to give poetic form to the unstable ground between body and language, while simultaneously preserving its revolting or form-resisting nature. The poem begins with a series of feminine absences, indeed with the figure of feminine absence as the negative model for the woman that the poet becomes: a woman in writing, the woman in the poem. But the poem also moves away from the more neutral feminine absence to a more active feminine negative reaction as the source of writing. The familiar women around her have a negative response to the poet's passion for reading, to her pleasure, and desire. In fact, the poet's desire for sounds and sweet airs that give her delight and pleasure at night make her sisters sick and provoke, quite by accident, a feminine revolt and maternal negativity. Her "ranting," and "the poems [she] recited ad nauseum" start a "nightmare fight" that brings on the maternal command to "Keep it to yourself!" (Alvarez 2004, 35–36).

But the maternal command to keep desire and pleasure to herself also has a similarly unexpected result. The feminine revolt and the maternal command turn back the reader to the page, literally making the reader in the poem inscribe herself on to the page. Feminine revolt and maternal negativity now become the accidents, the unintended, unforeseen, and undesirable origins of the writer, who in turn produces the woman in the poem. Feminine revolt and maternal negativity turn the reader into a poet, who now seeks her similarly disturbing pleasure and desire in writing. Poetic writing, in turn, becomes a repetition of the ambiguous effect of its unstable, accidental source: an ambivalent mode of expression adjusted to, or informed by the similarly ambiguous effect of pleasure and desire. Poetic writing becomes a silent practice that keeps secret its source in the disturbing interaction between pleasure and feminine revolt. It also becomes a practice that broadcasts its source in the same disquieting interaction between desire and maternal negativity. Alvarez's poetic writing gives form to the productive ambiguity of feminine pleasure and maternal desire while preserving its disturbed and disturbing effect.

But Alvarez's ambivalent poetry also tries to go beyond the mere repetition of the ambiguity of feminine pleasure and maternal desire in language. Her poetry also redeems the excess of *jouissance*, the disturbing but also productive nexus of body and language, a nexus that is both responsible for the self, and that leaves the self with an infinite responsibility, with an insurmountable debt. Alvarez's poet implicitly redeems *jouissance* by asking for forgiveness, hence the question that serves as a title for the last poem of the collection, "Did I redeem myself?" In that poem, Alvarez suggests both the need for (and the limits of) poetry as an unequal return or "tender" for the insurmountable debts incurred by the poetic self. The poem suggests its nature as a response to a call to service from "the truest after all," a "Beautiful" you "whose tongue wooed me to service" (Alvarez 2004, 155–156). Family, lovers, friends, and nation, are all figured as forms of this call in a beautiful tongue, a call that is the uncanny cipher for the unstable excess that is *jouissance*. But the poem also suggests it is indeed an answer that is unequal, and remains eternally indebted to, the strength and beauty of its source. And so, the poem, like the book, can only pose the question of redemption; it can only repeat the question, while leaving it necessarily open for the reader to experience as a similar call: a call to service, a call to interpretation, and a question of forgiveness. "Finally, my readers what will you decide / when all that's left of me will be these lines?" (Alvarez 2004, 155).

When many Latino authors in the United States write about their experiences, they often describe the temporal effects of growing up in a country that is both home and not home to them. They tend to describe contradictory pressures to both forget and return to the past, to both embrace and resist the present, pressures that often evoke and act on maternal symbols. Specifically, the mother figure and the mother tongue often appear in these works either as timeless symbols or as symbols of a lost past. Sometimes they are pushed to the past, deliberately forgotten or erased, sacrificed to the need to adapt, assimilate, and succeed in the present. Other times, the mother tongue and figure are nostalgically evoked, preserved, or frozen in suspended time, remembered as a timeless support for the hard work of surviving in time. Often they are both, as in this passage from the now classic *Hunger of Memory; The Education of Richard Rodríguez*: "The unspoken may well up within my mother and cause her to sigh. But beyond that sigh nothing is heard. There is no one she can address. Words never form. Silence remains to repress them. She remains quiet" (Rodríguez 1983, 185). Either way, these narratives either abject the maternal symbolically burying it in the past and silencing it, or idealize it as a timeless and silent symbol.[24]

Alvarez's writing in general, and her latest collection of poetry in particular offers an alternative response to this experience. Rather than indulging in a violently matricidal mode of identitarian discourse, Alvarez's *The Woman I Kept to Myself* avoids its catastrophic melancholy pitfalls by looking to the unstable ground of revolt as a model for poetic language. The disturbing nature of revolt as experienced in feminine pleasure/negation and maternal desire/abjection becomes the uncanny foundation that allows Alvarez to sublimate her losses. It is "the semiotic dimension of language through which bodily experience can make its way into language" (Oliver 2004, 170). But *The Woman I Kept to Myself* also goes beyond modeling poetry after the disturbances of revolt. Alvarez's collection of poetry is at its best when it suggests that the revolt of poetic language only makes sense in the service and redemption of a call from a lost m/other.

Notes

Introduction

1. I hasten to add that an increasing number of writers from diverse cultural, racial, and socioeconomic backgrounds are working on this attempt. Indeed, Maxine Hong Kingston in *The Woman Warrior* (1975), Jamaica Kincaid in *The Autobiography of My Mother* (1996), and Toni Morrison in *Beloved* (1988) among others are also engaging with the disturbing power of the maternal speaking body in their work. My intention is not to argue that this problem is a particular concern of Latin Americans, Chicanos/as or Latino/as. Nor do I claim that these writers give it a representative form. My intention is instead to call attention to their specific reinscriptions of a versatile matricidal imaginary that cuts across history, socioeconomic class, and culture, without abstracting their work from its historical socioeconomic and cultural context. My goal is to call attention to their reinscriptions as a possible way of coping, managing, and working through the twenty-first century versions of a symbolic matricide at the center of the limit-events of a globalizing and globalized capitalist market, and at the center of a culture of spectacle that flattens the psyche. My hope is to contribute to a change in the culture of interpretation that will make this culture more equal to the task at hand. A change that will allow us to occupy a transformative position that neither looks nostalgically back to a past transcendental subject, nor points nihilistically forward to a future ludic, but aggressively meaningless subject.

2. Perhaps the central concept of the maternal imaginary is what Kristeva calls the speaking body, a body that according to Oliver "is more than material" (Oliver 2002, xvii). So, exactly what is this more-than-material speaking body, and what is its relation to the maternal body and to the maternal imaginary? The speaking body is the least common denominator, or the irreducible part if you will, of our psychic lives and, of our sense of ourselves, both conscious and unconscious. It is the constellation of contradictory elements that makes us who we are, which gives us meaning in the broadest sense of that word. (For a discussion of the relationship of the speaking body and meaning, please see the introduction to Oliver's edition of Kristeva's works [Oliver 2002, xi–xxix].) As such, the speaking body exists as a thing out there in the material world. It is a subject that occupies a space and lives in time. But it also exists as a grammatical

person that does the action of the verb in a sentence, or rather in a set of statements that articulate our most commonly held myths, beliefs, fantasies, and
symbolic representations of the world.

As the term suggests, the speaking body combines linguistic with organic
material. In other words, the speaking body is Kristeva's challenge to a traditional notion of the body that circumscribes it to an organic and biological existence. When Oliver says that the body is "more than material," what she means
is that the body speaks. To the question of what does it mean for the body to
speak, Kristeva answers with a challenge to our traditional notion of what
speaking means. She does not circumscribe speaking to an abstract, instrumental,
and purely conceptual practice of signification. Instead, the speaking body performs what Kristeva describes as "an undecidable process between sense and
nonsense, between language and rhythm" (1980, 135). In Oliver's words, the
speaking body doesn't just speak the meaning of language; the speaking body is
by itself meaningful.

Oliver convincingly argues that Kristeva's account of the speaking body is a
more optimistic engagement with the problem of the relationship between
language and bodily experience than the efforts of her post-structuralist
contemporaries. Unlike philosophers such as Jacques Derrida, whose work suggests that language is but the dead remains of a living body, Kristeva marvels at
the "living drive force" that "makes its way into language" (Oliver 2002, xx).
Indeed, Oliver argues that Kristeva's reconnection of bodily drives to language
has the potential of opening the "impasse" of our postmodern world where we
face the meaninglessness of life or an "abyss between our fragmented language
and our fragmented sense of ourselves" (Oliver 2002, xxii).

The speaking body is meaningful because it is the heterogeneous foundation,
the unstable ground of the self. It is both an excess of signification and an
excess of organic material. It is both embodied language and a language of the
body. Indeed, the speaking body contains a logic of signification that is consti-
tuted by the bodily drives. "Kristeva takes up Freud's theory of drives as instinc-
tual energies that operate between biology and culture. Drives have their source
in organic tissue and aim at psychological satisfaction" (Oliver 2002, xvii). The
Speaking body defies and resists our insistent attempts at containing both its
excessive logic of signification and its heterogeneous bodily drives. It is the
process or flux caused by the movement and interaction between what Kristeva
calls the semiotic and the symbolic.

According to Oliver, the semiotic and the symbolic are Kristeva's most famous
contributions to language theory (Oliver 2002, xiv). Oliver argues that while the
semiotic provides language with movement or negativity, the symbolic provides
it with stasis and stability. Kristeva associates the former with rhythm and the
latter with grammar. Together the semiotic and the symbolic keep signification
dynamic and structured as well as coherent and meaningful (Oliver 2002, xv).
Together they produce the speaking body as a meaningful, but also unsettled,
questionable subject-in-process. It is a subject on trial that is outside the
symbolic law but is between the semiotic and the symbolic.

What is, then, the relationship between the speaking body or the subject-in-
process and the maternal body? According to Oliver, "the maternal body

operates between nature and culture, between biology and sociology. Neither the mother nor the fetus is a unified subject. Rather, the maternal body is the most obvious example of a subject-in-process" (Oliver 2002, 297–298). So, for Oliver the mother is a subject-in-process or an unsettled and questionable subject between the material world and language. Following the legal definition of "process," the mother is a questionable outlaw. She is outside the Law of the Father in traditional psychoanalysis. But to Oliver, who also follows the definition of "process" as a series of actions, changes, or functions, as a progress or a passage, the mother is also the source of a Law before the Law of the Father. If according to Freud and Jacques Lacan the child enters the social or language out of fear of castration, according to Oliver (following Kristeva) the child enters the social or language out of a love of signification or better yet out of a love of meaning both in its strictest sense as language and in its broadest sense as *raison d'être* or *élan vital*. In other words, the speaking maternal body endows its offspring with a process, a law of ambivalence (the pleasure of separation and the pain of identification and vice versa) that is necessary to generate identity, even as it simultaneously troubles the stability of identity. Or again, the maternal speaking body is responsible for the fact that the subject is always in a process of separation and identification that makes and troubles identity. In short, the maternal speaking body gives birth to the subject-in-process of Kristevan psychoanalysis.

This description of the maternal speaking body suggests its similarity to (if not its identity with) the process of signification itself. Oliver's provocative description of the maternal body as "the most obvious example of the subject-in-process" points the reader in this direction and her account of the body of the infant before it begins to use language confirms it. Following Kristeva, Oliver states that "the logic of signification is already operating in the body, and therefore the transition to language is not as dramatic and mysterious as traditional psychoanalytic theory makes it out to be," and she writes that "the principles or structures of separation and difference are operating in the body even before the infant begins to use language" (Oliver 2002, xxi, 134). She describes what she calls "the maternal function" in terms that remind the reader of the process of signification. "Unlike Freud and Lacan . . . who ignore the function of the mother [in language acquisition and socialization] Kristeva elaborates and complicates the maternal function. She insists that there is regulation and structure in the maternal body and the child's relationship to that body" (Oliver 2002, 296). Moreover, if the imaginary is the constellation of fantasies, myths, theories, and discourses that constitutes the core of our beliefs, which together are the linguistic and organic origins of our perceptions and experience of our bodies, then the imaginary is also a form of the process of signification. And if the imaginary is a form of the process of signification that generates the speaking body, then the maternal imaginary is the most obvious example of the imaginary.

3. Maternal writing defined here as a paradoxical, ambiguous, and hybrid practice that is always already structured by language, but that also makes language possible (even as it troubles language) approximates what Vanessa Vilches Norat has recently called "matergraphy." According to Vilches Norat, matergraphy arises when the autobiographical subject is "faced with the perception of

an irreparable separation, one that always confronts us with loss at the origin" (2003, 67; my translation). In other words, matergraphy is the symbolic wager at the center of all autobiographical writing for Vilches Norat. Matergraphy bets on the possibility of articulating what is not verbal, what is preverbal for Julia Kristeva (Vilches Norat 2003, 61). But similar to other Kristevan scholars such as Miglena Nikolchina, Vilches Norat also characterizes this wager as a mournful practice that is doomed from its inception, as a necessary symbolic matricide if you will. The object of matergraphy is the abject, perverse, unsayable, maternal void, position, or empty crypt mourned by the autobiographical subject. As the reader will see, my opinion on this point is quite different. For me, maternal writing has no "object," at least no object so defined. Maternal writing need not be matricidal, and it is instead a fundamentally productive (if uncanny) heterogeneous practice. It is aporetic, but it does not repeat the matricide implied in the reduction of the maternal imago to an always already lost object (Vilches Norat 2003, 67).

4. Licia Fiol Matta is right to suggest that "maternal discourse" (her name for what I call here a maternal imaginary) is a "thinking" or an "enunciation" belonging to both the state and the self and that it is neither uniform nor uniformly benign (2002, xxvi).

5. I borrow the term discourse from Michel Foucault, but I also elaborate it to mean something both organic and linguistic. For my definition of discourse please see the introduction to *Subjects of Crisis*.

6. For de Lauretis, heterosexually determined feminists such as Madelon Sprengnether, Julia Kristeva, Luce Irigaray, and Nancy Chodorow have dangerously reduced female sexuality to maternity. They have reduced feminine identity to the mother, and have erased the affirmation of difference by women. For de Laturetis, their mode of the maternal imaginary is a conservative and heterosexual response of feminists to the patriarchal account of the maternal imaginary. She argues that the heterosexual feminist maternal imaginary overempowers a pre-Oedipal mother and de-problematizes the contradictory and unsettling nature of the formative seduction scene. Its main pitfall is that this maternal imaginary reduces lesbianism to a metaphor and erases the difference between lesbian and heterosexual desire in feminist thought and writing. In other words, the heterosexual maternal imaginary falls prey to the essentialist traps of primary femininity. It produces the doxa of women's creative maternal power and already achieved enfranchisement from men.

Instead, de Lauretis praises the efforts of what she calls postfeminist theorists of female sexuality that includes Victoria Smith, Kaja Silverman, and Judith Roof. These writers develop a homosexual version of the maternal metaphor and a lesbian mode of the maternal imaginary that does not fall prey to the fantasy of mastery of the pre-Oedipal mother. Instead, these theorists address the lesbian nature of a mutual seduction in the pre-Oedipal scene and propose a different account of the maternal as always already lost. She proposes a lesbian account of female subjectivity based on the structural absence of maternal sameness (see de Lauretis, 163–175). It should be clear to the reader that I disagree with de Lauretis both in her characterization of Kristeva's work and in her description of the symbolic mother as always already lost, or as constitutively lost.

7. Although Oliver makes this argument through her work, it is most explicitly developed in *The Colonization of Psychic Space*.

8. In this respect, Oliver has taken a very different direction from other readers of Kristeva as well as from many of her critics. Critics of Kristeva such as de Lauretis ignore her emphasis on sublimation and transposition. Instead, they interpret Kristeva as arguing for a view of female subjectivity that is based on the equally dismal beginnings of matricide or primary (Pre-Oedipal) motherhood. Indeed, de Lauretis reads Kristeva's work as a mere "inversion" of a phallic economy of desire, as an even more insidious matricide made plain by her "dismal view of female subjectivity as structured by paranoia, exacerbated masochism, ever-lurking psychosis, and absolute dependence on the fruit of the penis" (1994, 180). Given this limited and limiting interpretation of Kristeva it is no surprise that she should wonder what could possibly be gained from it.

Like many readers of Kristeva, who appear to have stopped reading her after *Powers of Horror*, Miglena Nikolchina elaborates her theory of abjection into a theory of subversive feminine writing articulated into two specific rhetorical techniques that she names "abjectivity" and "merginality" (2004, 8–9). Nikolchina emphasizes the creative possibilities of writing from the reverberations, the wavering, and the after-shocks of the process of abjection described by Kristeva. She states that to do so can result in a more hopeful lineage of fantasies, symbols, and figures from the one that results from either uncritically engaging in cultural matricide or from disavowing it. In this way, Nikolchina criticizes both the phallic symbolic economy as well as the Feminist reaction to it for refusing to face and inhabit the unstable ground of what she calls a matricidal phantasmatics.

Though provocative, both readings of Kristeva (i.e., de Lauretis's and Nikolchina's) minimize or even erase what clearly appears to be its most promising and hopeful side for Oliver: the need to sublimate and transpose the maternal speaking body or the patriarchal abject.

9. Her object of analysis runs the gamut from the theories of Charles Taylor and Michel Foucault to those of Jacques Lacan and Judith Butler.

10. In *The Colonization of Psychic Space* (especially in chapter 7, "The Depressed Sex"), Oliver argues that feminine depression and maternal melancholy develop from a lack of social support structures.

11. The collection *La sartén por el mango* (1984) is widely held to be a watershed moment in this process. In the field of Chicana literature, Norma Alarcón's 1981 essay "Chicana's Feminist Literature: A Revision Through Malintzin/or Malintzin: Putting Flesh Back on the Object" represents an even earlier example of this turn.

12. Castro-Klaren's essay "La critica literaria feminista y la escritora en América Latina," (1985, 27–44) is an early example of this argument.

13. Alarcón's widely cited 1989 essay "Traddutora, Traditora: A Paradigmatic Figure of Chicana Feminism" is a landmark of this approach.

14. Franco's influential 1989 book *Plotting Women* is perhaps the most representative example of this mode of Feminist criticism. Other notable examples include the widely read 1984 essay by Josefina Ludmer "Tretas del débil,"

Doris Sommer's 1991 *Foundational Fictions*, as well as Mary Beth Tierney-Tello's more recent *Allegories of Transgression and Transformation* (1996).

15. Examples of this very popular approach range from Debra Castillo's *Talking Back* and Francine Masiello's *Between Civilization and Barbarism*, both published in 1992, to Adriana Méndez Rodenas' 1998 study of Cuban literature *Gender and Nationalism in Colonial Cuba*.

16. For an example of this unconscious or strategic (and defensive) erasure of psychoanalysis that nevertheless inflects concepts central to this tradition such as incorporation, projection, and transposition and even Freudian master narratives such as his interpretation of the primal meal in *Totem and Taboo* see Molloy's study of autobiography in Latin America, in particular her provocative study of the repeating image of the reader with the book in his hand (1991, 15–35).

17. For a representative example, see Kaminsky's insistence on the validity of a materialist approach to analysis in her 1993 book *Reading the Body Politic*. See also Castillo's lament about the directions taken by Latin American feminist criticism which according to her has fallen into one of two categories: either it is content-based and impressionistic or it is recuperative of work by women and informed by Anglo-American or French feminist thought.

18. See Castro-Klaren's early warnings against the sexist, antifeminist, and biological determinism contained in Freudian psychoanalysis. Naomi Lindstrom sees Castro-Klaren's observations as a sign of caution characteristic of Latin American Feminist criticism against the possible existence of Feminine writing (1998, 131–133). See also Kaminsky's criticism of post-Freudian psychoanalytic theoretical models for identifying women with traditional maternal roles in her 1993 book as well as Castillo's warnings against a mode of writing and criticism that is too personal and not social enough, that indulges in what she calls luxurious impulses and strange urges (Castillo 1992, 28).

19. For examples of this curious repetition please see Franco (1989, xxii), Castillo (1992, 18), Masiello (1992, see Introduction), and Tierney-Tello (1996, 6–7).

20. A sampling of a growing number of critics of Latin American literature who deploy Kristevan concepts would include Jill Albada-Jergelsma (1999), Ruth Silviano Brandão (1991), Nancy Cloutier (2000), Giulia Colaizzi (1996), Earl Fitz (2001), Nuala Finnegan (2001), Teresa Hurley (2003), Hilda Pato (1998), Cynthia Tompkins (1993) and Vilches Norat (2003). A similar list of Chicana and Latina critics would include Irene Brameshuber-Ziegler (1999) and Jeraldine Kraver (1997). See Emilie Bergmann (1998, 2000) and Cristopher Gascon (1999) for examples of Kristeva's concept applied to Spanish Feminist theory.

21. In that book, Prieto deploys Kristeva's early philosophical and psychoanalytic concepts (the semiotic chora, abjection, rejection, and repulsion) to suggest that a number of Latin American writers engage in a masculine mode or a phallogocentric writing composed with the unspeakable traces of an abject origin: an archaic maternal body. Armed with this idea, he offers provocative and suggestive readings of the different modes of ambivalent approximation to that body carried out by Julio Cortázar, Guillermo Cabrera Infante, Gabriel García Márquez, and Severo Sarduy in their writing. He concludes his book

with an account of Tununa Mercado's *Canon de Alcoba* (1989) as the manifestation in writing of a different libidinal economy, one that he also finds first
envisioned by Kristeva in *Revolution in Poetic Language*. "Insofar as women
do not experience the sense of loss that comes with castration, there does not
appear to be an inherent tendency to reject or lash out in feminine texts that are
free from the grip of patriarchy, that are truly a manifestation of the feminine"
(Prieto 2000, 233). Finding that Kristeva's later emphasis on the inescapable
nature of the symbolic (he reads phallic) domain is limiting, Prieto instead turns
to Hélène Cixous's notion of "writing said to be feminine" as a more promising
development of Kristeva's insight, and considers Tununa Mercado's text to be a
prime example of this mode of writing.

I   Transformative Witnessing: Clarice Lispector's Dark Ties

1. I use the term limit-event to mean something analogous to what Felman and
   Laub call a "limit-experience" (1992, 205). For a description of my elaboration
   of that term please consult the section "Matricidal Limit-Event" of the
   Introduction to this book.
2. All of the references in the text to *The Apple in the Dark* and *Family Ties* will
   be to the 1995 and 1997 editions translated by Gregory Rabassa and Giovanni
   Pontiero respectively.

   Following Hélène Cixous' "*écriture féminine*" (1979; 1990), and Maria
   Luisa Nunes's "*a questão da matriz*" (1984), Tace Hedrick has remarked that
   Lispector demands a witness to "the exposure of the female body," to a body
   that is both "essentialized" and "essentially feminized" (1997, 48, 45). She
   calls this body "the mother's place" (45). In this chapter, I argue for a different
   interpretation of Lispector's call for a witness, and for a different interpretation
   of the mother's place in Lispector's work.

   Cixous's theorization of a libidinal economy "said-to-be-feminine" famously
   emphasizes a non-appropriative and nonexclusive relation to an object of desire.
   Cixous developed her theory in the 1980s, and made important contributions to
   the scholarship on Lispector. She posed a convincing challenge to the criticism
   that inscribes Lispector's work within an existentialist tradition (for an example
   of rigorous scholarship from within this existentialist tradition see Lindstrom
   1989). Instead, Cixous interpreted Lispector's *The Apple in the Dark* as an
   unsuccessful attempt to enter into an alternative mode of knowing said-to-be-
   feminine, altogether different from the existentialist mode (1990).

   More recently, Mara Negrón-Marrero, a student of Cixous, has challenged
   her reading of Lispector's novel (1997). Negrón-Marrero forcefully claims that
   the novel is the foundation for Lispector's ethical effort to enter into this alternative mode of knowing, which Negrón-Marrero describes as an ethical form
   of knowledge we have forgotten and erased (44). Negrón-Marrero, however,
   follows Cixous's characterization of this knowledge as "said-to-be-feminine."

   Negrón-Marrero's and Cixous's characterization of the "Feminine," and
   Hedrick and Nunes' characterization of the maternal are limited by their

deployment of two problematic Freudian concepts. One could argue, in fact, that their apparent alternative to phallocentric knowledge (*savoir*) in fact repeats the "crime" of the phallocentric mode of knowledge. The libidinal economy "said-to-be-feminine," Nunes "question of the womb," and Hedrick's "female/maternal body" are based on the acceptance of the category of "object," and of the primacy of the castration threat and its profoundly wounding effect.

Kristeva instead suggests that the object of Freudian psychoanalysis is a screen for an archaic matricide (see chapters 1 and 9 of *Powers of Horror* and *Desire in Language* respectively). Transformative witnessing seeks to work through the melancholy effects of this archaic matricide. Transformative witnessing attempts to inhabit or imagine a third space that would allow us to challenge the categories of "object" and "subject," as well as the primacy of the castration threat. From this hopeful space, we would bear witness to the archaic matricide screened by the so-called lost object, and thus revise the accounts of subject formation implied by Hedrick, Nunes, Cixous, and Negrón-Marrero. From this hopeful space we might testify to the maternal speaking body at the center of the symbolic process of subject formation and transform the effects of a patriarchal maternal imaginary. For a definition of the concepts "maternal speaking body" and "maternal imaginary," please turn to the section titled "The Maternal Imaginary" in the introduction to this book.

3. "Since 1956, when she finished *The Apple in the Dark*, Clarice wrote no more novels until . . . 1963. The writer comments on this arid period thus: 'I could not live without writing. And yet, I experienced eight arid years. I suffered a lot. I thought I wouldn't write again. And then, I suddenly saw a whole book which I wrote with great satisfaction: *The Passion According to GH*. I didn't stop after that' " ([My translation], Gotlib 1995, 365).

4. For studies of Elisa Lispector's works that focus on her family's Jewish identity and traditions please see Peixoto 1994, xvii; Vieira 1995, 110; and Gotlib 1995, 121.

5. For example, Negrón-Marrero finds Lispector's "autobiographical" articles to be deliberate attempts (by Lispector) to force the reader to give up a search for her person, even her proper name, through the revealed biographical facts. In fact, Negrón-Marrero provocatively argues that Lispector wants her reader to turn to her works of fiction instead for a different way of knowing. This "impersonal" approach is based on painfully liberating the self from what is "proper" in order to arrive at something that is at once more particular and more essential (1997, 33).

6. For a useful review of the criticism that has struggled with Lispector's vexed relationship to her family's Jewish tradition and identity, please consult Lindstrom (1999). Contrary to this criticism, Lindstrom makes the case that Lispector's allusions to religious traditions are not limited to Judaism or to its sacred text. Instead, Lindstrom reminds us that Lispector also alludes to Christianity, its texts, and to a modern and secular type of mysticism. She argues that Lispector's allusions to religion are ironic and perhaps even parodical in nature; and that these allusions are in fact typical of twentieth-century experimental fiction.

But Lindstrom never denies Lispector's struggle with a Jewish identity. Indeed, she mentions that Lispector's "standard mode" of twentieth-century writing made her a mainstream success in an anti-Semitic and nationalistic literary environment. Moreover, she claims that this standard mode of writing reflects an acceptance of "the assimilationist ideology that held sway while she was launching her literary career" (1999, 119). Thus, while Lindstrom might argue against misguided readings that seek to find traces of a Jewish tradition in Lispector's writing, she nevertheless leaves open the question whether Lispector might have been responding to an anti-Semitic culture of readers. She suggests that Lispector's deployment of a consciously eclectic, ironic, oblique, ambiguous but accepted twentieth-century style, could be a defensive gesture against an environment that would not allow her to succeed as a writer otherwise, especially if she seemed "too Jewish" (1999, 112). In this way, Lindstrom hints that Lispector's ironic style could be a successful and defensive mask for a prohibited identity.

7. Getúlio Vargas committed suicide, when faced with imminent resignation or deposition by Brazil's military, following the investigation of a miscarried plot to assassinate the editor of an ultraconservative periodical that was highly critical of the regime (Keen 1992, 354).

8. A cantilena is a sustained, smooth-flowing melodic line. It is also associated with both prayer and poetry as in the canticle based on the biblical psalms.

9. The novel was originally titled *The Vein in the Pulse* (Gotlib 1995, 277).

10. The title of the story is a reference to *The Imitation of Christ*, a book Laura reads in school. First published anonymously in 1418, its authorship has been attributed to Thomas A. Kempis, among others. It is a widely read book designed to help the reader follow the "perfect" and "divine" Christian model through admonition, consolation, and explication of the Sacraments.

11. Lindstrom argues that the characters of *Family Ties* try to bear witness to an existentialist void that must be confronted by developing a "valid and effective voice" (1989, 36).

12. Cixous has described this repeated call in Lispector as an annunciation; a call to something beyond words (Cixous 1990, 69). Following Cixous, Negrón-Marrero refers to it as an undoing or as the zero-degree of self (30). For a forceful critique of Cixous's reading of Lispector please see Peixoto's book, especially chapter 3. In that essay, Peixoto draws from the postcolonial criticism of Gayatri Spivak to break the mirroring economy of identification violently limiting Cixous's readings of Lispector. She argues for the importance of a "third party" that would interrupt this mirroring economy that drives Cixous's work by standing inopportunely between her and Lispector, a position Peixoto ironically describes as "from another planet" (42). Peixoto describes this mediator as a necessary interrupting force that confronts the author with the absolute strangeness of the other that the author is unsuccessfully trying to reach (58–59). The reader is this mediator or third party from another planet pointing to the inassimilable violence in Lispector. Despite Peixoto's care to acknowledge the debt owed to Cixous's readings, her emphasis on the interrupting and violent nature of this third space also threatens to foreclose a response. I agree with Peixoto's attempt to open up a third space

to break the melancholy identification between writer and reader or between writer and characters. But rather than a challenge based on irony, on in-your-face cruelty, and on betrayal, I would instead emphasize the transformative promise of this intermediary position. Based on its exchange and inversion of opposites, on its dynamic movement, or affirmative energy, transformative witnessing cannot be reduced to the sustained refusal to be one or the other or both.

13. Gotlib devotes some pages to this accident in her biography (365–368). It appears that Lispector set herself on fire by accidentally falling asleep while smoking in bed.

14. After placing Anita at the head of her birthday table hours before the guests begin to arrive, her only daughter, Zilda, sprays her with a little cologne to hide "her musty smell" (Lispector 1997, 75). Following the exclamation of surprise "Eighty-nine today, my word!" her son Emmanuel says jokingly and nervously "She's only a youngster" (76). José, her oldest son, repeatedly refers to her in the third person despite the fact that she is sitting right in front of him. " 'This is Mother's day!' said José" (79).

2   Maternal *Jouissance*: Elena Garro's *Recuerdos*

1. Garro won the important Villarrutia prize for her novel in 1960 but she first denies it and later minimizes its importance in an interview with Michèlle Muncy (35).

2. All the references to *Recollections of Things to Come* will be to the 1991 University of Texas Press edition translated by Ruth L.C. Simms. All other translations into English will be mine unless otherwise noted.

3. The verb "to mend" (*remendar*) in Spanish can be turned into the noun *remiendo* a "patch" both of which words points to a menial task. *Remiendo* and *remendar* usually refer to patching up old clothes, as in mending socks.

4. In a postscript, Elena Garro writes to Carballo "My great loves: my father, my uncle Boni, my cousin Boni and my brother, who called me 'Saavedrita' to distinguish me from Cervantes. Helena Paz is my teacher. Deva, who was a bird, resembles the Playful Particle Paz: sometimes I get them mixed up. My mother is of another order: outside the real. Some day I will write about that character that called Helena 'Spirit of the North Wind' " (Carballo 1986, 505).

5. The mystery of the novel's memory has been the object of many critical studies, but its link to the dead maternal body at the beginning of the narrative has remained invisible to its readers. Nevertheless, Hurley has recently remarked on the importance of the mother–daughter bond to the narrative and to its outcome (2003, 145–150).

6. Kristeva calls this archaic joy maternal *jouissance*. It is the sexual desire felt for the maternal body and felt by that same body. "The language of art, too, follows (but differently and more closely) the other aspect of maternal *jouissance*, the sublimation taking place at the very moment of primal repression within the mother's body, arising perhaps unwittingly out of her marginal position. At the intersection of sign and rhythm, of representation and light,

of the symbolic and the semiotic, the artist speaks from a place where she is not, where she knows not. He delineates what, in her, is a body rejoicing [*jouissant*]" (1980, 242).

7. A note of caution here. I do not use the terms masculine and feminine as markers of an ontological essence or biological fact. Rather, they are used to differentiate between two representative types of psychic economies and modes of identification with the maternal that are traditionally based on a constellation of social, cultural, historical, economic, as well as biological markers.

8. For a different interpretation of the role of maternal pleasure in the novel, please see Hurley (146).

9. It is true that the maternal role holds the promise of a subversive matriarchy in the novel, but it only enjoys a Pyrrhic and temporary victory. The matriarchy ultimately fails in its efforts to challenge the authority of the strongman, but even before this failure the feminine societies in the novel prove catastrophic to the identity of its members, both male and female.

10. See Paz's discussion of the figure of the *caudillo* (1985, 315–318).

11. This moment dates the events in the novel. The narrative takes place during the Cristero rebellion in Mexico, between 1926 and 1928.

12. La Malinche is the name given in Mexico to Malinali or Doña Marina, the translator who according to legend fell in love with the Spanish conquistador Hernán Cortés and betrayed her people by aiding him in the conquest of Tenochtitlán, the capital of the Aztec empire, in 1519. Cuahutémoc was the last Aztec emperor (1495?—1525). He is credited with heroically defending the city and braving tortures before he was executed by Cortés.

13. "The fetish is a substitute for the woman's (mother's) phallus which the little boy once believed in and does not wish to forego" (Freud 1972, 215).

14. The tragic events of August, September, and October of 1968 have been recorded many times, perhaps most famously by Elena Poniatowska in her book of testimonies *The Night of Tlatelolco* (*La noche de Tlatelolco*, 1971). They are remembered as a brutal show of force by Mexico's military forces and one-party rule against antigovernment student-led popular demonstrations. Similar demonstrations happened in many other cities and universities around the world in a year of global political upheaval and unrest. In Mexico, they culminated in the violence of October 2, when the main plaza of Mexico City was invaded and occupied by the military in a show of force that left many students dead.

Garro was at that time a public intellectual identified with the movement to reform the political party that had ruled Mexico for more than 70 years. After October 2, she was publicly accused of helping the student movement. She was "panic-stricken" and reacted by making a set of public statements against other Mexican intellectuals, a reaction that would be her "hara-kiri" according to one of her biographers (Ramírez 2000, 50). The sensationalist account by the press of those meetings is documented in Ramirez's book *The Ungovernable* (*La ingobernable*, 2000). Garro never recovered from this set of interviews and was forced into exile for 20 years. Poniatowska writes that "the legend that was woven around her produces a fascinating attraction" (Ramírez 2000, 16). She became a mythical figure of treachery, an insane genius in the popular imagination, and a fetish symptomatic of its obsession. Ramírez's book is a good example of the way in which even writers with the best of intentions fetishized Garro. "The mythical stature of Elena Garro weaves itself together with a number of anecdotes and acts of defiance and insolence, with her enormously seductive power, but above all with the quality of her writing" (Ramírez 2000, 37).

15. The tale is told in Genesis 19.1–38. Garro makes a direct reference to this biblical story in *Testimonies for Mariana* (*Testimonios para Mariana*, 1981). In that later novel, Mariana, a mysterious and much maligned figure, is described as a returning version of Lot's wife (1981, 103).

16. A strong woman is at the helm of the town's brothel, which has a powerful influence over the military occupying force. The incestuous sisters Rafaela and Rosa are in control of Cruz (Rosas' second in command); they clearly represent the reach of the power of the outlaw female body. Another woman is in control of the town's landowning class and is the real power behind the "throne" of an infantilized Rodolfito Goribar. Finally, Ana Moncada is the head of the patrician Moncada family. She is both a protective and an ineffectual force that reminds Martín of his mother (77–78).

17. The conventional definition of nostalgia is the idealization of the past. Its effect is often described as lulling one into a false sense of security. Nostalgia is the phantasmatic experience of a past that never really happened, a past that was not lived as it is later remembered. Nostalgia is made of experiences that are "not lived" in a metaphorical sense. They are experiences that are only "lived" as memory.

18. Messinger Cypess mentions Garro's debt to Paz's notion of an indigenous mythical and cyclical temporality in *The Labyrinth of Solitude*. She also emphasizes the challenge of Garro to the "Malinche paradigm" that also emerges from Paz's book. In a similar feminist vein, Kaminsky has reluctantly compared the novel's paradoxical temporality to a problematic account of Kristeva's notion of women's time.

19. Kristeva has described monumental time in these very terms. She associates this time with an emerging memory of a phantasmatic completeness or wholeness, a "fusion state of pleasure" (1995, 211), a nostalgia for an archaic mother and for a mythical plenitude. Kristeva's account of motherhood and plenitude is ambiguous. On the one hand, she historicizes the appearance, intensity, and character of the nostalgia for this plenitude by referring to specific moments of religious schism and political upheaval. But her psychoanalytic paradigm also essentializes the primal scene of the maternal experience. Perhaps with good reason, this ambiguity has been the cause of much criticism leveled at Kristeva. And yet, it is this ambiguity that also gives Kristeva's account of psychic economies its promising reach. This ambiguous scene, both primal and inflected by individual and collective history, gives her theory and methodology the flexibility at the center of its explanatory power. It is also important to emphasize that Kristeva never idealizes this ambiguous scene. Indeed, her analysis is an attempt to demystify idealized plenitude and archaic motherhood by pointing to its material components. Significantly, she also

points to the dangers of an unmediated incestuous identification with maternal *jouissance*.

20. See Kristeva (1995, 205). That the circumscription of incestuous identification to the feminine is not justified does not prevent it from being a returning trope of our intellectual history and popular culture. The echoes of this long and sustained history can be heard in Garro's characterization of Martín and Conchita's relation to the maternal experience.

21. Kristeva writes, "If the archetypal belief in a good and sound chimerical substance is essentially a belief in the omnipotence of an archaic, fulfilled, complete, all-encompassing mother who is not frustrated, not separated, and who lacks the 'cut' that permits symbolism (that is, who lacks castration), the ensuing violence would be impossible to defuse without challenging the very myth of the archaic mother" (1995, 218).

22. If feminine identification is not limited to women, this masculine response is not limited to men either.

23. Ruth Simms' translation of the novel by Garro smoothes some of the roughness of the midwife's expression and misses the reach of the original. "Conceived with pleasure" suggests the pleasure of the reproductive act while emphasizing an abstract process of conception. The Spanish "*Hecha con gusto*" suggests instead something more organic. Perhaps a closer translation would read, "you can see that she was made with a taste for life." The midwife emphasizes that Isabel's liveliness and beauty are the result of the sexual desire and pleasure felt by her parents. Indeed, she hints at the effect of an enthusiastic and vigorous enjoyment, an overabundant vitality, once felt by the now *manqué* Moncadas.

24. Even Lola castrates as she invigorates her son. His emasculation is born out by the novel's repetition of the diminutive form of his name: Rodolfito.

25. Rodolfo enjoys a similar measure of independence, and will remain an individual force after his mother dies, while Conchita is expected to remain unmarried, a silent double of her mother.

26. Incestuous desire is a powerful force in the novel. Incest threatens to join Isabel with her brother, but also with her mother in a state of ecstasy with catastrophic consequences for her individuality.

27. Garro published "It's the Fault of the Tlaxcaltecans" in a 1964 collection of short stories and one year after the publication of her novel. In that short story, there are explicit references to Hernán Cortés's victorious war against the ancient Aztec City of Tenochtitlán in 1519 and to the Tlaxcaltecans, the indigenous people that according to Mexican history sided with the Spaniards against the Aztecs in that famous war. The main character in that story is a woman, Laura, living in modern Mexico, who finds herself trapped in a cycle of eternal return to that violent war. While there is no explicit mention of La Malinche, Laura's visions, her guilt, and her references to her "permanent betrayal" all suggest that she might identify with, and might even be possessed by the haunting figure of La Malinche. For a detailed discussion of the Malinche myth as it plays out in this short story, please see the essay by Messinger Cypess (1990).

3   The Mother Tongue: Rosario Ferré's Ec-centric Writing

1. Rosario begins an essay on the subject of the transition from wrath to irony in her own work, with a reference to Achilles. "When we think of wrath, Homer immediately comes to mind. Particularly, the beginning of the *Iliad*: 'Achilles wrath is my subject, that lethal wrath that, acceptant of the will of Zeus, brought so much suffering to the Achaeans, and sent so many courageous souls to the depths of hell' " (1992, 103).

2. For a sustained development of the thesis underlying my argument here, please see the concept of double alienation in Kelly Oliver's *Witnessing: Beyond Recognition*. See, especially, the first chapter of that book.

3. For detailed lists of these translations please consult the bibliography of *The Youngest Doll*, published in 1991.

4. Janice Jaffe's provocative essay on Rosario's self-translations describes these additions and reversals as attempts by Rosario to provide herself and Puerto Ricans with a new positive identity beyond colonialism. Jaffe goes a long way in pointing out Rosario's assault, through translation, on the binary principles of the colonial order. But her view that Rosario's reversals in translation are attempts to construct a new and positive identity for herself, as well as her concluding remark that this new identity is a dream-home of a future dwelling for "fellow Puerto Ricans," suggests the limits of Jaffe's commentary. Still attached to the symptoms of the process of subject formation, Jaffe continues to frame Rosario's work within a discourse of identity politics, a discourse that Rosario surely visits but has also attempted to escape throughout her work.

   Suzanne S. Hintz's essay on the question of whether Rosario's novel *Eccentric Neighborhoods* is a biographical or an autobiographical text reaches similar conclusions. Using narratological analysis, Hintz concludes that Rosario's novel is autobiographical despite the novelists' emphatic denials and claims that the novel is instead a fictionalized biography (Hintz 1995, 503). Unaffected by the differences between the Spanish and the English versions of a supposedly autobiographical text, Hintz argues that Rosario searches and discovers her own identity in her novel and that the biography of her mother is simply a means to this end (Hintz 1995, 505–506). In this essay, I suggest instead that, rather than find or discover her identity, Rosario interrogates, assaults, and manipulates the identity-making process itself.

5. For examples of defensive responses to Rosario's assault on the walls of fortified subjectivity, see Ana Lydia Vega's "Carta abierta a Pandora" and Aníbal González's letter to the editor of the *New York Times*, both published days after Rosario's editorial "Puerto Rico, USA."

6. Aponte Ramos maintains that Rosario's novels written in English are examples of a hybridity driven by a consumer market. The use of English is here reduced to a vexed marketing device within an economic system that turns the same into a facsimile of an exotic other (Aponte Ramos 1997, 37). For Aponte Ramos, Rosario's *House on the Lagoon* (1995) performs a solipsistic gesture that unsuccessfully hides itself behind a marketable cultural otherness.

Thus, Aponte Ramos concludes that Rosario's work in English is a mirrored "reflection" of the self in a "border situation" (Aponte Ramos 1997, 37). While Aponte Ramos seems to eschew the identity-driven rhetoric of writers like Ana Lydia Vega, her conclusion nevertheless presupposes an identity (if vexed) with a stable and intelligible core determined by market practices.

7. Curiously, Mozart also returns to his mother tongue in *The Magic Flute*. After composing the music for a number of operas in Italian, he composes the music for *Die Zauberflöte* with a libretto in German.

8. Kristeva suggests that the speaking subject emerges by cutting-off the maternal source of words, by stripping off the skin of the abject (1991, 16). In *Strangers to Ourselves*, she compares this painful cut both to a primal flaying and to a flight. "The word foreshadowed the exile, the possibility or necessity to be foreign and to live in a foreign country, thus heralding the art of living of a modern era, the cosmopolitanism of those who have been flayed" (1991, 13). The separation from the abject sets the subject in motion in two ways. On the one hand, the separation liberates and begins a new speaking subject. The skin of this new subject heralds exile and the subject emerges speaking a foreign language. On the other hand, the separation displaces and flays, an earlier skin (language) substituting it for another that works defensively as an anesthesia. The foreign language, then, is like a permeable but soothing skin that substitutes the old skin (language) and covers over the exposed material. Since the old skin and material are not entirely gone, the speaking subject not only emerges speaking a foreign language but s/he also emerges questioning inconsolably (1995, 219).

9. Inspired by Proust, Kristeva argues that all writing is translation, understood as the transformation of an archaic rumor that is irreducible to nature or to culture (the abject or *le sensible*) into a literary experience. Translation is the double labor that reproduces and recreates (transforms) that preexisting sensation or impression. The labor is double because of the fact that to translate is both to manifest creative agency and to make manifest something that is already created. Like Proust she compares translation to osmosis, the diffusion of a liquid through a semipermeable membrane, and, just as he does, she calls that translating membrane an intermediary region, a depth in the psyche, between material coiled in the body and the exterior intellect (Kristeva 2002, 382). For Kristeva, rough drafts in writing are similar equivalents of translation. They too are examples of the intermediary region before the final form that contains the notes, fragments, rhythms, and the monstrous intimacy of a region anterior to meaning and signification. Translation and rough drafts are not only metaphors for the literary experience but they are also processes that reveal the drama and process of individuation, of subject formation: an aperture to the other, to the abject, and a connection that both exalts and destabilizes identity.

10. I wish to thank Kelly Oliver for suggesting that my descriptions of Rosario's self-translations are similar to the process of working-through, as Freud understood it. For Oliver's emphasis on working-through over the emphasis on repetition by contemporary philosophy and critical theory please see "Identity as Subordination, Abjection, and Exclusion," the third chapter in her book *Witnessing*.

11. In her autobiographical work, Kristeva applies her ideas about this complex process of subject formation to translation. Paralleling Benjamin's views, Kristeva understands that translation is always rough and imperfect. The best it can hope for is to measure the distance from the original by endlessly asking the question "How far removed is hidden meaning from revelation, how close can it be brought by the knowledge of this remoteness?" (Benjamin 1968, 75). Similar to Benjamin, Kristeva finds imperfect access to truth, described by him as a mute deposit, a mysterious intention without tension, and an eternal process of supplementation, through translation. And again like Benjamin, Kristeva compares translation to a birthing process that gives life to material that is neither dead nor alive. Unlike Benjamin, however, Kristeva does not assume that translations are into the mother tongue, while the original material is pure disembodied language qualitatively different from the translation, a Spiritual (even Scriptural) language absolutely beyond words. Instead, she is interested in the translation *of* the mother tongue understood not as a Spirit but as a secret rumor of archaic tissue. And she emphasizes the connections between that rumor and the other language that contains it even as it separates itself from the original. For Kristeva, this double move constitutes the experience of writing. Finally, unlike Benjamin, Kristeva is less interested in the knowledge of the remoteness between the original and the translation; and she is more interested in the sensation of the intermediary region. For Kristeva, this region is not reducible to matter but is equivalent to life.

12. *Vecindarios excéntricos* was first published in *Diálogos* between 1989 and 1990 and another fragment appeared in Rosario's 1992 book *Las dos Venecias*.

13. It is perhaps fitting that the melancholy maternal voices haunting Rosario's essays should find their origin in a cemetery named after a mystic with a last name meaning mad in Italian. Born in Florence to a distinguished Florentine family (the Pazzis) Maria Magdalen entered a discalced Carmelite convent in 1582. Perhaps a victim of patriarchal social fortifications, she became ill and experienced numerous ecstasies and five years of spiritual depression. Her revelations were recorded, and she was canonized in 1669.

14. Rosario's personal connection with the cemetery and the link between the old man's curse and the mother's curse is only hinted at in another essay of the same collection. In an essay titled "Writing Between Two Edges," (*"Escribir entre dos filos"*) Rosario describes one of her first pieces of writing. She remembers publishing an article in her father's newspaper when she was 16 years old. That article had many things in common with "Meditation outside the City Walls." It too was a work of social commentary with a similar moral lesson. It too described and lamented the state of an old cemetery in Puerto Rico, though this time Rosario described the cemetery in Ponce, the town in the south of the island where she was born. Indeed, the 1989 essay seems to be a displaced version of that earlier journalistic article about the cemetery of Ponce. To hear Rosario tell it, the early article appears to have caused quite a stir, what with readers calling her father's newspaper to complain about it. And Rosario seems to have interiorized their criticism, as she describes that early piece as truculent, "pompously titled," and even "trash" (2001, 174).

The words against her own writing are harsh, and the reader wonders at their intensity. While Rosario does not describe her mother's reaction to the journalistic piece, her essay nonetheless helps the reader imagine the disturbing effect the piece must have also had on her. The reader can guess at her mother's anger, since Rosario begins her essay by saying that her mother disapproved of her husband's purchase of the newspaper to the point of cursing at it, calling it "sheer business madness" (2001, 175). By identifying her beginnings as a writer with the betrayal of the biographical mother, Rosario suggests that her life as a writer is indelibly associated with the metaphorical death of the symbolic mother. Like Pamina in Mozart's opera, Rosario sides with the father's voice against the mother's angry sounds (is this Orpheus standing against Ophelia?).

4 Accidents of Chicana Feminisms: Norma Alarcón, Gloria Anzaldúa, and Cherríe Moraga

1. Twenty years later, perhaps they can be viewed as founding figures of what Gabriela F. Arredondo, Aida Hurtado, and Norma Klahn have recently called Chicana Feminisms (2003).
2. Among the leading figures making up this group one could perhaps list Luce Irigaray, Hélène Cixous, Melanie Klein, and Nancy Chodorow. For a discussion of this maternal imaginary, please see Teresa de Lauretis' *The Practice of Love* (1994, 163–175).
3. For an example of a postfeminist reading see de Lauretis' reading of Moraga's play *Giving Up the Ghost* (1994, 203–253). Other examples might also include Madelon Sprengnether's *Spectral Mother*, Monique Wittig's *The Lesbian Body*, and Haunani-Kay Trask's *Eros and Power*.
4. The interstice in patriarchal language is analogous to what Kristeva calls the lability of the thetic or to the splitting disposition of the symbolic.
5. Consider, for example, the disturbing effect of the grammatical accidents in the following phrase: "That is, the drive to territorialize/authenticate/legalize and deterritorialize / deauthenticate / delegalize is ever present, thus constantly producing '(il)legal' / (non)citizen-subjects both in political and symbolic representations in a geographic area where looks and dress have become increasingly telling of one's (un)documented status" (2003, 360).
6. Consider, for example, Paz's representation of la Malinche in *Labyrinth of Solitude*, or Rudolfo Anaya's similar representation of la Llorona in *The Legend of La Llorona*.
7. The semiotic is the body's mode of signification. Kristeva argues that the semiotic is always already invested with the ability to make meaning (1984, 22). Indeed, the semiotic includes a structuring disposition, which Kristeva also finds in the maternal body. "The mother's body is therefore what mediates the symbolic law organizing social relations and becomes the ordering principle of the semiotic chora" (1984, 27).
8. Alarcón convincingly argues that the multiplicity of names for this maternal figure is an enabling reaction in its excess to the erasures performed by patriarchal discourse in the name of the Father (2003, 361).

9. Anzaldúa gives credit to James Hillman for her definition of the "archetype," which he describes as the unconscious *structure* in the process of subject formation (Hillman 1975, 148).

10. According to Kristeva, the semiotic chora's disposition to structure is commensurate with the similarly structuring operations of the unconscious, and in particular with displacement and condensation. Kristeva writes that the semiotic chora gives life to the subject by giving a particular structure to the death drive, a structure that is nevertheless haunted by its operations or accidents. The processes of condensation and displacement of the semiotic chora project or produce an "uncanny strangeness," but this strangeness is also "the first working out of the death drive" according to Kristeva (1991, 92).

11. Anzaldúa calls instinctive reasoning "*La facultad*" (1999, 60–61).

12. La Malinche, or doña Marina, is the Indian woman who served as Hernán Cortés' translator and was his mistress during his Conquest of Mexico in 1520. Described as an ontologically abject figure open to the exterior and passive, La Malinche is the natural object of Mexican myth, "an inert heap of bones, blood and dust" (Paz 1985, 85).

13. Anzaldúa, for example, places the wound both in the psyche and in the world. Indeed, Anzaldúa's lasting contribution to what has now become known as border studies is her compelling description of the border between Mexico and the United States as a bleeding, open, and hungry wound.

14. Together with works like *Beloved* by Toni Morisson, "*The Hungry Woman*" returns visibility, meaning, and humanity to acts reduced by other authors to a Feminine unintelligibility, if not irrationality. The play is a radical response to a well-established Mexican tradition of literary representation that simplifies and flattens out an otherwise heterogeneous maternal subject. "I had read Rudolfo Anaya's version of the story. I got really upset. I'm so tired of hearing how this woman killed her children because a man dumped her. Similarly, when I read Octavio Paz's work [*Labyrinth of Solitude*] on Malinche it made me angry . . . Their texts gave me the stimulus to respond" (Kevane, 106).

15. Felman's accident is an appropriation of Lacan's definition of "the real" as "what returns to the same place" (Lacan 1978, 42).

16. In an otherwise brilliant interpretation of the figure of "black milk" in Paul Célan's poem "Todesfuge," Felman associates the maternal body with a passive body possessed by a masculine master at the center of the accident. The maternal body performs the function of the concrete, material residue of the Lacanian real for Felman: a recalcitrant obscurity, unintelligibility, and insistent death of meaning. "The perversion of the metaphor of drinking is further aggravated by the enigmatic image of the 'black milk,' which, in its obsessive repetitions, suggests the further underlying—though unspeakable and inarticulate—image of a child striving to drink from the mother's breast" (Felman 1992, 30).

5   Memoirs for the Abject: Irene Vilar's *Memoria*

1. The interview by Ilan Stavans was broadcast in the WGBH program *La Plaza*, on September 2001. I would like to thank Ilan Stavans, Margaret Carsley,

Special Projects Assistant, and Joseph Tovares, Managing Producer of La Plaza at WGBH for making available a copy of this interview.

2. Lolita Lebrón, Rafael Cancel Miranda, Irvin Flores, and Andrés Figueroa Cordero fired on the United States' House of Representatives in 1954, wounding five Congressmen in a dramatic and violent effort to call attention to the issue of Puerto Rican sovereignty and independence.

3. In an interview with Irene Vilar conducted by Ilan Stavans.

4. But as Derrida's defensive moves in his essay suggest, deconstruction is also open, and just as susceptible to the resistance displayed by its objects of study. "Mnemosyne" is part of the Welleck Library Lectures Series, which Derrida delivered between January and February of 1984, shortly after the death of his friend, Paul de Man. The beginning of the essay includes an account or a history of the polemics surrounding deconstruction in the United States at that time, though significantly much of it is displaced to the endnotes. To the chagrin of his critics, and against the explicit wishes of the defenders of deconstruction who invited Derrida to give these lectures, he refuses to define or give a final and totalizing account of deconstruction. He refuses to do so because it would go against the grain and the spirit of deconstruction, and also because "to do so would be to . . . weaken it, to date it, to slow it down . . . to wear deconstruction out, exhaust it, turn the page." He says "You can well understand that in this matter I am not the one in the greatest hurry" (1989, 17). In short, to give a pithy definition of deconstruction is to already assume that its movement is over. The irony of the denial didn't escape Derrida. To deny exhaustion is also to have already recognized it and to recognize that one is already in its throes. Derrida brings this point home in his essay, not only home to his body and his self, but home to the maternal body, to the body that appears to be responsible for leaving and bequeathing the trace of death by his own account.

5. The *Odyssey* famously begins "Oh Goddess of Inspiration, help me sing of wily Odysseus, that master of schemes!" Odysseus lies about his identity and his origins to the Cyclops Polyphemus, Athena, and Eumaeus among others; he also lies about Skylla and Charybdis to his men and about pretty much everything when he returns to Ithaca in disguise. He was of course responsible for the cunning idea of the Trojan horse that eventually tricked the Greeks into defeat in the *Iliad*.

6. See Kafka's (1971) reinterpretation of the myth in "The Silence of the Sirens."

7. Renata Salecl has recently identified the mythical song of the Sirens in the *Odyssey* with the unspeakable, unutterable, empty point of Homer's narrative. According to Salecl, this point is but an instance of the death, the trauma, at the center of all subjectivity and of all compensatory narratives like Homer's narrative poem. It is a "deadly pleasure" around which both subjectivity and its defensive narratives are composed; a contradictory point that must be left unspoken. Like the Sirens, their song inhabits an in-between space. Citing Pietro Pucci and Tzvetzan Todorov, Salecl suggests that if the Sirens are figures in-between human and animal, in-between life and death, their song is both the beginning and the end (or failure) of narrative. She reminds us that on the one hand, the song incites the story. The myth of the mysterious song of the Sirens

is the pretext for the narrative that tells the adventure of Odysseus with them. On the other hand, the song is left un-narrated. The narrative leaves unanswered the question "What did the Sirens's sing?" The song is the leftover after narrative. The nature of the song of the Sirens as both pretext to (and surplus of) narrative puts the song always outside, and at the margins of, a displacing narrative. Salecl identifies the song of the Sirens with a knowledge that we do not want to know because it would unravel the compensatory and defensive narrative of subjectivity.

Following Lacanian psychoanalysis, Salecl associates the song of the Sirens with the "knowledge in the real," with drive, and with Feminine *jouissance*. Salecl defines Feminine *jouissance* as opposed to phallic *jouissance*: the fantasy that overcomes castration or the lack of the phallus. She suggestively calls Feminine *jouissance* an unexpected supplement to phallic *jouissance*, but she also condemns it to radical unintelligibility. Feminine *jouissance* is none other than the death drive, and to experience it is also to abandon oneself to suicidal impulses according to Salecl. In this essay, I suggest with Kristeva, that "Feminine" *jouissance* is a different event from the Salecl's account. It is not opposed to Phallic jouissance, but is in constant interaction and interdependent with its fantasies. In other words, it is a life-affirming force as well as a destructive power.

8. Lebrón and the other Nationalists involved in the shooting were granted clemency by President Jimmy Carter in 1979. In the Summer of 2001, at 81 years of age, Lebrón was again imprisoned (this time for 30 days) for trespassing military property in the island of Vieques. This smaller island off the coast of Puerto Rico became the displaced site of colonial struggle at the end of the twentieth century.

9. In *Powers of Horror*, Kristeva describes the rituals of defilement that constitute what she calls the clean and proper self. (The book is deeply indebted to the structural anthropology of Claude Lévi-Strauss and to the work by Mary Douglas on the relationship between purity and defilement.) These rituals, Kristeva argues, struggle to separate the clean stable subject from the sacred, defiled, and unstable object. Following Freudian psychoanalysis, Kristeva argues that these rituals produce taboos in order to achieve this, and these taboos are also the foundation of the social. But she also distinguishes her theory from Freudian psychoanalysis by underscoring Freud's inattention to the dread of the mother–child dyad at the center of these rituals and in particular at the center of the incest taboo. In her essay, she theorizes this dread, which she calls abjection, and finds that the confusion of its border state is what the rituals of defilement sacralize in order to separate it from the clean and proper body of the self.

10. Abjection for Kristeva is not simply something outside the rituals of defilement. Indeed, Kristeva emphasizes the correspondence between abjection and these rituals, just as she emphasizes the correspondence between social rituals and psychic economies, and between the resulting clean subject and defiled object. (In emphasizing this correspondence she distinguishes herself from Lévi-Strauss and Douglas.) She argues that the incestuous drive and the border state are already within the rituals of defilement. Abjection is both constitutive

of the rituals and the object of their dread. So the symbolic rituals are as prone to dissolving back into the undifferentiated drives and states that inhabit them as are the precarious oppositions they struggle to create between pure subjects and defiled objects.

11. In a critique of Freud's account of subject formation, and specifically of the suspicious role played by the object in his theory of primary narcissism, Kristeva writes "the abject is the violence of mourning for an 'object' that has always already been lost" (1982, 15). In other words, according to Kristeva, Freud first presupposes an object and then mourns it, finding it to be "lost." Kristeva's "abject" is the result of this double negative within Freud's theory. It is the aporia (or crisis) built-into the Freudian account of subject formation.

   According to Kristeva, Freud is not alone in the performative production of the abject. Indeed, for Kristeva all human knowledge driven by meaning is both dependent on and is productive of analogous aporias. "Crises, far from being accidents, are inherent in the signifying function and, consequently, in sociality" (1980, 125). All human knowledge based on meaning guarantees transcendence (transcendentalism, a bodily exclusion). This transcendence is located in a blind spot, an aporia, and a place we cannot see. Freud's and Derrida's lost and interred maternal bodies are examples of the aporia that determines the limits, the boundaries, and the form of their account of subjectivity. These aporias also determine the form that psychoanalysis and deconstruction take. Both are modes of knowledge that attempt to explain the processes of subject formation.

   Such aporias perform an ambiguous, double, function. On the one hand, they operate as purification rituals, or rituals of defilement, building hierarchical social structures, subjectivities, and theories. On the other hand, they also look back toward an archaic experience of parceling, separation and differentiation, reinscribing the crisis that they seek to erase. "As if purification rites, through a language that is already there, looked back toward an archaic experience and obtained from it a partial object, not as such but only as a spoor of a preobject, an archaic parceling" (Kristeva 1982, 73). According to Kristeva, we have an ethical responsibility to point out the debt of human knowledge to this aporia, to this already lost "object," to our rituals of defilement. Similar to Kristeva's analysis of the abject, Vilar's memoir reveals that this aporia, or archaic experience of parceling, is perhaps acoustically located in the maternal experience, where it is most violently silenced.

12. When Kristeva speaks of the "feminine" she does not mean an essence. The "feminine" is, instead, a limit, the limit of identity, the unnamable, otherness. It is the state, place and moment of *jouissance*, the foundation both of rituals of defilement, and of language in all its forms, including creative writing. The mother–child dyad is one representative instantiation of this archaic state, place and moment. Contact with the "feminine" is not idyllic for Kristeva. In fact, the Edenic image of that dyad is a defensive negation of its true nature. For Kristeva, "feminine" *jouissance* produces pleasure but also fear, impurity, and pain. It is attractive but it also reveals a horror, a terror, and a fear of being rotten, drained and blocked. She describes the state, place and moment of the "feminine" as imprecise and undifferentiated. The linguistic practice at

work where identity sinks into the ambiguity of the mother–child dyad is a language that does not name. She suggests that naming language breaks with the chaos and with the perviousness of the "feminine." She states that rituals of defilement and their linguistic derivatives ward-off the fear of sinking identity by coding or symbolizing the dual relationship's threat to the totality of the living being.

13. Kristeva draws from Freudian psychoanalysis for this definition of language. For Freud, the unconscious "speaks" in a language different from, but closely associated with consciousness. This is the "archaic" language of dreams, of jokes. In fact, in his essay on the unconscious, Freud uses the metaphor of translation to convey the passage from the unconscious to consciousness. This passage is crucial for Freud. In fact, it is the very support of subjectivity. When this linguistic passage breaks down, consciousness collapses into the unconscious and this produces what Freud calls the "organ speech" of schizophrenia.

14. Kristeva's use of the masculine and feminine pronouns here is both problematic and interesting. She seems to refer to the artist and to the rejoicing maternal body with gender specific pronouns. The artist is grammatically masculine, while the body is feminine. One reading of this opposition could be that the body needs interaction with a linguistic force of another order. Gender would be one marker, not a privileged one, of this facilitating difference. The playful slip in the phrase "the artist speaks from a place where she is not, where she knows not" would seem to support this interpretation. In that phrase, the artist is just as easily an opposing grammatical entity to the feminine body, as it could be the subject of the grammatical feminine "she." Given Kristeva's interpretation of the poet and the artist, "she" could very well be the one speaking from a place that is not and knows not, since the artist speaks from an unstable place it also possesses a similarly troubled knowledge. A similar (perhaps) inevitable slip can be detected both in Kristeva's and my own use of "feminine" *jouissance*, both as one pole in the process of subject formation and as the language that travels from pole to pole. Could this difference be explained temporally? Could the lost origin and the mourning memory of that loss be different moments of "feminine" *jouissance*?

15. Helen cries out to the Sirens in her distress: "To what spirit of music shall I appeal for a dirge,/ for a lament/ bitter enough to suit/ the burden of sorrow I feel?/ Come, deathly daughters of Earth,/ you sirens with bird-wings,/ and with your pipe or lyre or Libyan flute/ strike up a sad accompaniment,/ some grim, despairing strain/ in sympathy with my sufferings . . . a chant of blood, a black paean rising in unison/ with the tears I now let fall/ for the souls of the dead and gone" (Euripides 1981, 27–28).

16. If we compare Vilar's interpretation of the song of the Sirens to Salecl's, one can detect an important difference. Salecl's comments are based on "The Silence of the Sirens," a longer and slightly different text by Kafka. In that text, the song of the Sirens is indeed silence: the unspeakable, unutterable, empty point of narrative, the point of narrative's surplus and the pretext to narrative. In other words, the song is the antithesis of narrative, textuality, or language; and language can only exist in struggle if not in downright opposition to the Sirens's song. But in the shorter text quoted by Vilar, Kafka insists

that the song is not silence but a mournful music sung "aloud." In other words, it is still a sound: the sound not of silence but of mourning.

17. Iris Bruce tells part of the interesting history of *Parables and Paradoxes* in a recent article. Kafka never wrote a book with that title and the texts included in it are gathered from a variety of contexts such as a novel, a short story, aphorisms, autobiographical writings, and even personal correspondence. *Parables and Paradoxes* is a collection edited by Nahum Glatzer and originally published in 1946. There is a very interesting work written about Kafka's 1917 work "The Silence of the Sirens." However, the shorter text "The Sirens" has not been the object of much critical attention. Its relative obscurity might be due to the fact that Kafka never published it himself and that it is not included in the other collections of Kafka's work in English, German, or both, except, that is, for Glatzer's volume (Bruce 1997, 59). Sadly, Bruce does not give the source of the short text. Only that it was translated by Greenberg in the 1946 edition and was substituted by a new translation in Glatzer's 1961 edition of *Parables and Paradoxes*. Like many critics, Bruce focuses his critical comments on "The Silence of the Sirens."

6   From Revenge to Redemption: Julia Alvarez's Open Secrets

1. Melancholia is a psychosis for Freud. It is a revolt against a loved object that turns inward and transforms into an intimate cleavage between the component institutions of the ego. It is identification with an archaic love, with a narcissistic mode of love, for Freud, a feminine self-love. It involves regression to a preliminary stage of object choice, a stage of oral incorporation. As such, it entails a return to an archaic ambivalence that triggers a stage of sadism, violence, and punishment aimed at the self. For Freud, sadism against the self is an indirect way to overcome the overwhelming effect of the lost loved object on the self. In short, melancholia is a psychosis that disturbs and distorts judgment, or more specifically the mechanism of judgment: its painful reality-testing or "groping" that confirms the loss of the loved object. Instead, melancholia turns that judgment into a similarly painful and eternally repetitive process that insists on the loss of self, on self-reproach, on self-impoverishment, and on self-abjection.

Intimate revolt is a provocative mode of Freudian melancholia or an experimental psychosis according to Kristeva. "The semiotic chora, this infralinguistic musicality that all poetic language aims for, becomes the main objective of modern poetry, an experimental psychosis" (Kristeva 2002a, 10). It is a deliberate bringing to the fore the radical internal cleavage within the ego and its drives, a cleavage that puts unitary meaning to the test. It is a regression to a preliminary stage of subject formation that precedes narcissism: an archaic abjection or negation. It is an identification with Freud's account of negation; in other words, an identification with the very source of the mechanism of judgment: a constriction that informs language or gives language and judgment its form. It is a way to rediscover the place of the object within the subject. In short, reality testing, or the groping of judgment, is not opposed to revolt, psychosis, or melancholia for Kristeva. Instead, judgment is modeled after them. Following Freud's insights on negation and melancholia, Kristeva affirms that judgment is an experimental mode of psychosis, intimate revolt, or melancholia: "In sum, [Freud] maintains that the symbol and/or thought are a sort of negativity, which itself is but a transformation under certain conditions of rejection or of an unbiding proper to the drive, which he calls the death drive" (Kristeva 2002a, 9).

2. In her convincing analysis of Alvarez's novels, Oliver has forcefully described a form of this tradition and its fantasies as the colonization of psychic space. She reminds us in her book that oppression has consequences for the psyche and particularly on our "ability to imagine and create value and meaning in one's life. Oppression colonizes psychic space and cuts off affects from words and thereby undermines the possibility of sublimation" (Oliver 2004, 172). She goes on to show how Alvarez's novels open up the possibility of imagining otherwise by creatively turning the symbols of a patriarchal tradition against itself. But she also points out Alvarez's ability to show her readers "the semiotic dimension of language through which bodily experience can make its way into language, through which bodily sublimation is possible" (Oliver 2004, 170). I am indebted to Kelly for her insights into Alvarez's fiction both in her books and in our conversations. It is a debt I can only attempt to redeem by taking further her compelling argument as I try to do here. I am fascinated by the notion that literature in general, and Alvarez in particular, might show the semiotic dimension of language in language and by the contradictions and paradoxes such a claim might involve. In this essay, I try to show the difficulty of fleshing out, so to speak, this claim, the specific ways in which Alvarez sublimates the semiotic in language and practices the sublimation of maternal affect in her poetry.

3. In her compelling essay on women's time in Garro's *Recollections of Things to Come*, Méndez Rodenas argues that the neo-baroque tradition of Caribbean writing, best represented by the Cuban writer Alejo Carpentier (1904–1980), is built on the matricidal presupposition of a primeval and elemental woman who is lost and is impossible to recuperate in any deliberate way. Her central point is that Garro both repeats and transforms this tradition. Referring to the source of Garro's title in a novel by the Cuban writer she states "The—other— *recollections of things to come*, written ten years after *The Lost Steps*, refutes the Carpenterian (masculine) notion of a primeval origin, associated with an elemental woman (the jungle bound Rosario) and impossible to recuperate in any deliberate way" ([My translation] 1985, 850). In this chapter, I extend Méndez Rodenas's argument, and I characterize the writing of this tradition as a matricidal and epitaphial mode of writing, that is, as a mode of stonewriting or petrifaction. I also argue that Alvarez models her writing on the melancholy negativity that haunts this epitaphial tradition.

4. Intimate revolt is a complex term for Kristeva. It refers to the uncomfortable fluidity necessary at the foundation, center, and source of subjectivity. It refers to the disturbances that she locates in both space and time and that are

necessary in order to keep the speaking subject alive. For that reason, Kristeva defines the speaking subject not just as a subject that speaks, but also one that questions, interrogates, interprets, and writes.

5. Julee Tate repeats Alvarez's insightful remark about her mother in a recent article where she argues that the mother-figures of Alvarez's novels act as "cultural gatekeepers." They "raise their daughters in a manner that contributes to the perpetuation of traditional social and cultural codes, and . . . maternal authority is inextricably linked to national authority"; they stifle both the writing of their daughters and their exploration of identity (Tate 2003, 196, 199). But Tate also remarks on Alvarez's suggestion that her mother is an influence on her writing. She points out that, ironically, the mother-figure in Alvarez's novels has a negative influence on the process of identity formation and more specifically on the identity of the writer. Here, I take Tate's keen observation about the ironic effect of the maternal advice in a somewhat different direction. I argue that the influence of the mother figure is not so much a negative influence as it is an influence of negativity. In other words, the writer of Alvarez's novels is influenced by the intimate revolt contained within the maternal injunction to silence. Indeed, it is my claim that Alvarez's writing itself is modeled after that mode of maternal negativity.

6. For a rhetorically and symbolically seminal (and for that reason also troubling) account of autobiographical discourse as a privileged mode of the epitaphial writing that characterizes all literature please see the by now classic "Autobiography as De-facement" by Paul de Man.

7. My interpretation of Alvarez's mode of writing clearly owes an important debt to Josefina Ludmer's insightful analysis of the inversions performed by the subject whose symbolic context makes it painfully impossible to say what she knows. However, my interpretation also differs from hers in so far as Ludmer defines inversion as a reactive and defensive mode of silence, at least in the case of the famous Mexican intellectual Sor Juana Inés de la Cruz (Ludmer 1985, 47). This mode of silence includes the ironic deployment of rhetorical commonplaces to reveal the unequal power relations in the social context. It also includes a mode of writing encumbered or condensed with a strategic silence or resistance. In short, a writing that keeps quiet. But this mode of writing, ironic or encumbered by a strategic inversions, is also reactive by definition, and for that reason is potentially unproductive, as it is in the poignant case of Sor Juana. My analysis of Alvarez's writing insists instead on the difference between a defensive and reactive writing, and a productive transvaluation of the negativity of the maternal voice, a mode of the redemption to which Alvarez refers.

It is not surprising that Ludmer's essay begins with a disembodied maternal symbol hypostasized into a mathematical matrix in Sor Juana's calculating text (Ludmer 1985, 48). Ludmer is adamant in her association of the maternal with the superior symbolic position: "The maternal authority and the superior are closely linked" ([my translation], Ludmer 1985, 49). I take a different point of view. I attempt instead to return aporetic complexity to the maternal symbol in my account of its operations in Alvarez's writings and to find in that aporia a model that is more productive and enabling than the passive aggression described by Ludmer.

8. In her interview with Prida, Alvarez traces a direct line between socially conditioned bodily responses and her writing. "As a writer, I'm everywoman. I not only speak of myself; I give voice to the obsessions that afflict us all. In my youth I was so driven by those social forces to try to perfect my body. Whenever my world seemed to be falling apart, I'd control my eating. But I overcame that, or more honestly, let's say I transformed that need for control into poetry and vegetarianism" (Prida 2004, 128).

9. It is worth noting that Molloy has convincingly argued that Spanish American autobiographical discourse is marked by a tendency to dramatically perform the loss at the center of its practice and of all writing for that matter. Molloy emphasizes the public dimension that drives this sometimes defensive, sometimes authoritative (sometimes both) dramatic representation. Clearly Alvarez's autobiographical book of poems simultaneously repeats but it also transforms this tradition. Indeed, it is my claim here that to understand this all-important transformation, the public, social, and symbolic side of Alvarez's autobiographical performance must not completely eclipse the material, corporeal, and the intimate side as tends to happen in Molloy's readings of Spanish American autobiography.

10. In an essay on the significance of writing from her book *Something to Declare* (1998), Alvarez similarly describes the paradoxical feelings that poetry provokes in her. "As I write, I feel unaccountably whole; I disappear! that is the irony of this self-absorbed profession: the goal finally is to vanish. 'To disappear,' the young poet Nicole Cooley says in a poem in the voice of Frida Kahlo, 'I paint my portrait again and again' " (1999, 290).

11. The narrator of Alvarez's *In the Time of the Butterflies* (1994) suggests a similar transformation when she reverses Dedé's dark wish into the realization that even those wishes are the effect of the dark light. "Recently, in *Vanidades*, she had read how starlight took years to travel down to earth. The star whose light she was now seeing could have gone out years ago. What comfort if she counted them? If in that dark heaven she traced a ram when already half its brilliant horn might be gone? False hopes, she thought. Let the nights be totally dark! But even that dark wish she made on one of those stars" (Alvarez 1995, 190).

12. José, is the illiterate night-watchman in *¡Yo!*'s (first published in 1996) chapter by the same title whose ambiguous effect on Yolanda has as much to do with memory as it does with writing. He answers the sleepless Yolanda's questions about the Dominican Republic; he releases her from writer's block, making words flow, inciting her to remember poems; but he also makes her terribly sad. Rather unbelievably, José offers Yolanda his and his wife's unborn child, triggering in her a yearning for something "she herself could not get," a memory of loss and sadness (Alvarez 1997, 256). The night-watchman also appears in a story within the essay "Writing Matters" where he performs the same ambiguous double function. He accompanies the writer in her solitary mornings, and his responsibility is to remind her "of the quality of the writing" she is aiming for (Alvarez 1999, 287).

13. In *Tales of Love* (first published in 1983), Kristeva states that the "particulars" of the amatory, primal, identification with the mother/father conglomerate so

necessary to the process of subject formation can be detected (and perhaps recovered) through regression in analysis: "It is nonetheless true that by starting from Oedipal dramas and their failures—backwards in other words—one will be able to detect the particulars of primary identification" (47–48). Taking Kristeva further, I argue here that primary amatory identification might also be the principal effect of maternal *jouissance*. In other words, I suggest that regression in Kristevan analysis, and anamnesic narrative in Alvarez, are both modeled after the reverse (negative) temporality of maternal *jouissance*.

14. William Luis is right to trace the structure of Alvarez's first novel to a mode of Caribbean writing that includes Carpentier's 1944 short story "Journey Back to the Source," which is also narrated backward (Luis 1997, 269). As I have suggested here, Carpentier is part of an epitaphial tradition of writing that traces the maternal body from silent stone to radical loss. Such is indeed the case in Carpentier's story. "Journey Back to the Source" famously begins by describing a decaying and grotesque statue of Ceres "with a broken nose and discolored peplum, her headdress of corn veined with black" (Carpentier, 105). It ends with the foundational darkness of a dying maternal body "Then he shut his eyes—they saw nothing but nebulous giants—and entered a warm damp body full of shadows: a dying body" (Carpentier 1970, 129).

15. My analysis here seeks to go beyond, but also owes an important debt to the work of Idelber Avelar (1999) on post-dictatorial mourning, and to the work of Ranajit Guha (1998) on migrant time. Avelar's analysis of the sustained and open-ended melancholy gesture of post-dictatorial fiction is clearly on the right track, even if his account of Freudian melancholia is sorely lacking the provocative turn that attention to the vicissitudes of feminine sexuality can provide. Guha's notion of the temporal paradox that the migrant inhabits has been similarly helpful to my analysis. But, as in the case of Avelar, one can't help but ask what difference feminine sexuality makes to Guha's account of the temporal obstacles faced by the migrant.

16. The jelly from the olive-like fruit of the Anacahuita tree is used as cough remedy. Its leaves are used to treat rheumatism and bronchial disorders.

17. In his essay on the uncanny, Freud traces back this unfamiliar feeling to the archaic and familiar place of the maternal body. "This *unheimlich* place, however, is the entrance to the former *Heim* [home] of all human beings, to the place where each one of us lived once upon a time and in the beginning. There is a joking saying that 'Love is home-sickness'; and whenever a man dreams of a place or a country and says to himself, while he is still dreaming: 'this place is familiar to me, I've been here before,' we may interpret the place as being his mother's genitals or her body. In this case too, then, the *unheimlich* is what was once *heimlisch*, familiar; the prefix '*un*' ['un-'] is the token of repression" (Freud 1953–1973, Vol. 17, 245).

18. In what is clearly a provocative reading of Freud's account of the uncanny, Kristeva refers to Freud's discovery of an uncanny temporality that is both linear and not linear. She calls this temporality the timeless (*Zeitlos*) and associates it with the maternal body, with the drive, and also with the time of analysis, of transference and beyond transference, and of forgiveness. "Freud underscored the unprecedented timeless (*Zeitlos*), which no philosophy had

isolated before him and which characterizes the unconscious: while human existence is intrinsically linked to time, the analytical experience reconciles us with this timelessness, which is that of the drive, and more particularly the death drive. Unlike any other translation or deciphering of signs, analytical interpretation emerges as a secular version of forgiveness, in which I see not just a suspension of judgement but a giving of meaning, beyond judgment, within transference/countertransference" (Kristeva 2002a, 12).

19. Alvarez's account of the paradox of familial time, its simultaneous existence outside and inside the self, can shed a light backward, or a shadow if you will, on the changing emphasis of Kristeva's thought. If Kristeva emphasizes monumental women's time in her famous 1977 essay "Women's Time," she moves instead to the intimate revolt of the semiotic timelessness in her later work.

20. Guha warns against a similar confusion in his account of what he calls the "future-oriented past" of the migrant, an attitude different from nostalgia in its focus on the anxiety about a future in an unfamiliar world rather than a radically lost past. "It is not uncommon for the necessary inadequacy of such translation [of the past] to be diagnosed wrongly as nostalgia. The error lies not only in the pathological suggestion it carries, but primarily in its failure to understand or even consider how the migrant relates to his own time at this point. Driven on by anxiety, he has only the future in his horizon. 'What is going to happen to me? What should I do now? How am I to be with the others in this unfamiliar world?' These are all cogitations oriented towards what is to come rather than ruminations about what has been so far" (Guha 159).

21. In assuming this negative mode of identity, Alvarez, together with other Latino writers, challenges the tendency of the publishing industry in the United States to search for, overdetermine, and market an unproblematic bilingual cross-over identity (see, for example, Gustavo Pérez-Firmat's *Tongue Ties* (2003) among others). By doing this, Alvarez also joins in, and transforms a long-standing Latin American discursive tradition that monumentalizes the mixed race, turning it into a universal symbol of national identity. José Vasconcelos' *The Cosmic Race* (first published in 1925) remains as the emblematic text of this still powerful discursive gesture.

22. Writing about *Homecoming* (1984), an earlier collection of poems by Alvarez, Kathrine Varnes insightfully writes "even as [Alvarez's] poems query identity, shaping a self before our very eyes, they also show how precarious and continuously evolving identity, of necessity, must be" (Varnes 1998, 67).

23. The story of Salomé is the infamously compelling Christian story of the beheading of St. John the Baptist. According to Christian mythology, Herodias exacts a deadly revenge on St. John the Baptist for declaring that her marriage to the tetrarch of Galilee, Herod Antipus, was outside the law. The Biblical narratives of the Evangelists St. Mark and St. Matthew condemn Herodias's adultery, compounding it with her command to her nameless daughter to dance for her stepfather, and with her homicidal demand for the death of the Christian prophet. The historian Flavius Josephus develops the narrative and writes that Herodias simultaneously married two of her uncles, adding incest to her perversity. Josephus is also the historian who remembers the name of the nameless daughter, Salomé, in his *Jewish Antiquities* (ca. 94).

The ancient story clearly holds the European imagination and Herodias becomes an explicitly anti-Christian figure in the medieval folktale about a covenant of witches that worships her namesake. Since then, the combined story of Herodias and Salomé has become a familiar narrative in the Western artistic canon. The story includes an always ambivalent account (both repulsive and attractive) of a perverse maternal desire circumscribed to the feminine, displaced only to her daughter, and catastrophic to her identity. In fact, the narratives tell the displacement of the perverse maternal desire to the seductive movements of the body of her once nameless daughter, turning Salomé into an organic puppet of her mother's desires. In the Biblical narratives, Herodias's nameless daughter even voices her mother's demand for "the head of John the Baptist" (St. Mark 6:25), suggesting that she is possessed by her mother's perverse voice and body, and has no identity of her own. Adulterous, incestuous, homicidal, and even necrophiliac, the maternal possessive and lawless desire is similarly represented in painting (e.g., Titian's 1515, *Salomé*, and Gustave Moreau's 1876, *Salomé*), narrative (e.g., Gustave Flaubert's 1877 short story "Hérodias," and Oscar Wilde's 1893 one-act play *Salomé*) and in opera (e.g., Jules Massenet's 1881, *Herodiade*), culminating perhaps in Salomé's seductive dance of the seven veils by Richard Strauss in his 1905 one-act opera *Salomé*.

In the Name of Salomé repeats and reverses this long lasting representation of an overwhelming maternal body and voice, of a perverse and seductive maternal desire outside the law, and of its catastrophic effect both on her daughter's identity and on the fate of mankind. But her perspective is also radically different from that of these canonical and male writers, painters, and musicians. Alvarez not only remembers but also insistently identifies, albeit ambivalently, with the seductive voice and body of the maternal, while similarly transforming the maternal material, potentially catastrophic to the identity of the daughter, into a redemptive poetic language.

24. Despite their claim to an exceptional story, authors like Rodríguez follow a fairly traditional narrative pattern that bases the achievement of sociality on the foundation of matricide. This pattern follows the matricidal fantasies at the center of nationalistic, authoritarian, and identitarian social narratives that split a fundamentally heterogeneous maternal experience into conflicting and irreconcilable halves. The good mother or the *femme fatale*, the Virgin of Guadalupe or La Malinche of Mexican myth, the National icon of Motherhood or the perverse pair of Herodias and Salomé in Christian myth, are some examples of this widely disseminated fantasy, which gives way to catastrophic and suicidal modes of being as I claim here and have argued elsewhere in this book.

Bibliography

Alarcón, Norma. 1981. "Chicana's Feminist Literature: A Revision Through Malintzin/ or Malintzin: Putting Flesh Back on the Object." In *This Bridge Called My Back: Writings By Radical Women of Color*. Ed. Cherríe Moraga and Gloria Anzaldúa. Watertown: Persephone Press. 182–190.

———. 1985. "What Kind of Lover Have You Made Me, Mother?: Towards a Theory of Chicanas' Feminism and Cultural Identity Through Poetry." In *Women of Color: Perspectives on Feminism and Identity*. Ed. Audrey T. McCluskey. Bloomington: Women's Studies Program Occasional Papers Series Indiana University. 85–110.

———. 1989. "Traddutora, Traditora: A Paradigmatic Figure of Chicana Feminism." *Cultural Critique* 13: 57–87.

———. 1996. "Making Familia From Scratch: Split Subjectivities in the Work of Helena María Viramontes and Cherríe Moraga." In *Chicana Creativity and Criticism: New Frontiers in American Literature*. Ed. Maria Herrera-Sobek and Helena María Viramontes. Albuquerque: University of New Mexico Press. 220–232.

———. 1999. "Chicana Feminism: In the Tracks of 'The' Native Woman." In *Between Woman and Nation: Nationalisms, Transnational Feminisms, and the State*. Ed. Caren Kaplan et al. Durham and London: Duke University Press. 63–71.

———. 2003 (1996). "Anzaldúa's Frontera: Inscribing Gynetics." In *Chicana Feminisms: A Critical Reader*. Ed. Arredondo, Gabriela et al. Durham and London: Duke University Press. 354–369.

Albada-Jelgersma, Jill. 1999. "Mourning, Melancholy and the Millennium in Martin Jay, Julia Kristeva and Pablo Neruda." *Literature and Theology: An International Journal of Theory, Criticism, Culture* 13. 1 (March): 34–35.

Alvarez, Julia. 1984. *Homecoming*. Berkeley: Grove Press.

———. 1992 (1991). *How the García Girls Lost their Accent*. New York: Plume.

———. 1995 (1994). *In the Time of the Butterflies*. New York: Plume.

———. 1997 (1996). *¡Yo!* New York: Plume.

———. 1999 (1998). *Something to Declare*. New York: Plume.

———. 2000. *In the Name of Salomé*. Chapel Hill: Algonquin Books.

———. 2004. *The Woman I Kept to Myself*. Chapel Hill: Algonquin Books.

Anaya, Rudolfo. 1984. *The Legend of La Llorona: A Short Novel*. Berkeley: Tonatiuh-Quinto Sol International.

Anzaldúa, Gloria. 1981. "Speaking in Tongues: A Letter to 3rd World Women Writers." In *This Bridge Called My Back: Writings by Radical Women of Color*. Eds. Cherríe Moraga and Anzaldúa. Watertown: Persephone. 165–173.

———. 1999 (1987). *Borderlands/La Frontera: The New Mestiza*. San Francisco: Aunt Lute Books.

Aponte Ramos, Lola. 1997. "Recetario para el novelar híbrido: Esmeralda Santiago y Rosario Ferré." *Nómada* 3: 33–37.

Arredondo, Gabriela et al., eds. 2003. *Chicana Feminisms; A Critical Reader*. Durham and London: Duke University Press.

Avelar, Idelber. 1999. *The Untimely Present; Postdictatorial Latin American Fiction and the Task of Mourning*. Durham and London: Duke University Press.

Benjamin, Walter. 1968 (1923). "The Task of the Translator." In *Illuminations*. Ed. Hannah Arendt. Trans. Harry Zohn. New York: Schocken. 69–82.

Bergmann, Emilie. 1998. "Narrative Theory and the Mother Tongue: Carmen Martín Gaite's Desde la ventana and El cuento de nunca acabar." In *Spanish Women Writers and the Essay; Gender, Politics and the Self*. Eds. Kathleen M. Glenn and Mercedes Mazquiarán de Rodríguez. Columbia and London: University of Missouri Press. 172–197.

Bergmann, Emilie and Paul Julian Smith, eds. 1995. *¿Entiendes?: Queer Readings, Hispanic Writings*. Durham and London: Duke University Press.

Bhabha, Homi K. 1994. *The Location of Culture*. London: Routledge.

Bierhorst, John. Ed. 1984. *The Hungry Woman: Myths and Legends of the Aztecs*. New York: William Morrow and Company.

Brameshuber-Ziegler, Irene. 1999. "Cristina García, *Dreaming in Cuban* (1992): Collapse of Communication and Kristeva's Semiotic as Possible Remedy." *Language and Literature*. 24: 43–64.

Brandão, Ruth Silviano. 1991. "Feminina mãe imperfeita." *Tempo Brasileiro*. 104:83/100 (January–March): 101–110.

Bruce, Iris. 1997. "Seductive Myths and Midrashic Games in Franz Kafka's Parables and Paradoxes." *Carleton Germanic Papers*. 25: 57–77.

Bruzelius, Margaret. 1999. "Mother's Pain, Mother's Voice: Gabriela Mistral, Julia Kristeva, and the Mater Dolorosa." *Tulsa Studies in Women's Literature*. 18.2: 215–233.

Burch, Dianne. 1999. "Language. It's like a Second Skin." *College Park*. Winter. 26–31.

Butler, Judith. 1990. *Gender Trouble*. New York: Routledge.

Carballo, Emilio. 1986. *Protagonistas de la literatura mexicana*. México, DF: Consejo Nacional de Fomento Educativo.

Carpentier, Alejo. 1970 (1944). "Journey Back to the Source." In *War of Time*. Trans. Frances Partridge. New York: Alfred A. Knopf.

———. 2001 (1953). *The Lost Steps*. Trans. Harriet de Onís. Minneapolis: University of Minnesota Press.

Castillo, Debra A. 1992. *Talking Back: Toward a Latin American Feminist Literary Criticism*. Ithaca: Cornell University Press.

Castro-Klaren, Sara. 1985 (1984). "La crítica literaria feminista y la escritora en América Latina." In *La sartén por el mango; encuentro de escritoras latinoamericanas.* Ed. Patricia Elena González and Eliana Ortega. Río Piedras: Ediciones Huracán Inc. 27–46.

Cisneros, Sandra. 1984. *The House on Mango Street.* New York: Vintage Books.

Cloutier, Nancy. 2000. " 'no me gusta' de Montserrat Alvarez. La negatividad como manifestación de un proceso femenino de afirmación." In *Celebración de la creación literaria de escritoras hispanas en las Américas.* Eds. Lady Rojas-Trempe and Catharina Vallejo. Ottawa: Girol Books. Inc. 157–164.

Cixous, Hélène. 1989 (1979). "Vivre L'Orange: To Live the Orange." Trans. Ann Liddle and Sarah Cornell. Paris: Des femmes. 7–110.

———. 1990. *Reading with Clarice Lispector.* Ed., trans., and introduction by Verena Andermatt Conley. Minneapolis: University of Minnesota Press. Volume 73 of the series Theory and History of Literature.

Colaizzi, Giulia. 1996. "Abyección y escritura: Del yo a la no-identidad del cyborg." *Feminaria* 9.16: 1–7.

De la Campa, Román. 1999. *Latinamericanism.* Minneapolis: University of Minnesota Press.

De Lauretis, Teresa. 1994. *The Practice of Love: Lesbian Sexuality and Perverse Desire.* Bloomington: Indiana University Press.

de Man, Paul. 1979. "Autobiography as De-facement." *MLN* 94.5: 919–930.

Derrida, Jacques. 1989. *Memoires for Paul de Man.* Trans. Cecile Lindsay et al. New York: Columbia University Press.

Euripides. 1981. *Helen.* Trans. James Michie and Colin Leach. Oxford: Oxford University Press.

Felman, Shoshana and Dori Laub. 1992. *Testimony: Crises of Witnessing in Literature, Psychoanalysis, and History.* New York: Routledge.

Ferré, Rosario. 1976. *Papeles de Pandora.* México: Joaquín Mortiz.

———. 1980. *Sitio a Eros.* México: Joaquín Mortiz.

———. 1982. *Fábulas de la Garza Desangrada.* México: Joaquín Mortiz.

———. 1991. "On Destiny, Language, and Translation; or, Orphelia (sic.) Adrift in the C. & O. Canal." In *The Youngest Doll.* Ed. and foreword by Jean Franco. Lincoln: University of Nebraska Press. 153–165.

———. 1992. *El coloquio de las perras.* México: Literal Books.

———. 1995. *The House on the Lagoon.* New York: Farrar, Straus and Giroux.

———. 1998a. "Puerto Rico USA." *New York Times.* March 19.

———. 1998b. *Eccentric Neighborhoods.* New York: Farrar, Straus and Giroux.

———. 1999. *Vecindarios excéntricos.* New York: Vintage, Español.

———. 2001. *A la sombra de tu nombre.* México: Alfaguara.

Finnegan, Nuala. 2001. "Reproducing the Monstrous Nation: A Note on Pregnancy and Motherhood in the Fiction of Rosario Castellanos, Brianda Domecq, and Angeles Mastreta." *Modern Language Review* 96.4: 1006–1015.

Fiol Matta, Licia. 2002. *A Queer Mother for the Nation: The State and Gabriela Mistral.* Minneapolis: University of Minnesota Press.

Fitz, Earl E. 1985. *Clarice Lispector.* Boston: Twayne Publishers.

———. 2001. *Sexuality and Being in the Poststructuralist Universe of Clarice Lispector; The Différance of Desire.* Austin: University of Texas Press.

Foster, David William. 1997. *Sexual Textualities: Essays on Queer/ing Latin American Writing*. Austin: University of Texas Press.

Foster, David William and Roberto Reis, eds. 1996. *Bodies and Biases: Sexualities in Hispanic Cultures and Literature*. Minneapolis: University of Minnesota Press.

Foucault, Michel. 1982. "The Subject and Power." *Critical Inquiry* 8.4: 777–795.

———. 1988. "Technologies of the Self." In *Technologies of the Self*, ed. Luther H. Martin et al. Amherst: University of Massachusetts Press. 16–49.

———. 1997 (1983). "Self Writing." In *Ethics: Subjectivity and Truth*. Ed. Paul Rabinow. Trans. Robert Hurley et al. New York: The New Press. 207–221.

Franco, Jean. 1989. *Plotting Women: Gender and Representation in Mexico*. New York: Columbia University Press.

Freud, Sigmund. 1953–1973 (1901). *The Psychopathology of Everyday Life*. Vol. 6. *The Standard Edition of the Complete Psychological Works of Sigmund Freud*. Ed. James Strachey in collaboration with Anna Freud. Assisted by Alix Strachey and Alan Tyson. London: The Hogarth Press and the Institute of Psychoanalysis.

———. 1953–1973 (1915). "The Unconscious." *The Standard Edition of the Complete Psychological Works of Sigmund Freud*. Vol. 14. Ed. James Strachey in collaboration with Anna Freud. London: Hogarth Press and the Institute of Psychoanalysis. 161–204.

———. 1953–1973 (1917). "Mourning and Melancholia." *The Standard Edition of the Complete Psychological Works of Sigmund Freud*. Vol. 14. Ed. James Strachey in collaboration with Anna Freud. London: Hogarth Press and the Institute of Psychoanalysis. 237–258.

———. 1953–1973. (1919). "The Uncanny." In *The Standard Edition of the Complete Psychological Works of Sigmund Freud*. Vol. 17. Ed. James Strachey in collaboration with Anna Freud. London: Hogarth Press and the Institute of Psychoanalysis. 219–252.

———. 1959 (1919). "The Uncanny." In *Sigmund Freud: Collected Papers*. Vol. 4. Ed. Joan Riviere. New York: Basic Books. 368–407.

———. 1961 (1930). *Civilization and its Discontents*. Trans. and ed. James Strachey. New York: Norton & Co.

———. 1963 (1913). "The Theme of the Three Caskets." In *Character and Culture; Psychoanalysis Applied to Anthropology, Mythology, Folklore, Literature and Culture in General*. Ed. Philip Rieff. New York: Collier Books.

———. 1963 (1905). *Jokes and Their Relation to the Unconscious*. Trans. and ed. James Strachey. New York and London: Norton & Co.

———. 1972 (1927). "Fetishism." In *Sexuality and Psychology of Love*. Introduction by Philip Rieff. New York: Collier Books. 214–219.

———. 1997 (1925) "Negation." In *General Psychological Theory*. Ed., and introduction by Philip Rieff. New York: Touchstone. 213–217.

———. 1997 (1917). "Mourning and Melancholia." In *General Psychological Theory; Papers on Metaphsychology*. Ed. and introduction by Philip Rieff. New York: Touchstone. 164–179.

García Márquez, Gabriel. 1999 (1962). "Big Mama's Funeral." In *Collected Stories*. Trans. Gregory Rabassa and J.S. Bernstein. New York: HarperPerennial of HarperCollins.

Garro, Elena. 1963. *Los recuerdos del porvenir*. México: Joaquín Mortíz.

———. 1981. *Testimonios para Mariana*. México: Editorial Grijalbo.

———. 1986 (1964). "It's the Fault of the Tlaxcaltecas." In *Other Fires; Short Fiction by Latin American Women*. Trans. and ed. Alberto Manguel. New York: Clarkson N. Potter.

———. 1987 (1964). *La culpa es de los Tlaxcaltecas*. México: Editorial Grijalbo.

———. 1991 (1963). *Recollections of Things to Come*. Trans. Ruth L.C. Simms. The Texas Pan American Series. Austin: The University of Texas Press.

Gascon, Christopher D. 1999. "The Heretical and the Herethical in Angela Azevedo's *Dicha y Desdicha del juego y devoción de la Virgen*." *Bulletin of the Comediantes* 51. 1–2: 65–81.

Goldsmith, Oliver. 1939. *The Vicar of Wakesfield*. New York: The Heritage Club.

González, Aníbal. 1998. "Puerto Rico Statehood." Letter to the Editor. *New York Times*. March 26.

González, Patricia Elena and Eliana Ortega, eds. 1985 (1984). *La sartén por el mango: encuentro de escritoras latinoamericanas*. Río Piedras: Ediciones Huracán Inc.

Gotlib, Nádia Battella. 1995. *Clarice Uma Vida Que Se Conta*. Sao Paulo: Editora Atica SA.

Guha, Ranajit. 1998. "The Migrant's Time." *Postcolonial Studies* 1.2: 155–160.

Hamilton, Edith. 1969. *Mythology: Timeless Tales of Gods and Heroes*. New York: Meridian.

Hedrick, Tace. 1997. "Mother Be You Among Cockroaches: Essentialism, Fecundity, and Death in Clarice Lispector." *Luzo-Brazilian Review* 34.2: 41–57.

Hillman, James. 1975. *Re-visioning Psychology*. New York: Harper & Row.

Hintz, Suzanne S. 1995. "The Narrator as Discriminator in (Auto)Biographical Fiction: Rosario Ferré's 'Vecindarios Excéntricos.' " *Romance Languages Annual* 7. West Lafayette: Purdue Research Foundation. 503–508.

Hirsch, Marianne. 1989. *The Mother / Daughter Plot: Narrative, Psychoanalysis, Feminism*. Bloomington: Indiana University Press.

Homer. 1963. *The Odyssey*. Trans. Robert Fitzgerald. New York: Anchor Books.

Hong Kingston, Maxine. 1989 (1975). *The Woman Warrior: Memoir of a Girlhood Among Ghosts*. New York: Vintage International.

Hurley, Teresa. 2003. *Mothers and Daughters in Post-Revoutionary Mexican Literature*. Woodbridge: Tamesis.

Irizarry, Guillermo. 2001. "Travelling Textualities and Phantasmagoric Originals: A Reading of Translation in Three Recent Spanish-Caribbean Narratives." <http://www.lehman.cuny.edu/ciberletras/v04/Irizarry.html>

Jaffe, Janice. 1995. "Translation and Prostitution: Rosario Ferré's *Maldito Amor* and *Sweet Diamond Dust*. *Latin American Literary Review* 23.46: 66–82.

Kafka, Franz. 1971. *Parables and Paradoxes*. Ed. Nahum N. Glatzer. Trans. Clement Greenbert et al. New York: Schocken Books, Reprint.

Kafka, Phillipa. 2000. *Saddling La Glinga: Gatekeeping in Literature by Contemporary Latina Writers*. Westport: Greenwood Press.

Kaminsky, Amy K. 1993. *Reading the Body Politic: Feminist Criticism and Latin American Women Writers*. Minneapolis: University of Minnesota Press.

Kaminsky, Amy K. 1999. *After Exile: Writing the Latin American Diaspora*. Minneapolis: University of Minnesota Press.

Keen, Benjamin. 1992. *A History of Latin America*. Boston: Houghton Mifflin Company.

Kevane, Bridget and Juanita Heredia. 2000. *Latina Self-Portraits: Interviews with Contemporary Women Writers*. Albuquerque: University of New Mexico Press.

Kinkaid, Jamaica. 1996 (1975). *The Autobiography of My Mother*. New York: Farrar, Straus, and Giroux.

Kraver, Jeraldine R. 1997. "Revolution Through Poetic Language: Bilingualism in Latina Poetry from la Frontera," *Literature, interpretation, theory: LIT* 8.2: 193–206.

Kristeva, Julia. 1980. *Desire in Language: A Semiotic Approach to Literature and Art*. Trans. Thomas Gora, Alice Jardine, and Leon Roudiez and ed. Leon Roudiez. New York: Columbia Press.

———. 1982 (1980). *Powers of Horror; An Essay on Abjection*. Trans. Leon S. Roudiez. New York: Columbia University Press.

———. 1984 (1974). *Revolution in Poetic Language*. Trans. Margaret Waller. Intro. Leon S. Roudiez. New York: Columbia University Press.

———. 1987 (1983). *Tales of Love*. Trans. Leon Roudiez. New York: Columbia University Press.

———. 1989 (1987). *Black Sun: Depression and Melancholia*. Trans. Leon S. Roudiez. New York: Columbia University Press.

———. 1991 (1988). *Strangers to Ourselves*. Trans. Leon S. Roudiez. New York: Columbia University Press.

———. 1995 (1993). *New Maladies of the Soul*. Trans. Ross Guberman. New York: Columbia University Press.

———. 2002a (1996). *Intimate Revolt: The Powers and Limits of Psychoanalysis*. Trans. Jeanine Herman. New York: Columbia University Press.

———. 2002b (1997). *The Portable Kristeva*. Ed. Kelly Oliver. New York: Columbia University Press.

Lacan, Jacques. 1978 (1973). *The Four Fundamental Concepts of Psychoanalysis*. Trans. Alan Sheridan. New York: W.W. Norton & Co.

Lanzmann, Claude. 1985. *Shoah*. New York: Pantheon Books.

Lindstrom, Naomi. 1989. *Women's Voice in Latin American Literature*. Washington DC: Three Continents Press.

———. 1998. *The Social Conscience of Latin American Writing*. Austin: University of Texas Press.

———. 1999. "The Pattern of Allusions in Clarice Lispector." *Luzo Brazilian Review* 36.1: 111–121.

Lispector, Clarice. 1986 (1969). *An Apprenticeship or The Book of Delights*. Trans. Richard A. Mazzara and Lorri A. Parris. Austin: University of Texas Press.

———. 1992 (1984). *Discovering the World*. Trans. and preface by Giovanni Pontiero. Manchester: Carcanet Press Limited.

———. 1995 (1961). *The Apple in the Dark*. Trans. Gregory Rabassa. New York: Book of the Month Club.

————. 1997 (1960). *Family Ties*. Trans. and introduction Giovanni Pontiero. Austin: University of Texas Press.

Lowe, Elizabeth. 1979. "The Passion According to C.L." *Review* 24. New York: The Center for Inter-American Relations. 37.

Ludmer, Josefina. 1985 (1984). "Tretas del débil." In *La sartén por el mango; encuentro de escritoras latinoamericanas*. Eds. Patricia Elena González and Eliana Ortega. Río Piedras: Ediciones Huracán Inc. 47–54.

Luis, William. 1997. *Dance Between Two Cultures: Latino Caribbean Literature Written in the United States*. Nashville: Vanderbilt University Press.

Manguel, Alberto. Ed. Trans. 1992 (1986). *Other Fires: Short Fiction by Latin American Women*. Canada: Vintage.

Marting, Diane E. Ed., 1993. *Clarice Lispector: A Bio-Bibliography*. Westport, London: Greenwood Press.

Masiello, Francine. 1992. *Between Civilization and Barbarism: Women, Nation and Literary Culture in Modern Argentina*. Lincoln: University of Nebraska Press.

Mayoraga, Irma. 2001. "Homecoming: The Politics of Myth and Location in Cherríe L. Moraga's The Hungry Woman; A Mexican Medea and Heart of the Earth: A Popol Vuh Story. In *The Hungry Woman*. Cherríe Moraga. New York: West End Press. 155–165.

Méndez Rodenas, Adriana. 1985. "Tiempo femenino, tiempo ficticio: *Los Recuerdos del Porvenir*, de Elena Garro." *Revista Iberoamericana* 51: 843–851.

————. 1998. *Gender and Nationalism in Colonial Cuba*. Nashville: Vanderbilt University Press.

Mercado, Tununa. 1988. *Canon de alcoba*. Buenos Aires: Ada Korn Editora.

Messinger Cypess, Sandra. 1990. "The Figure of La Malinche in the Texts of Elena Garro." In *A Different Reality; Studies on the Work of Elena Garro*. Ed. Anita K. Stoll. London and Toronto: Bucknell University Press. 117–135.

Molloy, Sylvia. 1985 (1984). "Dos lecturas del cisne: Rubén Darío y Delmira Agustini." In *La sartén por el mango; encuentro de escritoras latinoamericanas*. Eds. Patricia Elena González and Eliana Ortega. Río Piedras: Ediciones Huracán Inc. 57–69.

————. 1991. *At Face Value; Autobiographical Writing in Spanish America*. Cambridge: Cambridge University Press.

Mora, Jorge Aguilar. 1978. *La divina pareja; historia y mito en Octavio Paz*. México: Ediciones Era.

Moraga, Cherríe. 1983. *Loving in the War Years: lo que nunca pasó por sus labios*. Boston: South End Press.

————. 1993. *The Last Generation*. Boston: South End Press.

————. 1995 (1986). *Heroes and Saints and Other Plays*. New York: West End Press.

————. 1995 (1989). *Giving Up the Ghost*. In *Heroes and Saints and Other Plays*. New York: West End Press.

————. 1997. *Waiting in the Wings: Portrait of a Queer Motherhood*. Ithaca: Firebrand Books.

————. 2001. *The Hungry Woman*. New York: West End Press.

Moraga, Cherríe and Gloria Anzaldúa. 1981. *This Bridge Called My Back: Writings by Radical Women of Color*. Watertown: Persephone Press.

Moreiras, Alberto. 1999. *Tercer Espacio: Literatura y Duelo en America Latina*. Santiago: LOM Ediciones.

Morrison, Toni. 1997 (1988). *Beloved: A Novel*. New York: Vintage.

Muncy, Michèle. 1990. "The Author Speaks . . ." In *A Different Reality; Studies on the Work of Elena Garro*. Ed. Anita K. Stoll. London and Toronto: Bucknell University Press. 23–37.

Navarro, Mireya. 1998. "Bilingual Author Finds Something Gained in Translation." *New York Times*. Cultural Desk. September 8. 2.

Negrón-Marrero, Mara. 1997. *Une Genèse au Feminin; Etude de La Pomme Dans Le Noir de Clarice Lispector*. Amsterdam: Rodopi.

Nikolchina, Miglena. 2004. *Matricide in Language; Writing Theory in Kristeva and Woolf*. New York: Other Press.

Nunes, Maria Luisa. 1984. "Clarice Lispector: Artista Andrógina ou Escritora?" *Revista Iberoamericana* 50: 126. 281–289.

Oliver, Kelly. 1993. *Reading Kristeva: Unraveling the Double Bind*. Bloomington: Indiana University Press.

———. 2001. *Witnessing: Beyond Recognition*. Minneapolis: University of Minnesota Press.

———, ed. 2002 (1997). *The Portable Kristeva*. New York: Columbia University Press.

———. 2004. *The Colonization of Psychic Space; A Psychoanalytic Social Theory of Oppression*. Minneapolis: Minnesota University Press.

Ortega, Eliana. 1985 (1984). "Desde la entraña del monstruo: voces 'Hispanas' en EE.UU." In *La sartén por el mango; encuentro de escritoras latinoamericanas*. Ed. Patricia Elena González and Eliana Ortega. Río Piedras: Ediciones Huracán Inc. 163–169.

Pato, Hilda. 1998. "The Power of Abjection: Reinaldo Arenas in his Palacio." *Revista Canadiense de Estudios Hispánicos* 23.1: 144–154.

Paz, Octavio. 1983 (1950). *El Laberinto de la soledad*. México: Fondo de cultura económica.

———. 1985. *The Labyrinth of Solitude and Other Writings*. Trans. Lysander Kemp, Yara Milos, and Rachel Phillips Belash. New York: Grove Press.

Pérez-Firmat. Gustavo. 2003. *Tongue Ties: Logo-Eroticism in Anglo-Hispanic Literature*. New York: Palgrave Macmillan.

Peixoto, Marta. 1994. *Passionate Fictions; Gender, Narrative, and Violence in Clarice Lispector*. Minneapolis: University of Minnesota Press.

Plato. 1956. *Phaedrus*. Trans. W.C. Helmbold and W.G. Rabinowitz. Indianapolis: The Bobbs-Merrill Company, Inc.

Poniatowska, Elena. 1971. *La noche de Tlatelolco*. Mexico: Ediciones Era.

Prida, Dolores. 2004. "Being Julia Alvarez: the award-winning (and famously private) author opens up about the things she regrets, her passions, and what keeps her writing." *Latina* 8.8: 128.

Prieto, René. 2000. *Body of Writing: Figuring Desire in Spanish American Literature*. Durham: Duke University Press.

Ramírez, Luis Enrique. 2000. *La ingobernable: Encuentros y desencuentros con Elena Garro*. México: Raya en el Agua.

Ramos, Julio. 1993. "Cuerpo, Lengua, Subjetividad." *Revista de Critica Literaria Latinoamericana*.19.38: 225–237.

Rodríguez, Richard. 1983 (1982). *Hunger of Memory: The Education of Richard Rodríguez*. New York: Bantam Books.

Santiago, Esmeralda and Joie Davidow. Eds. 2000. *Las Mamis: Favorite Latino Authors Remember their Mothers*. New York: Alfred A. Knopf.

Salecl, Renata. 1997. "The Sirens and Feminine *Jouissance*." *Differences* 9.1: 14–35.

Schmidt-Cruz, Cynthia. 1997. "Writing/Fantasizing/Desiring the Maternal Body in 'Deshoras' and 'Historias que me cuento' by Julio Cortazar." *Latin American Review* 25.49: 7–23.

Sommer, Daris. 1991. *Foundational Fictions*. Berkeley: University of California Press.

———. 1999. *Proceed With Caution, When Engaged by Minority Writing in the Americas*. Cambridge: Harvard University Press.

Spivak, Gayatri Chakravorty. 1994. "Can the Subaltern Speak?" Ed. Patrick Williams and Laura Chrisman. *Colonial Discourse and Postcolonial Theory*. New York: Columbia University Press. 66–111.

Stockton, Sharon. 1994. "Rereading the Maternal Body: Viramontes' *The Moths* and the Construction of the New Chicana." *The Americas Review: A Review of Hispanic Literature and Art of the USA* 22.1–2: 212–229.

Tate, Julee. 2003. "Maternity and Mobility: The Search for Self in the Novels of Julia Alvarez." *Proceedings of the 23rd Louisiana Conference*. Baton Rouge: Department of Foreign Languages and Literatures, Louisiana State University. 195–200.

Tierney-Tello, Mary Beth. 1996. *Allegories of Transgression and Transformation: experimental fiction by women writing under dictatorship*. Albany: State University of New York Press.

Tompkins, Cynthia. 1993. "El Poder del Horror: Abyección en la narrativa de Griselda Gambaro y de Elvira Orphee." *Revista Hispánica Moderna* 46.1: 179–192.

Traba, Marta. 1985 (1984). "Hipótesis de una escritura diferente." In *La sartén por el mango; encuentro de escritoras latinoamericanas*. Ed. Patricia Elena González and Eliana Ortega. Río Piedras: Ediciones Huracán Inc. 21–26.

Trigo, Benigno. 2000. "Thinking Subjectivity in Latin American Criticism." *Revista de Estudios Hispánicos* 34.2: 309–329.

———. 2000. *Subjects of Crisis: Race and Gender as Disease in Latin America*. Hanover: University Press of New England.

———. 2002. Ed. *Foucault and Latin America*. New York: Routledge.

Valenzuela, Luisa. 1986. "The Other Face of the Phallus." In *Reinventing the Americas; Comparative Studies of Literature of the United States and Spanish America*. Ed. Bell Gale Chevigny and Bary Laguardia. 242–248.

Varin, Claire. 1990. *Langues de feu: essai sur Clarice Lispector*. Quebec: Editions Trois.

Varnes, Kathrine. 1998. " 'Practicing for the Real Me': Form and Authenticity in the Poetry of Julia Alvarez." *Antipodas: Journal of Hispanic Studies at the University of Auckland* 10: 67–77.

Vasconcelos, José. 1997 (1925). *The Cosmic Race / La raza cósmica: A Bilingual Edition.* Ed. and Trans. Didier T. Jaén. Baltimore: John Hopkins University Press.

Vega, Ana Lydia. 1998. "Carta abierta a Pandora." *El Nuevo Día.* Perspectiva. March 31. 57.

Vieira, Nelson H. 1995. *Jewish Voices in Brazilian Literature: A Prophetic Discourse of Alterity.* Gainesville: University Press of Florida.

Vilar, Irene. 1996. *The Ladies' Gallery; A Memoir of Family Secrets.* New York: Vintage.

Vilches Norat, Vanessa. 2003. *De(s)madres o el rastro materno en las escrituras del yo.* Chile: Editorial Cuarto Propio.

Yarbro-Bejarano, Yvonne. 2001. *The Wounded Heart: Writing on Cherríe Moraga.* Austin: University of Texas Press.

Yeats, W.B. 1928. *The Tower.* New York: The Macmillan Company.

Index